VOLUME 2

PLACES TO FLY

AOPA's second collection of travel articles, selected

from recent issues of The AOPA PILOT, which

were written to help you get more pleasure

from your airplane

PUBLISHED BY THE
AIRCRAFT OWNERS & PILOTS ASSOCIATION

First printing, May 1967
Aircraft Owners and Pilots Association
Washington, D.C. 20014

"Places To Fly, Volume 2" was prepared for publication by the staff of The AOPA PILOT. Joyce J. Carter, Editorial Supervisor.

Preface

The heavy demand for copies of "Places To Fly," published by the Aircraft Owners and Pilots Association in 1965, provides convincing proof of the desire of owners and pilots of private airplanes for information about interesting places to which they may fly for pleasure. The edition went into four printings, totaling 60,000 copies. This proves again that most private planes are used very much as the owners use their private automobiles— for both business and pleasure.

It is because of this need that AOPA is particularly pleased to present "Places To Fly, Volume 2." In several ways, Volume 2 surpasses its predecessor. For one, it is fatter, containing 160 pages as compared to the 120 pages in the 1965 edition. Also, you will find many of the articles in this book illustrated with color photographs, as compared to only a handful of such illustrations in the 1965 edition.

All of these articles have appeared in The AOPA PILOT during the last two years. An effort has been made to select articles describing interesting places to fly to throughout the country, and nearby places abroad. It is by no means intended to be a resort directory, but the editors believe there will be some places you will want to visit after reading this book.

Every effort has been made to update information in Volume 2 where necessary, but we again caution the reader to check other sources, such as current charts, airport directories, and the operators of the establishments mentioned in the articles, before taking off on a trip. It is always best to write ahead to the establishment you plan to visit and get the latest information on facilities and prices for accommodations. AOPA's Flight Department will be glad to assist AOPA members in obtaining late information if it is needed.

Here are more Places To Fly. Why not get out and try a few of them?

CONTENTS

❧ *CANADA AND ALASKA* ❧

8 Destination Mt. McKinley, Alaska | MAY 1967 | *Richard Owens, Jr.*

11 Fly North Of The Border | MAY 1965 | *Alice S. Fuchs*

14 New Brunswick | AUGUST 1965 | *Matilda J. Metcalf*

18 Fishing For Fun | SEPTEMBER 1965 | *Miner W. Seymour*

21 Fly To The Finest Fishing | MAY 1965

23 A Wilderness Adventure | MARCH 1967 | *H. Jack Bartels*

❧ *LATIN AMERICA AND THE CARIBBEAN* ❧

28 Serenidad, Mulege | APRIL 1965 | *Ruth and Don Downie*

30 Mañana Land Beckons Pilots | JANUARY 1967 | *Don Downie and Dana Downie*

34 Isla Mujeres | NOVEMBER 1965 | *Anne Bremicker*

36 Beachcombing In The Bahamas | MARCH 1967 | *Gilbert F. Quinby*

42 Island Hopping Around The Caribbean | JUNE 1966 | *Max Karant*

48 Caribbean Crossroad | AUGUST 1966 | *Max Karant*

54 Latin-American Byways | JANUARY 1966 | *Richard Owens, Jr.*

59 Planning A Flight To Latin America | MARCH 1966 | *James H. Hamersley*

62 Around South America On One Engine | APRIL 1966 | *Lena and Gunnar Brune*

❧ *UNITED STATES* ❧

70 Fly The Byways | AUGUST 1965 | *Ruth and Don Downie*

76 The Bluegrass State | SEPTEMBER 1966 | *Irene Sullivan*

79 Golf In North Carolina Sandhills | MARCH 1965 | *Page Shamburger*

81 Indians And Smokies Attract Tourists | AUGUST 1966 | *Jane M. Dacus*

83 A Report On Some Interesting Texas Vacation Spots | FEBRUARY 1966 | *Gunnar Brune*

84 Let's Go Flying — North | SEPTEMBER 1966 | *Robert N. Moorehead, Jr.*

85   A Maine Discovery | JUNE 1966 | *Kenneth A. Young*

87   Three East Coast Ocean Beaches | JULY 1965
        Virginia Beach, Ocean City, Md., and
        Delaware's 'Gold Coast' | *William L. Hill, II*

90   'Spellcaster' Islands — The San Juans Of Washington | SEPTEMBER 1965 | *Dolly Connelly*

93   Fly To St. Augustine — Historical City Restored | DECEMBER 1966 | *Anne L. Carling*

95   Fly To Year-Around Fun | OCTOBER 1965 | *Jane Mahon*

101   A Pleasant Florida Island | AUGUST 1966 | *George R. Reiss*

102   Airport Hopping Through The Arkansas Ozarks | OCTOBER 1966 | *Joe Boyd and Mary Boyd*

105   Fly To South Louisiana Bayous | APRIL 1967 | *Nola Mae McFillen*

107   Mackinac Island: Gem Of The Great Lakes | NOVEMBER 1965 | *Allen F. Edwards, Jr.*

111   Aviation Greats At Henry Ford Museum | FEBRUARY 1966 | *Vincent R. Courtenay*

117   Flying The 'High Desert' | SEPTEMBER 1965 | *Ruth and Don Downie*

123   Flight Plan To 'Levis And Spurs' | JUNE 1965 | *Chuck Banfe*

126   Take A Carefree Flight | NOVEMBER 1966 | *H. V. Miller*

128   Saddleback Ranch | DECEMBER 1966 | *Joan Standlee*

130   Leadville: Country's Highest Landing Spot | OCTOBER 1966 | *Don Downie and Dana Downie*

134   Williamsburg, Virginia | MAY 1966 | *Richard A. Repp*

137   Mattamuskeet, N.C. | MARCH 1967 | *Anne H. Cutler and Richard A. Repp*

139   The Clipper-Ship Country | JULY 1966 | *Charles H. Ball*

144   Fly To Four Oklahoma State Parks | JUNE 1965

146   A Skier's Paradise | FEBRUARY 1966 | *Allen F. Edwards, Jr.*

150   Durango, Colorado | APRIL 1966 | *Don Downie*

153   Mammoth Cave National Park | APRIL 1967 | *Ira Harkey*

156   Flying To Mountain Campgrounds | FEBRUARY 1966 | *R. E. Pendley*

159   Pilots Invited To Desert Resort | SEPTEMBER 1966 | *Allan Palmer*

Photographs on the front cover by H. Jack Bartels, Don Downie, Allen F. Edwards, Jr., and Don Sullivan.

Photos on the back cover by Gerald S. Curhan, Don Downie, and Max Karant.

Page 7 Stormy weather over Cassiar Mountains, Canada, photo by Don Downie.

Page 27 Bay at Panama, photo by Charles P. Miller.

Page 69 Grand Canyon, photo by Max Karant.

CANADA & ALASKA

Mt. McKinley, towering up to 20,320 feet, is the main attraction in the McKinley National Park, which was established in 1917. Wildlife is abundant in the 1,939,319-acre reserve, and game was clearly visible from the air.

The author photographed these moose at a lake in the park.

This is the runway at the Fairbanks International Airport. The photograph was taken when the author was on final for landing there.

My wife, Peggy, swept her oxygen mask off long enough to remark simply and seriously, "I really don't think we should be up here." Looking out alongside the wild contortions of ice and snow of Mt. McKinley's gigantic slopes and the endless rivers of glaciers below, I was somewhat tempted to share her sentiments. But to see Mt. McKinley was the ultimate purpose of our trip north, and we were certainly doing just that.

Changing over from floats to wheels some 14 years ago necessitated a number of sacrifices, one of the most frustrating being the loss of a safe and practical means of flying the coast route to Alaska from our home in Washington state. That is, safe and practical from a single-engine point of view. However, after flying all over the wilds of Canada and jungles of Central America, this coast route seemed less and less formidable, and we decided to trust our one engine and the weather long enough to retrace our old seaplane route to Anchorage. To be more specific, we were most interested in the Mt. McKinley country, and our destination was Mt McKinley National Park north of Anchorage.

We were allowing only five days for the trip. Since our departure was late June, we knew our hours of daylight flying were mostly limited to our endurance and not darkness, which really doesn't exist in the latitudes of McKinley at this time of year. Peggy and I departed Port Angeles, Wash. in our *Cherokee 180* at 7 a.m. with Anchorage, some 12 hours flying time away, as our first day's destination. The weather reports were mostly good except for some 5,000-foot overcast in the Juneau and Gulf of Alaska regions; but with the 4,500–6,000 feet scattered and broken elsewhere and apparently nothing higher, we assumed it was clear above and hoped to top this for a look at the Fairweather and St. Elias Ranges along the Gulf of Alaska. Anchorage was reporting only a scattered layer so we were fairly well assured ideal conditions in the Mt. McKinley area if nothing else.

From Port Angeles to Ketchikan is approximately 540 statute miles, which is well within the *Cherokee's* range. With very few alternates in the event weather became a problem, we decided to stop at Port Hardy on the northern tip of Vancouver Island to refuel and relax a bit before striking out on the remaining 300 miles to Ketchikan, which are mostly over water. After climbing out of Port Hardy, we topped a scattered and broken layer at 4,000 feet and climbed to 10,000 feet in the clear. The broken deck below obscured most of the en route water and islands, which was comforting in some respects since we weren't being reminded constantly of the lack of suitable terrain for a forced landing.

The broken clouds changed to scattered as we approached Ketchikan. We landed at the Coast Guard Air Station on Annette Island for Customs, lunch and fuel. North at Ketchikan the scattered went to broken again, then to a solid overcast as advertised at Juneau. We stayed under this time because there was a solid overcast at our destination. This caused another two hours of concern since the beaches are skimpy and the islands completely covered with a dense growth of forest. We spotted our first big blue icebergs in the waters north of Petersburg which originated from glaciers on the

*Couple flies Cherokee to our Forty-Ninth State
via the coast from Washington. McKinley National Park
covers over 3,000 square miles of unspoiled wilderness
and claims the highest mountain in North America*

Destination

Mt. McKinley

Alaska

mainland protruding into the water.

From Juneau we filed to Cordova, 450 miles up along the Gulf of Alaska. There are probably no more spectacular mountains in the world than the giants of Alaska, so the overcast conditions of Juneau and the Gulf were rather depressing since the Fairweather and St. Elias Ranges of this area were apparently obscured by clouds. However, after rounding Cape Spencer and heading up the gulf shores there were breaks visible out over the water, so we climbed up through into a world of clouds below and ice, snow and rock above that defies description. With the Yakutat VOR ahead for navigation and reported broken ceilings at Cordova, we felt secure on top despite the solid deck below and headed inshore to get a closer look at the ramparts of the St. Elias Range protruding above the clouds. This range is culminated by 19,850-foot Mt. Logan and 18,008-foot St. Elias. There are higher mountains in the world, but there are few as formidable and awe inspiring as these ice-sheathed monsters. Besides the unbelievable upthrusts of the peaks themselves, the St. Elias Range breeds a system of glaciers that is surpassed only by the ice caps of the polar regions. For example, the Seward Glacier, which originates on the flanks of Mt. St. Elias, is nearly 150 miles long and the Malaspina Glacier is as large as Delaware.

Upon reaching Cordova, we called friends and accepted an invitation to stay over for the night rather than continue on to Anchorage. We had logged 11 hours of flying time this first day.

The following morning we filed to Anchorage via the Columbia Glacier, which is one of the largest emptying into salt water in the area. It is two miles wide and over 300 feet high above the water where it ends its many thousand year journey to Prince William Sound. We traversed its face 200 feet above the water and as close to its vertical ice face as my wife would allow. We thought the engine vibrations might collapse the wall in places, as the boat whistles do for the tourists, but either our pitch was wrong or it just wasn't the right day since the glacier remained intact along its entire face.

We arrived over Anchorage at 10,000 feet with Mt. McKinley, 130 miles to the north, clearly visible. We refiled to the McKinley Park strip with a dogleg over to the mountain. Already above 13,000 feet, we hooked up our oxygen and climbed to 17,000 feet

as we passed it close to the south. Anyone who has the vaguest interest in mountains cannot help being overwhelmed by the size and spectacular grandeur of McKinley. Unlike the giants of the Himalayas which rise from extremely high plateaus of already dizzy elevations, McKinley has no such assistance and is all mountain from its 20,320-foot summit to the lower reaches of its huge glacial system which winds down to below 1,000 feet in places. Also, being so close to the Arctic Circle, these elevations, temperatures and precipitation tend to create a chaos of ice, snow and glaciers unmatched anywhere else in the world.

After leaving McKinley, we tuned in on Summit radio and wound down to the more docile terrain of the Chulitha Valley and headed for the McKinley Park strip. This strip is adjacent to the McKinley Park Hotel and is contrary to the usual park policy prohibiting landing fields within park boundaries.

The slopes north of McKinley is the tundra, the great Arctic meadow that covers thousands of square miles between the Arc-

By RICHARD OWENS, JR. | *AOPA 46578*

Author Owens and wife, Peggy, beside the Cherokee in which they made this trip to Mt. McKinley National Park, Alaska.

A stretch of the Alaska Highway, which was built during World War II. The now partially paved highway runs between Dawson Creek (B.C., Canada) and Fairbanks (Alaska).

COLOR PHOTOGRAPHS BY THE AUTHOR

tic Ocean and Arctic mountains. It is inhabited by the constantly moving caribou herds, wolf, fox, grizzly and many smaller creatures that abide in the fearsome Arctic. The caribou migrate from their winter feeding grounds to higher summer terrain during the last of June and while doing so gather in herds sometimes numbering in the thousands. We hoped to find these herds from the air prior to climbing over the mountain so we struck out towards McKinley just above the terrain. It wasn't long before a herd was spotted and in rapid succession we also saw Dall sheep, moose and a grizzly. Caribou were just about everywhere. With the absence of growth of any consequence on the tundra, it is extremely easy to spot the herds from the air.

Approaching the Alaska Range and Mt. McKinley from the north over the tundra the spectacle that greeted us suggested a panorama from another planet: dark seren-

ity of rolling tundra in the foreground savagely broken by the brilliant blue-white of McKinley and its giant neighbor. Leaving the tundra and beginning our long flight up the Muldrow Glacier toward the summit, we donned oxygen masks; so the problem of our loss of words was solved — all we could do to express ourselves was widen our eyes and point. We climbed to 18,000 feet, made a complete circle below its 20,320-foot summit and exhausted nearly all our film in two cameras trying to record everything we could see. The round trip, hunting game and circling the mountain, took 2½ hours and we both agreed that it was the most thrilling flight we had ever made together. However, my wife's enthusiasm was a bit on the apprehensive side since she still prefers coconut palms and the white beaches of the tropics to the hostility of the ends of the earth.

We returned to the hotel, checked out, and began the homeward flight (via Fair-

banks and the Alaska Highway because of questionable weather along the coast). We spent that night at Whitehorse on the Yukon after arriving there at 10:30 p.m. in bright daylight.

Flying the Alaska Highway was more interesting than we had anticipated, especially the northern portion which is quite mountainous with numerous lakes and beautiful scenery. We were delayed by a stretch of bad weather north of Prince George which put us a bit behind schedule and necessitated another overnight stop at 100 Mile House just south of Williams Lake. Ordinarily, in clear weather we could have continued home from there after dark, but thunderstorm activity with accompanying buildups made night flying over the mountains somewhat hazardous. Early the next morning it was an easy 2½-hour flight home to Port Angeles and back to work before noon. ◆

By *ALICE S. FUCHS* | *AOPA 58615*

FLY NORTH Of The BORDER

Floatplane flying over the Lake Of The Woods area, Ontario. Lake Of The Woods is a 1,000-square-mile body of water dotted with thousands of islands.

Heading northward this summer? Canada offers a land of enchanting variety. From the stately Parliament Buildings of Ottawa to the grandeur of the Canadian Rockies, you'll find an abundance of places for fun flying.

Nowhere is there an international border that is so easy to cross and where you will be greeted with such friendly courtesy as that extended in Canada.

In turn you will want to make yourself a welcome guest by observing Canadian regulations and informing yourself about Canadian procedures, compliance with which will make your trip more pleasant by avoiding embarrassment or a situation which might be downright dangerous.

Thanks to border proximity and ICAO standardization, flight within Canada is conducted with procedures so similar to those of the United States that you will immediately feel at home. There are, however, a few differences which should be noted and observed.

Flight Altitudes. The Canadians do not fly at the "plus 500 feet" altitudes. When flying on a magnetic track of 0° to 179° in Canada, fly odd thousands of feet (1,000 feet, 3,000 feet, 5,000 feet, etc.), and when flying on a magnetic track of 180° to 359°, fly at even thousands (2,000 feet, 4,000 feet, 6,000 feet, etc.). These flight altitudes are mandatory for flights over 3,500 feet above terrain and should be followed wherever possible below that altitude. With no distinction between the flight altitudes for VFR and IFR flight, an IFR flight which encounters VFR conditions must exercise greater caution in Canada than in the United States to avoid conflict with VFR traffic. In Canada, as in the United States, the best anticollision device is a pair of sharp eyes.

Block Airspace. The area on Canadian airways at an altitude between 9,500 feet and 23,000 feet, east of 114° west longitude, and between 12,500 feet and 23,000 feet, west of 114° west longitude, is designated as Block Airspace. In order to fly here, a pilot with a U.S. pilot certificate must have a valid instrument rating and must file IFR. The holder of a Canadian license may fly VFR in Block Airspace if he has passed the instrument written and has had his license endorsed for Block Airspace. A licensed American pilot can take the Canadian instrument written and get a Block Airspace endorsement on it. This procedure, however, seems a bit complicated. If you are a VFR pilot flying on Canadian airways, stay below 9,500 feet in eastern Canada and below 12,500 feet when west of the 114° west longitude line.

VFR On Top. This is not permitted in Canada. If you want to fly on top of an overcast, it is necessary to have a current instrument rating and to file an IFR flight plan, obtaining either an altitude clearance that you know will put you on top or else a 1,000-feet-on-top clearance. The 1,000-on-top clearance is not permitted in Block Airspace.

Here are some tips on making

your Canadian flying trip pleasant

and as trouble-free as possible

Radio. No trouble here. You'll occasionally get a French Canadian or British accent that may slow your comprehension, but you'll have less difficulty coping with Canadian accents than a Canadian will have with yours if you come from one of the more distinctive speech regions of the United States. Terminology is virtually the same. (The word "circuit" is used in place of "traffic pattern.")

Radio frequency allotment is approximately the same as that in the States. The frequency 122.2, which is a ground-to-air frequency in the United States, is also an air-to-ground frequency in Canada, and a very useful one there. It can be used for contacting radar units and range stations and is the frequency used for Unicom at an airport which has a control tower. The frequency is utilized by pilots operating outside of controlled airspace to pass position reports to aeradio stations or other ground stations, and it is recommended that pilots monitor this frequency when operating in uncontrolled airspace.

Weather Broadcasts. Scheduled weather sequences are given at 22 and 52 minutes past the hour at some radio stations, and at 25 and 55 past the hour at others. If you wish to find out the time of weather sequences for a particular station, consult the communications panel on the Canadian Enroute-Low Altitude Radio Navigation Chart for that area or the aerodrome directory of the Canada Air Pilot. The weather sequence form is virtually the same as that given in the United States except that cloud coverage is indicated by number. Thus "strato-cumulus six" indicates that the sky is six-tenths covered with strato cu.

Flight Plans And Flight Notifications. Procedures for IFR flight plans are the same as in the States. For VFR flight in Canada, both flight plans and flight notifications are used. A flight plan must be closed within 30 minutes after arriving at destination. If you know that you will be unable to close a VFR flight plan within 30 minutes because of lack of communication facilities, a flight notification should be filed instead of the flight plan. This requires closing within 24 hours of the time the pilot states on the flight notification and may be filed with any responsible person if communications facilities are inadequate to permit filing with an appropriate air traffic control unit. A flight plan is required for all night flight in Canada as well as any flight to or from a military airport.

An IFR flight plan, DVFR flight plan or Defense Flight Notification must be filed for any flight to be conducted within a Security Identification Zone at a TAS of 180 knots or more (except that southbound flights in the Mid-Canada Identification Zone must file regardless of airspeed). Transborder flights into eastern Canada will not encounter an identification zone, and those into western Canada need have no concern about an identification zone if traveling under the specified air speed.

Flight In Sparsely Settled Areas. The northern portion of Canada, an area defined by an irregular line which sets off most of the area north of 50° latitude, is designated as a "sparsely settled area." Aircraft operating wholly or partially within a sparsely set-

tled area must carry radio equipment capable of two-way communication with a ground station in the area where the aircraft is operated, or a portable emergency transmitter capable of operation on the ground independently of the aircraft battery and transmitting on a distress frequency or a frequency used by the RCAF for search and rescue purposes. A SARAH emergency radio is commonly used in Canada for this purpose, and in some areas can be rented by transient pilots.

In addition to the required radio equipment, pilots going into sparsely settled areas are required to carry five pounds of concentrated food for each person aboard, cooking utensils, waterproof matches, a portable compass, an ax, 30 feet of snare wire, a knife, fishing equipment and mosquito nets

Terminal of the Calgary Airport, Alberta. The Calgary Stampede is reported to be an exciting event for American visitors. Be sure to get advance reservations.

in the summer. Furthermore, in the wintertime, tents, sleeping bags and snowshoes must be carried. Flights within 25 miles of an airport or operating base and multi-engine flights within controlled airspace are exempt from the emergency equipment rule. It has been said that the best survival equipment you can carry for flight in the Canadian North is an Eskimo. Lacking such a companion, you'd better carry plenty of man-made survival gear.

For flight within a sparsely settled area, a flight plan or flight notification must be filed with an air traffic control unit or, if communications facilities are inadequate, with a responsible person.

There is a vast amount of unbelievably wild country in Canada, especially if you head very far north of the border. Visiting pilots should carry along a healthy respect for the wilderness. As much as possible, it is well to stick to established airways and never head off without letting someone know where you are going. Flight over lake country, with one lake looking pretty much like

every other, can be especially confusing, and there are some regions where you'll do best to park your wheelplane and go on by chartered floatplane. If you're flying on floats yourself, there are wonderful areas of water flying for you to enjoy. Whether you're on wheels or floats, there are some places where it is inadvisable for you to fly. Before starting into any primitive area, make sure your plane is in top condition and seek the advice of experienced local pilots.

Navigation. The farther north you fly, the less reliable your magnetic compass becomes. There is greater lead on southerly turns and lag on northerly turns, and the northern regions of Canada have rightly been designated as regions of compass unreliability. A directional gyro is a must for northern flights, and an ADF is extremely valuable. Although Canada has proportionately more low frequency ranges than does the United States, many of the ranges are being converted to nondirectional beacons. In many places the ADF is the only radio navigational aid of any value. The Canadian omni network is rapidly expanding, but is limited mainly to the southern part of Canada. If you're heading north, an ADF will be indispensable.

Customs And Border Crossing Formalities. The first landing in Canada must be at an airport where Customs service is available. Of the many Customs airports in Canada, 40, located at the principal cities of Canada, are authorized to receive Customs notification through pilot flight plans. The pilot need only include on his flight plan a request for notification of Canadian Customs and Immigration at these points and tell the number of persons aboard. Customs will be notified through the Canadian airport tower or range station. If landing is to be made at any other Customs Airport of Entry, advance notice must be sent to the Customs officials by telephone, telegram or letter. Pilots flying to Canada by seaplane may, after proper notification, land at any place where Customs is available for boats. This includes numerous places along the St. Lawrence and Great Lakes.

There are no exorbitant charges for crossing into Canada after regular Customs hours or on weekends as there are in the United States. For off-duty periods a special service charge of $2.50 an hour or portion thereof, with a minimum payment of $5, may be levied at some airports after 5 p.m. or on Sundays, and you may be required to pay for transportation of the Customs officer if he must make a special trip to the airport. If there are any extra charges, however, you will be surprised at how reasonable they are. Twenty-four-hour Customs service is avail-

and procedures. If you fly into Canada frequently and wish to get a more permanent Canadian pilot license, it is necessary to take the same written and flight tests as Canadian pilots, since there is no reciprocal agreement on licensing between the two countries. The private flight test (but not the written) is sometimes waived for a U.S. commercial pilot seeking a private license.

Money. The comparative value of U.S. and Canadian currency varies from day to day. At time of writing the rate is approximately 7% in favor of U.S. currency (that is, $1 Canadian is 92¢ American). While this extra credit will usually be given if you offer U.S. currency for Canadian purchases, you will find it much more convenient to change your money at a bank and to carry Canadian currency in that country.

with some adjoining Canadian charts, you may find a slight discrepancy in making them fit. The reason is that Canadian charts are in the process of being converted from the old eight miles per inch to the 1:500,000 scale and from 16 miles per inch to the 1:1,000,000 scale. The small discrepancy in matching charts won't bother your navigation, but may make you wonder.

Various Canadian provinces publish their own aeronautical charts, which are available free of charge (Ontario, British Columbia, Alberta, Manitoba, etc.). Write COPA if you wish any of these charts. You may also write COPA for free copies of any Air Regulations that you are concerned about.

Subscribers to Jeppesen Service who fly frequently into Canada will do well to extend their subscriptions to include Canadian coverage. For a single trip, Jeppesen will supply a subscriber with complimentary charts for the approximate area.

The Canada Air Pilot, issued by the Surveyor General, Surveys and Mapping Branch, Department of Mines and Technical Surveys at 615 Booth Street, Ottawa, Ontario, contains a description of all major land airports in Canada as well as instrument approach procedures. It comes in two volumes, East and West, priced initially at $7.50 apiece including one year of amendment service ($4 yearly amendment charge thereafter). Enroute-Low Altitude Radio Navigation Charts are available from the same source at 25¢ each or an annual subscription rate of $1.50 per sheet (six sheets to cover the country).

Two useful publications, the Water Aerodrome Supplement, containing information about seaplane bases in Canada, and the Airport and Aerodrome Directory Supplement, are issued annually at prices of $1 and 75¢, respectively. These may also be obtained from the above address. Mail orders must be accompanied by a check or a money order payable to Receiver General of Canada.

The RCN/RCAF FLIP Enroute Supplement, Canada and North Atlantic costs $5 per year subscription and is available from Queen's Printer, Publications Branch, Ottawa, Canada. Order direct.

The AOPA Flight Department will assist members in flight planning a Canadian trip, and the AOPA Flight Report on Canada is available. While you are in Canada, the Canadian Owners and Pilots Association extends a friendly hand to visiting pilots. They can be reached at the above-mentioned mail address or, if you're in a hurry, phone Ottawa, CE 6-4901. Bill Peppler, COPA manager, runs an extremely efficient and helpful organization. The Information and Publications Section, Civil Aviation Branch, Air Services, Department of Transport, Ottawa, will also on request supply free copies of Canadian Air Regulations and a useful booklet, Admission Of Aircraft To Canada. The Canadian Government Travel Bureau, Ottawa, offers a gold mine of information about vacation and travel facilities in any area of Canada.

Canada is a land of infinite variety, and each region has its special charm — from the beautiful Vancouver area to the picturesque Maritime Provinces, from the historic sights of Quebec City to the primitive regions of the Canadian wilderness. Whatever your tastes, you will find a rewarding experience when you visit our friendly neighbor to the north. ◆

Air service at a buffalo-hunting camp in the Fort Smith area of Canada's Northwest Territories.

PHOTOS BY CANADIAN GOVERNMENT TRAVEL BUREAU

able at Edmonton, Montreal, Saskatoon, Toronto, Vancouver and Winnipeg. Service from 0800 to 2400 is available at London, Ottawa and Victoria.

Be sure to have with you your pilot certificate, Certificate of Airworthiness and aircraft logbooks when crossing the border, and file a flight plan for all transborder flights.

Cruising Permit. If you are flying a U.S.-registered aircraft which is to be used for purposes of health or pleasure only, and not for trade or profit, you will receive a cruising permit for a period not exceeding three months. Unless goods which require documentary control are being carried on the outward flight, if you have a valid cruising permit, you need not report to Customs at time of departing Canada.

Pilot Certificate. A valid U.S. pilot certificate is all that is necessary to fly U.S.-registered aircraft in Canada. If you wish to fly Canadian-registered aircraft, you can obtain a Temporary Private Pilot Permit (Tourist) by taking a written examination on the Air Regulations and air traffic rules

Gasoline Taxes. You may save a bit on your trip by making application for fuel tax refund. U.S. flying tourists should consult with fuel vendors at the points where they purchase their fuel. Taxes vary from province to province, and the vendor can give guidance about tax refunds. Incidentally, if Canadian gasoline prices seem high, remember that you are getting an imperial gallon, which contains 20% more than an American gallon.

Charts And Publications. U.S.-issued Sectional and WAC charts are available for all areas of Canada and can be obtained from the AOPA Chart Department. Similar charts issued by the Canadian government can be ordered from the Canadian Owners and Pilots Association, Box 734, Ottawa, Ontario. COPA offers one-day service versus a much longer time for charts ordered direct from the Canadian government. Since Canadian charts cost 50¢ each, it is cheaper to buy U.S. charts for the desired area before the flight if possible. In matching some Canadian charts with American charts or

NEW
BRUNSWICK

By MATILDA J. METCALF | AOPA 256817

Since my husband wrote his report for AOPA members entitled "Places to Fly: The National Parks" (three parts, December 1963 and January and February 1964), a lot of land and water have passed under our wings. We reluctantly traded off our faithful Cessna N5771A. In her place we now fly N2666U, a trim red and white *Skyhawk* which has taken us as far south as the island of Antigua in the West Indies.

Our agent asked us to fly to Fredericton, New Brunswick, Canada, to give a travelogue lecture. This presentation was to be the first of a series of such travel film lectures to be given each year in Fredericton, Moncton, St. John and other towns in the province.

We were familiar with nearby Nova Scotia because of having filmed there for a four-month period, but our acquaintance with New Brunswick had been limited to a hasty trip down the coast of the Bay of Fundy on a gray, foggy, miserable drive. This upcoming trip was to open our eyes to the charm and beauty of the province.

Our home airport at Dowagiac, Mich., might well be substituted for any departure point in the United States, but since Detroit and Windsor, Canada, Customs personnel are old friends, we chose to enter Canada there. Besides, it was directly on the route we had planned.

Knowing that we would have tail winds for some time, we started early in the morning, hoping to go all the way in only one day. If that proved impossible, we intended to go as far as weather and daylight permitted. Our flight to Windsor was routine, and we landed for Customs in the usual gusty conditions normal at their airport. Customs procedures are quick and pleasant, although we always have the added chore of listing serial numbers of our professional equipment, such as tape recorder, projector, etc., that we take along to present our lecture program. Planes entering Canada can often save much time by listing make, model and serial numbers of such equipment in advance, and the Customs men simply copy these down on the appropriate form.

When airborne again, we skirted over the southeastern corner of Lake St. Clair to London VOR, overflying it and Toronto's International Airport. Both these locations have fine general aviation facilities, should you wish to make a leisurely stopover. Lunch is served at Toronto's beautiful terminal building.

Crossing over Toronto's VOR, our route was Victor 98 to Sterling VOR. After leaving Toronto, the landscape gradually changed from level, cultivated farms to light rolling and forested terrain which seemed to be about 50% lakes and rivers. We were surprised to learn that many of the aforementioned farms turned out to be tobacco farms! We never imagined that tobacco could be grown in southern Ontario.

From Sterling we proceeded toward Massina VOR. Off to our right we could see the St. Lawrence River snaking its way north-eastward, and on checking the Burlington Sectional chart, I saw that the famous Thousand Islands lay in the river directly south of Victor 98. Never having seen them, I begged Jim to leave our course and overfly them. It was well worth the few extra minutes, for, since it was spring, they were alive with bright new greenery. I have heard that many of these small islands are for sale, and I want to go back there sometime. There is a small airport — Paddock — on the U.S. side of the river and it would be very easy to do. Imagine owning your own island!

We followed the St. Lawrence to Massina, which is five miles south of the U.S. border, and continued along Victor 98. We knew that from Massina VOR on to Fredericton, New Brunswick, our route would be a fairly straight and well-ordered one, but a glance at the air charts showed we would be in and out of the United States and Canada airspace because of the irregularities and twistings of the border between the two countries. Since we had already cleared into Canada, we could overfly the United States at any point along the border, but we could land only in Canada if we wished to remain legal with Customs authorities of both countries!

Because of tail winds and good fuel management, we made our first gas stop, since leaving home, at St. Jean, just south of Montreal. We could see that great city to the north as we "finaled" at St. Johns Municipal Airport, St. Jean, and remarked that we'd take a closer look at it on our return trip. We taxied up to the office as a gentleman in Customs uniform pedaled up on a bicycle. We were required to fill out some papers and have those in our possession inspected, and then we were asked to pay 50¢ — no doubt the equivalent of our U.S. landing fee. Tiny St. Johns was the only place where such a "user tax" was collected.

Gas was obtained there, after which Jim asked me to remain with the plane: a strange aircraft was apparently a novelty for a few Sunday airport visitors at St. Johns. A dozen or so French-speaking civilians had gathered and busily poked, wiggled, turned, and pushed and pulled controls inside and outside the plane until Jim locked the cabin and left me to do police duty outside! After paying for our petrol we departed, east and slightly north on Victor 300N to Sherbrooke VOR (113.2).

Millinocket VOR is in the state of Maine, and keeping to a heading of 104° takes the pilot across some interesting but primitive country. Megantic Mountain rises almost 3,700 feet, and beyond it Lake Megantic sprawls northward with great areas of marshland running to the south. At about 3,500 feet we blithely flew over once more an unseen U.S.-Canadian border. Incidentally, that border is part of the longest undefended international border in the world. There isn't a gun emplacement or fortress on any of it, a fact that we and our Canadian friends can be proud of!

We now thought it advisable to climb up for greater altitude in case of emergency, for airstrips are few and far between across this part of Maine. Our route led us on across the southern tip of great Moosehead Lake where we noted both a seaplane base and a 3,000-foot hardtop strip located near the resorts. We commented that had we the time, and proper Customs clearance, this too would be an enjoyable stopover. But on we

Overflying Fredericton, New Brunswick, the capital of New Brunswick. This city is the cultural center, the industrial leader and the educational hub for eastern Canada.

LEFT: St. John Harbour. Arriving over the city of St. John, the Metcalfs looked across the Bay of Fundy and could see the distant shore of Nova Scotia.

flew; and, for the next 50 miles, roads of any description were nonexistent, as were signs of human habitation. On rare occasions we saw a dwelling near a lake's edge far below, and we could only conclude that such establishments were reached either by packing-in or by floatplane.

Reaching Millinocket VOR, we gently swung a little north to 97°. This would take us directly to Fredericton VOR, 103 miles farther on. The balance of the trip was uneventful, and the terrain below gradually changed from wilderness forest to small cleared fields and then to larger cleared provincial farms.

The airport at Fredericton is large, but is mainly devoted to Trans-Canada and other commercial and military traffic. The tower, weather and other government people were wonderful and friendly. A brand-new terminal building was under construction when we were there and is now open to the public. Since the airport is 12 miles southeast of town, a taxi has to be hired (we paid $3.50 per head) unless the private flyer is lucky enough to have his arrival coincide with that of a commercial flight, at which times there is limousine service.

The ride into Fredericton is very pleasant, and we were quite surprised to learn how ignorant we were of this corner of our continent. To begin with, Fredericton is the capital of the province. It is the cultural center, the industrial leader and the educational hub for eastern Canada, for it is the home of the University of New Brunswick. The town itself reminded us of our Michigan towns of like population, the midtown section having shops, markets and services comparable to any in the United States. Government buildings, park areas and streets are shaded with hundreds of great elm trees. The St. John River, largest in the province, forms a majestic watery highway which rolls past Fredericton to the mighty Bay of Fundy and the Atlantic.

Three buildings in the town interested us most. They are all named after the same man, the renowned Lord Beaverbrook. A well-run hotel, a modern art museum and the new Playhouse all bear the name of this distinguished New Brunswickian and were gifts from the great man. The Playhouse, where the future travelogue lectures were to be presented, was a fabulous building outfitted with the newest electronic theatrical equipment — a building in which it is a great joy to present a program.

The morning after our presentation we were held up in our departure from the Fredericton Airport due to mist and fog, for which the Maritime Provinces of Canada are famous. It was 12:30 p.m. before we could legally depart, but the ceiling was rapidly rising and the white, steamy ball of the sun worked diligently to burn away the dissipating mists.

We had decided to take another more scenic route home, first traveling southeast following the serpentine St. John River to the Bay of Fundy, a distance of about 50 air miles. It is Saint John, the second largest city in the province, that the visiting pilot from the eastern United States would use as a port of entry to New Brunswick. Arriving over that city, we looked across the Bay of Fundy to the distant shore of Nova Scotia. The bay, which regularly has the highest tides in the world (58 feet) was at low ebb,

The terminal of the Fredericton Airport.

The Playhouse at Fredericton, where the Metcalf's travelogue lectures were presented. Equipped with the newest electronic theatrical equipment, the Playhouse was a gift to Fredericton from Lord Beaverbrook.

PHOTOS BY NEW BRUNSWICK TRAVEL BUREAU

and the vista of great stranded ships, mud flats and mist made a most impressive scene.

Turning northwestward, we retraced our flight from Fredericton, arriving back over the city in about 22 minutes. From there we intended to continue following the St. John River west and northward to the St. Lawrence River.

The valley of the St. John is most beautiful and is dotted with frugal fields and farms of old world French flavor. Bridges were few, but ferry crossings along the river were many. Airstrips were also in short supply. Occasionally, a short, newly bulldozed strip lay along the river, used by commercial sprayers controlling the diseases of the Canadian forests.

At an altitude of 2,000 feet our plane purred like a contented kitten up the St. John Valley past Meductic, Peel, Maliseet, Aroostook, and St. Leonard, over which we could look back out of our Cessna's "greenhouse window" to Loring Air Force Base. The active runway was directly behind us, and we watched the great jets climb out toward us and then rise up and over our tiny plane long before they came up with us.

Loring is the northernmost Air Force Base in the eastern United States, and on it is also the northernmost omni in the eastern United States. Here, along the St. John River, we once again met up with that U.S.-Canadian boundary.

Although it is not shown on the air charts, there is a good airstrip at Edmundston (still in New Brunswick). It is the property of timber interests. Over the town itself we turned to 330°, leaving the course of the St. John River to follow instead the Madawaska. This smaller stream, and a hardtop road below, led us to 15-mile-long Lac Temiscouata, which we skirted to the west, coming thus upon the towns of Cabano and St. Louis du Ha Ha. All along our route from Edmundston to the St. Lawrence, sawmills and great rafts of timber were testimonials to New Brunswick's forest wealth.

For the pilot who might not wish to "rubberneck" and follow rivers and roads as we did, there is Riviere du Loup radio for navigation. The town of Riviere du Loup lies along the shore of the St. Lawrence, and it is here, if the visitor would care to extend his visit to the provinces, that you could fly

St. John, New Brunswick, Canada, as seen from Kings Square. It is St. John, the second largest city in the province of New Brunswick, that the visiting pilot from the eastern United States would use as a port of entry to New Brunswick.

northeast to follow the coast line of the Gaspé Peninsula to the town of Gaspé itself. The scenic beauties of the peninsula's French countryside and Gaspé Park's 4,160-foot Mount Cartier peak are a pleasant introduction to Quebec Province. Instead of turning northeast to the Gaspé country, we swung to the southwest heading of 250° to follow the St. Lawrence River to where it narrows and meets the heights of Quebec.

Here we stopped at Ancienne Lorette, Quebec City's airport. The pilot can almost imagine himself in Paris because French is the predominant language of the province. However, there are no language problems, for aircraft information personnel are bilingual. Beautiful Quebec should be a stopover when in this part of the world, but take along some tiedowns, as the man who gassed us told us that the airport had none for small planes! This we found hard to believe but didn't have time to pursue the point.

It is hardly necessary to advise the overnight visitor to Quebec that lodgings are readily available and fine food can be had practically anywhere, there being many restaurants, large and small, to choose from.

Exploration of Quebec's old city is the great outdoor sport for the tourist.

After our stopover in Quebec, we again took off in bright VFR conditions, although weather forecasts predicted a "low" moving across Lake Michigan and Detroit, directly on our route. We hoped we might beat it.

Again following the St. Lawrence River southwestward, we flew over locks, dams, the city of Montreal, and at Kingston, Ontario, kept to the north shore of Lake Ontario. At Kingston the atmosphere became hazy and, as we proceeded westward, it worsened, so we advised Toronto tower of our decision to terminate our flight at Toronto International. We were so intent on our approach, which was that given us by approach control, that it was not until we were coming "over the fence" that we noticed we were not at the right airport! Through the haze we could see far too many aircraft, all with the letters RCAF on their sides. Gunning the motor, we quickly advised Toronto that we had just missed landing on Downsview, the Royal Canadian Air Force Base, five miles east of Toronto International. The answering voice matter-of-factly replied,

"Join the club. You're the fourth one this week, and one of those was a commercial flight!" With red faces, we proceeded on to International, landing not a "front" too soon, for the visibility dropped to less than a mile as we taxied to Field Aviation, which, by the way, has excellent facilities.

Being grounded is sometimes a dreary, weary situation; but on the ramp next to us, unloading their *Bonanza* N513R, we met Juanita and Ollie Sturdy (AOPA 143189) of Fort Worth, Tex. They very kindly offered to share their rental car, so the four of us joined forces to get a motel, dine, and spend a most pleasant time together at Toronto.

It was two days before our front of thick fog, thunderstorms and low ceilings moved on enough to let us squeeze under and move west to clear skies and Windsor, our port of exit. There our friendly Canadian Customs man greeted us by remarking "You're a few days late!"

During our "late" trip we had flown safely and in a leisurely manner for 2,360 miles and had thoroughly enjoyed visiting a wee corner of France in America as well as our Canadian neighbors of New Brunswick. ◆

Being a fisherman first and a physician second during the past 25 years has led to a constant conflict between fly rods and stethoscopes. My father, having been an avid fisherman and also a doctor, found the answer by being a full-time teacher in a medical school and thus was able to be off most of each summer to cast, troll, and fly-fish to his heart's content. When his son was only seven, he was introduced to a fly rod and, until the demands of college, medical school and residency training made it impossible, the son spent hundreds of hours wading the streams of Michigan.

After father became a pediatrician and added a family, trips to the cabin in northern Michigan and its many trout streams came on a once-a-year basis. The first two children being girls was no real disadvantage, since they had no chance to discover that vacations consisted of anything other than trout fishing. A private trout club membership in northern Ohio sharpened the whole family's fly-fishing techniques but never took the place of wild stream fishing in Dad's heart.

The years rolled on and a son arrived who at six was started with the family rods and was soon wading with Dad on the yearly trips. But the years and the superhighways were rapidly more than Michigan trout could stand, in spite of the valiant efforts of the Michigan Conservation Department. The long drive to Mason and Lake Counties in Michigan, from Columbus, O., became more and more unproductive of trout.

Then came the airplane. Until 1958, Dad's idea of planes consisted of an occasional commercial flight to a medical convention or a quick trip to New York with Mom. Anyone who flew his own small plane was either nuts or an old fighter pilot or both. Then came the awakening. The local Piper distributor was touted on the unsuspecting doctor by a Michigan fishing companion who just happened to manufacture airplane instruments. The phone call came: "Ace Cockrill told me to call you and tell you that fishing is lots closer by air than by road." It came at a weak moment; Mom and the kids were in Michigan and Dad was sweating out the family income in 100° August weather. "At least come out and let us take you for a ride — free," sounded innocent enough. So out he went and up he went — first being introduced to the pilot, Ray Jayjohn (AOPA 129146), but not being told he was to be his instructor for the next year. Then the greatest selling job on record started. Being completely innocent of flying anything but a kite (and it doesn't have front seats), he didn't know most planes are flown from the left front seat. He was introduced to *Tri-Pacer* 9308D and told to climb over into the left seat. This seemed like a normal precaution, for the pilot to sit nearest the door, so he could depart first when something fell off in the air. However, close inspection of the interior failed to turn up any parachutes, so it was assumed they were under the seats as life-jackets are in most boats.

After being shown how to "look over" an airplane (it looked smaller each time around), the passenger was allowed to set the brakes, call out "clear" and start the motor. Steering with the feet was explained. Some unintelligible jargon was exchanged by the pilot with some unseen person named Roger. Suddenly we were rolling grandly down a runway and the right seat was calmly telling the left seat to pull back gently on the wheel. A question quickly arose: "Who is flying this thing?" "You are; look out the side window" — and there was the ground falling away under the wing. Several careful turns and a landing later, Dad was as completely hooked as a trout on a worm.

Many hours stolen from a busy medical practice later (and after enough turns to have added up to at least 111,000°) came the solo. These hours were many and varied and old Jayjohn became more and more of a perfectionistic grandfather as they progressed. The middle-aged student was soon black and blue from elbow to shoulder on the right arm where the elbow of the instructor was constantly nudging him, pointing out such things as: airplanes fly better if the wings are level, and you get places

FISHING FOR FUN

Doctor solves conflict between rods and stethoscopes by learning to fly

By MINER W. SEYMOUR | *AOPA 174467*

more quickly if the altitude is maintained within 1,000 feet rather than porpoising up and down constantly. Landing soon became fun after a few caustic remarks such as, "That would have been a good landing, if the runway had been in a 10-foot ditch"; "That is a good flare-out, but how do I get out of the plane? I didn't bring a ladder!" Several times the student nearly gave up, especially when it came to something called "short-field emergency landings." It was soon obvious that this middle-aged student couldn't comprehend the approach necessary to accomplish one satisfactorily.

Then, suddenly, it was solo day. After 40 minutes of "touch and goes" with Jayjohn, each landing of which was obviously much worse than the one before, a full stop was finally accomplished. Open went the door and out climbed the instructor. "I'm afraid to ride with you any more. So take it around by yourself three or four times. I'll be standing beside the approach end of the runway, and it would be nice if you look at me as you come in; if I have fainted, go around — you're probably too high or too low. See you later." Having no time to review my insurance program and my many responsibilities, suddenly I was roaring down the runway. Two things quickly became apparent: an airplane is lighter with only one in the front seat, and, second, at 150 feet it is very lonely. Lots of solo hours later,

Dad made a solo cross-country to Michigan (complete with tackle box and rod), where he made a passable landing, only to be promptly deflated when the field operator approached him and said "Do you want your logbook signed?" "How did you know I was a student?" said the pilot. "Pretty easy, because most pilots don't circle the field three times before entering the landing pattern and landing."

Dad was told several times, "You will probably get lost before you have flown very far." This seemed like a ridiculous statement to a professional man with a college education who had lived in central Ohio all his life. However, on a nice sunny day coming down from Lake Erie to Columbus, suddenly all the towns began to look alike. There are probably 50 towns in northern Ohio which have a railroad going in the east end and coming out the west end which are equipped with a white church and a grain elevator. But by persistently sitting still and holding a shaky heading, suddenly the reservoir north of the airport appeared right where it should, even though the student was convinced he had departed Ohio and was somewhere over Kansas by that time.

A written exam and a flight test soon were accomplished, and Dad had a brand-new, shiny private pilot license. It was three years before Mom would accept the fact that Dad probably could wrestle the airplane into the

air and back on the ground without maiming or destroying the passengers. It was soon obvious (as I am sure the Piper agency knew) that if you are going to fly, you are going to need an airplane in which to fly. So the old training *Tri-Pacer* became the official property of Dad. After several trips to Michigan to fish, which were delightful in that Dad could go for a weekend of fishing and come home to the office on Monday, it was soon apparent that one more passenger or one more piece of luggage always seemed to want to go on the trips. So more lift was needed. The natural progression followed: the *Tri-Pacer* was traded in on a *Comanche 180* and one year later the 180 grew up to a 250, which was completely IFR equipped. Jayjohn was back in the right front seat and we were off to try for an instrument ticket. The friendly little dials on the dashboard that were so easy to keep lined while VFR soon became very unruly, and it was quite obvious to the student that, while he could keep any three of them lined perfectly, one always wanted to sneak off someplace by itself.

For the past few years, fishing has again become a way of life. Dad and son are off at any opportunity to fish any place within 800 miles of Columbus, O. A whole new horizon of fishing possibilities rapidly appeared. It is well known to all fishermen that, under present-day circumstances, any

The Seymour's camp on Opichuan River, northern Ontario, Canada. Since Dr. Seymour got his pilot's license, he and his son are off at any opportunity to fish anyplace within 800 miles of Columbus, O.

place there is a road there are now no fish. The *Comanche* released us from the need of fishing next to roads, and most of our expeditions are now into Canada. After a series of trials of the areas from the Laurentides Park in the east through Sudbury, Northbay, and Sault Ste. Marie, finally the ideal fishing was found.

Superior Airways with headquarters on the Lakehead Airport at Ft. William, Ontario, was discovered, along with its extremely friendly manager, Jack Cameron. Superior has floatplanes scattered across Canada, north of Ft. William, and for reasonable rates will take you into streams and lakes that are rarely, if ever, fished.

The pattern is now complete. We fly the *Comanche* by way of Traverse City, Marquette, and Houghton, Mich., across Lake Superior over Isle Royale and land at Lakehead. Customs is quickly cleared, and straight north to Armstrong we go. Armstrong on the Canadian National Railway has no access by road but has a beautiful, two-hardtop-runway airport. Its homer leads you along the west shore of Lake Nipigon over the beautiful wild Canadian lakes and forests. Two large hangars previously used by the Canadian Air Force are now, for all practical purposes, abandoned, and the custodian is only too glad to store the plane in one of them. A most friendly weather and flight service man is on duty during the daylight hours.

Superior Airways picks us up by truck and takes us 10 miles to Lake McKenzie where they have two floatplanes stationed. A one-hour flight north from Armstrong in the floatplane deposits us on the Opichuan River, a tributary of the Albany, which flows into the Hudson Bay. Fishing there is fast and furious. The variety is exceptional. Brook trout, up to six pounds, are caught on fly rods. Walleye and large northern come easily in the lakes connected by this stream, and in the spring whitefish can be caught at up to six or seven pounds on dryflies in the fast water. A small tent, sleeping bags, dried food and the fishing accessories needed come to about 100 pounds.

On the day appointed to depart, we are picked up promptly soon after daylight and we return to the floatplane dock at Armstrong, truck again to our airplane, take off and depart for the United States. With about seven hours' flying time including a gas stop, Columbus is reached well before dark. Entering and leaving Canada is now much easier than it was originally. Now it is unnecessary, on a private flight, to check out of the United States; however, it is, of course, mandatory that a flight plan be filed to enter Canada. Requesting Customs on this flight plan insures the Customs man's meeting the flight at Ft. William. He now gives you a "cruise and depart" certificate which makes it unnecessary to check with Customs again on leaving Canada. Of course, on departure it is again necessary to file a flight plan (which is easily done at Armstrong) to cross into the United States. Houghton, Mich., on the tip of the upper peninsula, with an excellent airport, has Customs service from 8 a.m. to 5 p.m. each weekday. The man who gasses your plane goes back into the building and comes back with a Customs hat and makes out a Customs clearance. The charge is a minimal $2. Not being able to quite stretch the *Comanche* from Houghton to Columbus, a further gas stop is usually made at either Traverse City or Jackson, Mich.

The whole new concept of "getting away from it all" has been possible only by air. The family now is well addicted to flying. Mom now rides, somewhat reluctantly but without any backseat comments. Of course, the amateur doctor-pilot has made all the usual amateur mistakes in an airplane, but certainly, after now over a thousand hours, respects weather and his own limitations, perhaps more than he did at 200 hours. He has certainly adapted to the 180° and the "get the hell out of here" approach to weather. Several nights have been spent in towns not on the original flight plans, but never has weather been a problem as long as this respect has been maintained.

So, to all fishermen, this advice is given: if you really want to fish, learn to fly. ◆

Superior Airways Otter — a real load carrier which took six people and all their gear out in one trip. After a one-hour flight north from Armstrong, Ontario, the fishermen reached the Opichuan River, a tributary of the Albany, which flows into the Hudson Bay. Fishing there is fast and furious.

Dr. Seymour's son helps with the preflight check of the Comanche 250. The Seymours graduated from a Tri-Pacer to a Comanche 180 and then to a 250 as more passengers wanted to go on their fishing trips.

PHOTOS BY THE AUTHOR

The Seymours unload at their camp site.

*The Kenora area of Ontario, Canada,
promises to gladden the hearts of all but the unluckiest
of fishermen. Two camps are described*

FLY TO THE FINEST FISHING

*Grassy Lodge as seen from the lake. The area around Grassy Lodge consists of dozens of lakes and islands, and
there are hundreds of miles of shore line.*

Dr. W. R. Washick (AOPA 58054) of Kuttawa, Ky., caught this lake trout on one of his trips to Grassy Lodge. He flew the Seabee to the lodge, landed on the lake, put the wheels down, and pulled up to the sloping rock in front of the main lodge.

The Ontario Department of Tourism and Information claims that the fisherman's luck would have to be inordinately bad for him to leave the fishing waters of the Kenora area empty handed. Between 30,000 and 40,000 lakes dot this wilderness region 1,250 miles northwest of Toronto, and the larger ones are reported to teem with the "fightingest" game fish to be found anywhere in Canada. The walleye is king in this region. Great northern pike, lake trout that run to 50 pounds, kingsize smallmouth black bass, muskellunge and whitefish also abound.

Flying visitors have their choice of sliding their boats into the Lake Of The Woods, a 1,000-square-mile body of water dotted with thousands of islands, or going to one of the many fly-in camps reached from Kenora. Detailed rundowns on two of these camps follow. Kenora itself, a frontier town which typifies Ontario's romantic northland, boasts four good hotels, each with its own cocktail bar and live entertainment, and a dozen motels on its outskirts.

GRASSY LODGE

Grassy Lodge, 31 air miles northeast of Kenora, claims "the best in fly-in fishing and hunting." George Hohnstein, Jr. (AOPA 128568), owner, also says that a few guests "come just for rest and relaxation, to get away from it all."

The closest airfield, Kenora Airport, is an airport of entry with Customs for tourists only. Services available are 80/87 and 100/130 fuel; 80, 100 and 120 oil; weather information by continuous MET teletype service, and lights. You have to bring your own tiedowns. From the airport, one can take a taxi to the Second Street dock in downtown Kenora, where flights (on floats) to Grassy Lodge originate. The exact location of Grassy Lodge is shown on WAC

Chart 219 (it is listed as Grassy Narrows).

The area around Grassy Lodge consists of dozens of lakes and islands, and there are hundreds of miles of shore line. The fishing and hunting "menu" at Grassy Lodge is as follows.

Lake trout are near the surface in May and early June and move into deeper water as the weather becomes warmer, moving back into shallow water late in September. Northern pike can be caught throughout the season and are reported to be particularly good in July and August. The season on bass and walleye opens around May 15. Walleye are reportedly especially good in July and August. Muskie season runs about June 20 to Oct. 15. Spring bear season runs approximately from April 1 to June 15. Fall bear season opens about Sept. 15, as does the season on duck and partridge. The season on moose and deer opens about Oct. 1.

Grassy Lodge provides experienced guides who can take the fisherman or hunter to more than half a dozen lakes without portaging as well as to a number of others with a short portage. Boats are kept on the lakes at all times.

Evening activities for guests include croquet, badminton, volleyball and horseshoes.

Accommodations at Grassy Lodge are rooms on the second floor of the main lodge and in modern cabins. (Check for 10% discount to AOPA members on daily rates.)

A freezer keeps fish and game fresh until guests depart.

Grassy Lodge opens about May 15 and closes about Oct. 20. Winter address for the lodge is George Hohnstein, P.O. Box 195, Trumbull, Neb. 68980; phone (402) 743-2351. Address at the lodge is P.O. Box 265, Kenora, Ontario, Canada; phone (through long-distance operator only) (807) Grassy Narrows 1-4402.

CAT ISLAND LODGE

Jack Mitchell's Cat Island Lodge on Trout Lake, 22 air miles northeast of Red Lake, Ontario, claims to have excellent fishing and hunting.

Red Lake Airport at Cochenour, 93 statute miles north-northwest of Kenora, is the closest field. After arrival at Red Lake, arrangements can be made with Holiday Airways to fly directly to Cat Island Lodge. Services available at Red Lake Airport, which has a 4,000-foot gravel runway, are 80/87 and 100/130 fuel, 80 and 100 oil, and telephone at field. You have to bring your own tiedowns. Snow is compacted on the field in winter. Lighting is available on a one-hour request. There is also a nondirectional beacon. To reach the airport, you can phone Cochenour 2581 from 8 a.m. to 5 p.m.; other times, phone Cochenour 3171.

Trout Lake has about 400 square miles of water and hundreds of miles of shore line, with 142 islands, reefs and bays. Walleye (season begins about May 15) and northern pike (no closed season) are plentiful. For those who prefer lake trout, spring and late fall are best. Moose (Oct. 1), fall bear, duck, grouse (all Sept. 15) are reportedly plentiful. Deer (Oct. 1) can also be found, but in limited numbers.

Cat Island Lodge has facilities to accommodate 24 guests (make your reservations early) and provides boats and Indian guides. A cooler for storage of game is also available.

There is a recreation room for guests to use in the evening which has horseshoes, Ping-Pong and darts. There's a large sand beach for swimming in warm weather.

Winter address for Mitchell's Cat Island Lodge is c/o Jack B. Mitchell, 3 Central Avenue, West Carrolton, O. 45449; phone (513) 859-8451. After May 15, it is Red Lake 60, Ontario. ◆

By H. JACK BARTELS | AOPA 37153

A **W**ILDERNESS ADVENTURE

Author Bartels' rod seeks out Arctic char at remote Lake Tessioriak.

This trip to Quebec and Labrador in an amphibious aircraft could be an outdoorsman's dream; however, caution should be a byword when flying into the areas described

23

THE WAY OF AN EAGLE

She stood vacant off the ramp, like the empty shell of a chambered nautilus, beautifully formed but lifeless. She had always been beautiful, but had been lifeless for only a short time. It had happened after returning from a tryst with a wild, clear body of water, horizons away in Canada. When she had come back to the airport, as a gull coming back to its island, the pilot had reached out his hand, drawn back the mixture controls and slowly starved her into a shuddering death.

*This was predestined to be the pattern of her existence, yet she didn't really seem to mind. Conceived by aeronautical engineers, carefully formed and finished by skilled hands, she was named at birth after the migratory waterfowl—***Mallard.***

Now we were making ready to bring her back to life. The canvas covers were taken off the throat of her nacelles, tethers removed from her wings, controls unlocked. Ailerons and empennage once more free, flexed as idle forces played against them. One could almost hear her sigh as life again nuzzled her body, suggesting a new experience. This rendezvous would be with the George River, a brawling stream in the Ungava wilderness area of northern Quebec. It would be across the curve of the earth to a land of sparkling air and dazzling sunlight, a place for man and ship to be transposed into another short span of ecstasy.

by H. Jack Bartels

Beautifully formed — yes — but only temporarily lifeless. The Grumman Mallard used on this expedition to the far north wilderness rests at Lake Tessioriak where a party of adventurers has gone in quest of char.

Her tanks are topped with gas; oil to the full mark; men and baggage aboard to the fore and aft of her center of lift, weight and balance checked and within limits. Electrical systems on. Booster pumps on. Fuel mixtures rich. Starters engage, engines cough and gulp and life surges again through the entire body of the craft!

After a brief communication with ground control for taxi instructions, throttles are advanced slightly and the aircraft moves forward. At the approach end of the assigned runway we stop for the final, routine check of all systems. Controls are free, propeller pitch changes, magnetos, oil pressure, oil temperature, on and on. You fight back the tendency to glance at a gauge without really interpreting what it is reading. You check, double check and finally advise the tower you are ready to go.

You're cleared to the active runway. Excitement wells up, but you control it. Thoughts jump like drops of water on a hot skillet, marking an awareness of the welfare of your passengers back of you, who complacently accept the takeoff, the wind, its velocity, its direction. Throttles full forward now, mixtures full rich, propellers in low pitch, manifold pressure rising, the acceleration, propellers snarling and grabbing for the air ahead, the craft becoming light and then airborne.

The taboo which nature had so long exacted against man is again flaunted. The airport drops away like the shell of a chrysalis in the sunlight. We enter another existence. A long climb to our altitude and course is completed and our face is set toward the northeast. King Solomon was so right: "Three things are too wonderful; the way of a man with a maiden; the way of a serpent on a rock and the way of an eagle in the sky."

Our destination is approximately 1,800 miles distant — the northern tip of Labrador and Quebec, between the Bay of Ungava and the Labrador Sea. Passengers and baggage we are carrying are limiting factors with regard to the fuel we may take on. In order to stay within our gross weight limit, we may carry enough to provide us with a maximum range of approximately 1,000 miles — 800 miles with a margin of safety. Adequate airports are limited in that region, and this fact governs our decision as to where our fuel stops will be made. The first will be in the province of Quebec at the Quebec City Airport, four hours away.

At Quebec Airport we clear Customs and refuel. From here our course is north by northeast. As we proceed, we become more alert to corrections for compass variation which will increase to 38° westerly.

Schefferville, our next stop and the last airport on our way north, is 570 miles, three hours away. It is also the last ADF fix point, the last point to which we will navigate by an electronic device, the last landing where an instrument approach could be even remotely considered. Fortunately, the weather remains friendly, our navigation accurate and we arrive as scheduled.

The town of Schefferville is at the end of the railroad. It exists because of a huge iron ore deposit. The size and coloration of the stripped earth are mute testimony to the extent and richness of the lode. The sporadic fringe of slums is inhabited by the Indians who have drawn close to the material benefits of civilization.

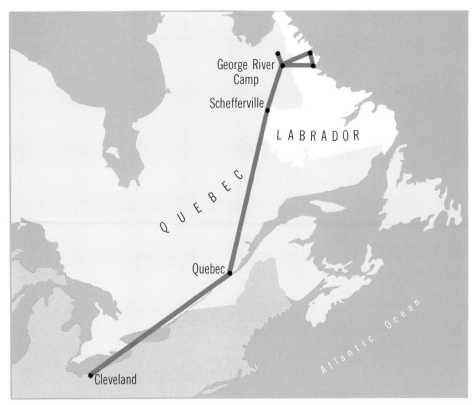

Route followed by these wilderness adventurers.

North from here 185 miles is our destination, the George River Camp. Navigation from this point must be a combination of pilotage and dead reckoning. It must be perfect also. The rolling terrain has changed in appearance from forest to tundra, with sparse stands of stunted spruce. The coloration has changed from an even shade of deep green to hues of light beige, grays and soft greens. Streams and chain lakes form a lacework pattern spreading to the horizon. Occasional eskers, bulldozed into being by glaciers ages ago, lie strung across the earth.

Now the charts state bleakly, "topographical information unreliable," which causes a fleeting sense of insecurity. Without compensating for vagaries of drift, we steer a compass course of 53° to make good a true heading of 15°. The sameness of the landmarks makes positive identification of position very difficult. We dare not let our eyes or minds wander and so we keep our charts before us constantly to pinpoint our position. Finally, the contour of the river ahead indicates that the camp, consisting of three log cabins, should be on the left bank of a large quiet area. We have found it and now circle to look over the water, noting the current, checking again the wind direction and mentally marking the dangerous shallows. When we are sure of that portion of that surface which we will use, we prepare for the water landing. The check list is gone through again with one important difference to remember — the landing gear stays *up*.

The bottom of the hull kisses the water softly, almost hesitantly. The spontaneous sigh of the meeting increases in a crescendo of rushing water and spray, then subsides. The plane wallows briefly, then settles, as it is transformed from aircraft to watercraft.

Ahead of the copilot's seat is a passageway through which he goes to the bow. A hatch is opened and lines are readied to be cast to those on shore who have come to assist. As

we approach slowly, the landing gear is lowered to protect the hull from the bottom and to afford more maneuverability to the craft. The lines are made fast, and a canoe is launched from shore to transport passengers and baggage. The crew secures the aircraft, then joins the others.

This is a severe land of great beauty and of many extremes. The weather changes constantly from sparkling sunshine to fog, then to rain and back again. It brings with it impressive rewards in the form of scintillating aurora borealis and brilliant rainbows.

Along the northern tip of the Labrador coast the brooding mountains stand up from the sea to heights of above 5,000 feet. With austere visage, they ignore the sea which extends inland between their feet to form quiet fiords. The blue depths of the water add breathtaking contrast. Even in August, shimmering icebergs on the sea and great snowdrifts cradled in the arms of the hills make it clear that winter is never really defeated here. It merely retreats a little to regroup its forces for another determined assault.

As we fly above, one can see water from melting snow increase its flow from trickle to brook to river. Occasionally it runs off the edge of a mountain and plunges a thousand feet to be dashed to spray on the rocks below. In this very sparsely populated land, one is impressed with the thought that some of the more remote rivers and lakes seen from the air haven't been visited by man since the beginning of history — possibly never.

Excepting for the upper reaches of the mountains, the surface of the land is carpeted with cream-colored reindeer moss and waist-high scrubby green bushes. Their colors blend subtly with the grays of the lichen which cover the rocks and boulders. Caribou trails, made clear and firm by annual migrations, are everywhere. Thousands upon thousands of these animals have recently passed through, leaving the usual very old or

very young stragglers. The wolves, always present, sometimes heard but seldom seen, are huge and well fed. Ptarmigan flush in large coveys from the heath. Their predominantly brown plumage shows patches of light gray when the birds are in flight, evidencing the beginning of the change to a camouflage of all white.

When we first arrived at the George River Camp, which was to be our base camp, one of the men who had assisted us in beaching the aircraft looked to us as though he had lived there for years. A red full beard covered his suntanned face; his hair had not been cut for months. The one thing that arrested my attention immediately was his perfect English. I surmised that it would be interesting to know more about him. As planning would have it, we sat on the same bench having dinner which was served direct from a wood burning iron stove. Our conversation revealed that his name was Bill Splake and that he was a professor of chemistry at one of the colleges in the states. With him was Wolfgang Streisand, a professor of sculpture associated with the same school.

These two had left Schefferville 49 days earlier and had arrived at this place the same day that we had. We had left one hour before. For transportation each had a Fiberglas kayak 15¾ feet long with a 38½-inch beam and a depth of 14 inches. They had traversed more than 360 miles of lakes and streams and had crossed two watersheds using only an aerial chart and a compass. One of the French Canadians and an Indian who knew something of that country said that, to their knowledge, seven men had been drowned during the past few years along that same waterway. When Splake was asked how he avoided being drawn into the many awesome whitewater rapids along the way, he said he carefully studied the apparent drop of the riverbed ahead, and more important still, he listened to the sound of the water. A

These large brook trout were taken from the George River. Sixteen miles of this river have been leased from the Canadian government, and a private camp is being run there.   PHOTOS BY THE AUTHOR

Bartels shows off his lake trout and proudly so. That was a 33-pounder.

THE AUTHOR

Jack Bartels' flying career began when he enlisted in the Air Corps during the war and has had, he said, "its periods of tears and smiles." Presently the pilot-owner of a Cessna Skyhawk, Bartels occasionally flies co-pilot on amphibious charter trips. Such trips allow him "splendid opportunities to hunt, fish and photograph in wilderness areas," he reported. For the past 17 years, Bartels has specialized in aircraft insurance.

floatplane picked up Streisand the next day; however, Splake remained determined to continue all the way north to Ungava Bay, a distance of another 130 miles.

Henri Culos, who operates the George River Camp, has leased 16 miles of the river from the Canadian government. They began taking parties four years ago, using tents for accommodations until recently. Now they have three log cabins and have added some of the more primitive comforts.

The Atlantic salmon begin to run up the rivers from the sea during the first week in August. Their numbers increase in the rivers until about the first week in September. When the number of salmon in the stream reaches its peak, the brook trout begin to move into smaller streams to spawn.

This section of the river is restricted to fly rods only, or to spinning lures with a single hook. Fishing with only a fly rod and with wet or dry flys, I took and released as many as 28 brook trout, salmon, char, lake trout and whitefish on one fly in one afternoon. The size ranged from two to 10 pounds. Others, fishing with spinning tackle, took lake trout up to a little more than 33 pounds. The camp records show that on Sept. 8, 1964, Tone Hounsel, a guest from New Hampshire, caught a salmon weighing 31 pounds, two ounces, and one which weighed 28 pounds. Both of these were taken with a fly rod.

Being adventuresome and wishing to see more of this country, we took off one morning in search of Lake Tessioriak. In the plane with us was "Smudge" Grant, who had flown his single-engine seaplane to the camp from his home in Bangor, Me. He had fished for char at the outlet of this lake the year before and had made some unbelievable claims about the place. The exact location was a little vague, but we narrowed it down to a place about 150 miles to the northeast along the Labrador coast. Finding one lake among hundreds just like it takes a little bit of doing.

Our charts showed a seaplane base in the general area and our first move was to locate this and to, perhaps, stop for fuel. We did

locate the place marked on the map. If there was ever a base there, it had been long abandoned, because no evidence existed that there had ever been anything there other than a place to land a seaplane. On an inlet from the sea, about 40 miles south of our position, the chart indicated a village called Nain. In wilderness areas one is always conscious of a diminishing fuel supply, so we headed there, hoping that some might be available.

Nain, as do most villages in this coastal area, lies inland several miles on the shore of a protecting fiord. Its population is Eskimoan; its industry is fishing. The men form small units of two or three, usually relatives, to a boat and are often away three or four weeks at a time. The boats principally in use were double ended and of lapstreak construction, approximately 20–25 feet in length. The engines were inboard. Toward the stern of these boats, in place of cabins, shelters were formed of canvas. Fish are taken in gill nets and cleaned immediately. We learned that the catch would vary greatly from year to year.

We were fortunate in that aviation fuel was available. Although it is not normally for sale, the villagers understood our need and many friendly hands helped to roll the drums out onto the wharf. We were unable to pay for it but were made to understand that, eventually, through proper government channels, we would receive a bill.

Within a 20-minute flight of Nain we found Lake Tessioriak. It was a lake of unbelievable beauty, a span of liquid sapphire surrounded by protecting black and green hills. Twice we came in low though the pass at the outlet to look over the surface, then landed. We had come for char and had found them. They were coming up through about a quarter of a mile of white water rapids to enter the lake. These were sea-run char. Their bodies were hard and firm and colored a light silver which darkened to include shades of light green and blue toward the dorsal section. In the same water were a great number of brook trout and lake trout which led us to marvel that the water could produce, during the summer, enough food to sustain the high fish population.

From this lake, which is not more than 200 feet above sea level, we climbed out between peaks showing 3,000–5,000 foot elevations on our chart. The mountains appeared almost black in large areas of the country as through composed of volcanic rock. As we flew to the west we could see reindeer, but only on the snowdrifts. We wondered if they were there to escape the blackflies, or whether we could see only those on the snow because they stood out against the white background.

Our return to the George River was a westerly flight of about 150 miles. It was across hundreds of lakes and dozens of streams; across another immense area in which there was no apparent sign that a man had ever passed through. This great wilderness area and the gigantic arctic barrens of the Northwest Territories are among the last areas to be penetrated on the North American continent. As the population and the mobility of man increase, these remote, pristine wonderlands will inexorably diminish. Struck by the vastness and the beauty of this land with its abundant wildlife and promise for posterity, the thoughtful man will leave no mark of his passing but the game taken for food and the ashes of his campfire.   ◆

LATIN AMERICA
& THE CARIBBEAN

The town of Mulege, midway down the peninsula of Baja California, has some 800 permanent residents — and five flight strips. One of these landing spots is the 3,000-foot airport (including 200-foot, soft, overrun area) at Serenidad, which means "serenity."

It's just 450 air miles down the coast line from the border-crossing town of Mexicali to Mulege. We counted no less than 16 landing strips along the coast line, and more in the making. Into a 12–15 knot head wind, the flight from Mexicali took two hours and 50 minutes in a Piper *Cherokee 235*, N8934W.

This was our fourth trip to Baja in just two years, and each had included a stop at Mulege. During research for the original tour of Baja (July and August PILOT, 1963), the airport at Serenidad was not in existence. Like so many of the thriving resorts on the peninsula, this flight strip and expanding resort grew out of the desire of a few pilots from Redondo Beach, Calif., to establish a place to land, put up a simple building and keep a boat or two available. The group included Lee Center (AOPA 218641), former mayor of Redondo Beach; Dick Fitzgerald, manager of the Redondo Beach Chamber of Commerce, and Drs. William A. Taylor (AOPA 214447) and Robert A. Ronnie.

the walk a bit. We took the "grass shack" and found it most comfortable. These cabañas rent for a minimum of $11 per day, for up to four people, each additional bed at $2.50 per day extra. Four people have plenty of room, and cabañas with eight beds (Mexican style heavy canvas stretched taut over a wooden frame) are not at all crowded. Meals are $1.25 for breakfast, $1.50 for lunch and $2.50 for dinner. Thus, a family of four can live in a comfortable grass shack and include meals for $32 per day total.

There are two complete two-bedroom houses with bath, kitchen and living room available at $25 per day, and others nearing completion. With a kitchen available, a visitor can either bring his own food (if there's space in the baggage compartment) or, if he's a good angler, eat off the many varieties of fish that can be caught either right off the beach or from boats that Serenidad has available. The river which adjoins the Serenidad property on the north provides excellent river fishing, small sailboating, etc., and contains many species of pargo, some of which are of record size and often caught within 300 feet of the hotel.

Year-around deep-sea fishing is especially good in the Gulf of California, and the fishing grounds are within 10 minutes of Serenidad. Rooster fish, dolphin, yellowtail, ca-

4,000 and then 5,000 feet. All that's in the way of this runway extension is a low hill of fairly soft sand. Serenidad is attacking the problem with a D-5 Caterpillar tractor. However, pilots planning to visit Serenidad should be qualified to use the existing 2,800 feet, since Mulege is a considerable distance from Caterpillar spare parts, and there's always plenty of other work for the 47 full-time employees to do. A great part of the charm of Mexico is still "mañana land," despite the best efforts of stateside management.

However, Serenidad's directors affirm that the airport extension will come, and with it will come expanded airline service. At present Lockheed *Lodestars* from Baja Airlines in Tijuana land at the airport west of town. Serenidad/Mulege reports that it has one of the few lighted flight strips between Mexicali and La Paz. The strip is outlined by 16 smudge pots, and the location is easy to define after dark because of the marine lighthouse located within a mile of the resort. Pilots should remember that there is a Mexican restriction against flying single-engine aircraft at night, although it is completely legal for twin-engine craft.

There is a Unicom at the resort. Use of the 122.8 Unicom party line is a great safety factor, not only along the beaches en route but also in the vicinity of the complex of air-

By RUTH and DON DOWNIE | AOPA 188441

SERENIDAD, MULEGE

Thriving Baja California fly-in resort grows from desire of California pilots to fly to simple 'serenity'

The site they picked was just south of the mouth of the Santa Rosalia River at Mulege and directly across the stream from Hotel Mulege (formerly Club Aero de Mulege). As the original buildings were completed, an ever-increasing number of pilots landed to take a look at the new facility. In a period of 32 months, beginning in March 1962, Serenidad grew from a single adobe building adjoining a tiny flight strip to its present size that can handle 84 guests.

Serenidad's flight strip is surfaced with "blue earth," a mineral composition dug from a mountain site near the city of Mulege. When soaked with salt water and rolled, the blue earth makes a surface almost as hard as cement. "We learned that from Kaiser on Guam," said the Serenidad manager.

Eighty- and 100-octane fuel are available at 70¢ per gallon, oil at 70¢ per quart. Cost of overnight accommodations varies, depending on whether you want to live in the main adobe building or in a thatched palm-leaf cabaña with the showers and such down

brilla, red snapper, sierras and garrupa can be caught. Many marlin and sailfish are usually caught in each season.

Boats range all the way from Sabot sailboats at $10 per day to 28-foot inboard cabin cruisers with the Mexican skipper (required by law) at $55.

In addition to the hotel and houses and family style cabañas at Serenidad, Mulege is the site of the Hotel Mulege, just across the river, where some 50 guests can receive fine tourist accommodations. The in-town Hacienda Hotel, now under new management, has also been refinished and has 11 rooms for tourists.

The main products of Mulege, aside from the "crops" of fly-in tourists, are primarily dates and olives. However, all sorts of lush tropical fruits are grown by the rancheros who live nearby. Included on the menu are local grapefruit and oranges, sweet limes, figs, bananas, mangoes and papayas.

If plans materialize, the 2,800-foot airport at Serenidad will soon be lengthened to

ports at towns such as Mulege. Normal landing at Serenidad, for instance, is directly over the top of two of Hotel Mulege's three flight strips, and it's more than just a courtesy to call Hotel Mulege's Unicom to advise what you're going to do. Takeoff from Serenidad, usually made toward the north, is again over the top of Hotel Mulege's close-in fields, but aircraft departing Serenidad should have sufficient altitude by the time they cross the river to clear any Hotel Mulege traffic. However, four of the five flight strips are in sight of each other, and pilots can see other aircraft in the runup area merely by taking a look.

At present, the fifth and largest flight strip is 4,400 feet long and large enough for the *Lodestars* flown by Baja Airlines. It is located up the river and some five miles northwest of town. This airstrip is able to accommodate, also, a Martin 202 owned by Baja Airlines.

The only border crossing fee, as such, was a 64¢ landing charge at the Mexicali Airport.

However, pilot Gene Burget, Serenidad's former aviation and general management consultant for the booking offices (located at 448 W. Broadway, San Diego, Calif.; phone 714-232-0815), flew the company's Aero Commander frequently to Mulege. Pilot Burget reported that the normal — though not required — procedure is to pay $1 for the landing fee and associated paperwork. Immigrations officials who fill out tourist cards right on the spot charge no fee, but regular travelers have established an unofficial gratuity of 50¢ per person. Then the normal gratuity to the inspector who looks over your aircraft and baggage is $1. Thus, the three of us in N8943W paid $3.50 according to this unofficial standard. We were on the ground less than 30 minutes outbound and, on our return two evenings later, we weren't stopped in Mexicali long enough to smoke a cigarette.

At this writing, RAMSA fees were still in effect. [This article appeared originally in the April 1965 issue of THE PILOT; therefore, readers should beware that RAMSA charges and controls may not be in effect as described by Author Downie at that time. For example, as of publication time, a two-month RAMSA card costing $8 may be obtained. Our sources say all cards can be purchased in person at any airport of entry (provided that airport has not run out of cards) or by writing the main office: Radio Aeronautica, S.A., De C.V., Melchor Ocampo #469-101, Mexico, D.F., Mexico. To save yourself some possible trouble, time and money, we advise that when you are planning your trip, write the Mexico City office for information concerning controls in effect; and, if necessary, obtain your RAMSA card from there.—Ed.] However, we paid nothing for nonexistent RAMSA services on our Serenidad/Mulege flight. In a Dec. 20, 1963, memorandum from the FAA Flight Service Station at Imperial, Calif. (where we filed an in-flight two-day round-robin flight plan), local regulations on RAMSA fees were clarified.

The FAA station advised in part, "Mexican RAMSA cards cost $24 for one year. . . . There are only four locations in all of Mexico where RAMSA controls and operates the Traffic Control Towers, and at these locations, the rates and charges . . . are strictly adhered to and enforced: Tijuana, Matamoros, Guadalajara, and Mexico City . . .

"At all other Airport Control locations, the control towers are usually controlled and operated by the airline companies serving those airports. At these locations they are required to charge the same fees as are charged by RAMSA operated locations, but in most cases this is not so, and their fees are considerably less.

"They will charge for this first control tower service, and for every radio range or radio aid to air navigation you fly over, and/or land at your destination within 160 miles of one of these stations. . . . If you were to land at Mulege, or Bay of Los Angeles, you would only have to pay for the use of Tijuana Tower Services, radio range, as you will be over 160 miles from any radio aid to air navigation."

Since the Mexicali tower, listed at 118.1 mc, seldom answers unless a scheduled air carrier is approaching or departing, the visitor has not used the tower and is not charged for its availability. As long as the tourist flies to a point at least 160 miles distance from the RAMSA radio-range-beacon at La Paz, Baja, there's no RAMSA charge. Most seasoned air travelers to Baja California plan a fuel-and-eat stop at either Bay of Los Angeles or Mulege and promptly forget about RAMSA.

Serenidad is a fine example of the ever-expanding list of comfortable, easy-to-reach resorts that pilots are discovering on the peninsula of Baja California. This "forgotten peninsula of Baja" still has the relaxing isolation away from the freeway and TV, it has excellent drinking water from nearby springs, the fishing is fabulous, and it's virtually impossible to reach except by air. What more can a pilot and his family wish for? ◆

Serenidad with the Hotel Mulege, its hangars and three flight strips clearly visible across the Santa Rosalia River. In 32 months, Serenidad grew from a single adobe building adjoining a tiny flight strip to its present capacity to handle 84 guests. **PHOTOS BY THE AUTHOR**

A 180 h.p. Piper Cherokee on final approach over the Santa Rosalia River for the flight strip at Serenidad, Mulege. Serenidad's flight strip is surfaced with 'blue earth,' a mineral composition dug from a mountain site near Mulege.

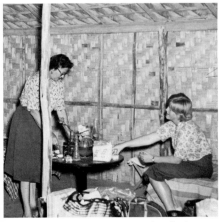

Ruth and Dana Downie in thatched cabaña ("grass shack"). Cabañas rent for a minimum of $11 per day for four people.

Native fisherman returning up the Santa Rosalia River in Mulege.

MAÑANA LAND
Beckons Pilots

This Skymaster, flown by Sunset Magazine's Travel Editor, Martin Litton (AOPA 150594), circles low for a landing at Punta Chivato at sunset.

COLOR PHOTOGRAPHS BY THE AUTHORS

By DON DOWNIE | *AOPA 188441* *and DANA DOWNIE*

Baja California plays host to relaxation-hungry pilots at new fly-in resort. There are modern facilities at Punta Chivato, located in an area where fishing is excellent

W ant an isolated, brand-new fly-in resort with excellent year-around fishing, air-conditioned rooms with style and comfort, scenery out your front window, and two flight strips long enough to present no problem to the newer pilots?

Then try Punta Chivato, just north of the twenty-seventh parallel on the peninsula side of Baja California. "Chivato" is brand new. In fact, some sections weren't quite completed when we made this summer discovery flight.

If you don't have a brand-new chart, you probably won't find this $600,000 resort listed. However, it's 10 miles north of Mulege and just over 30 miles south of Santa Rosalia. If you flew over the peninsula two years ago, there was nothing at Punta Chivato except a picturesque point of land, white sandy beaches, shallow turquoise water and a sheltered harbor. It took up to 150 laborers over 18 months to bring this new resort to completion. During our visit, we saw plenty of manpower and heavy machinery at work completing the job. [Late summer, 1966. — Ed.]

The 3,000-acre Punta Chivato resort is the brain child of two Covina, Calif., pilots. Dixon Collins (AOPA 259117) and his wife, Barbara (AOPA 255655), are devoting all their time and energy — except that taken with three growing youngsters — to developing the resort. Mrs. Collins, who has a commercial license and multi-engine rating, has designed the landscaping and is handling stateside reservations. (The office is located at 2096 Buenos Aires Dr., Covina, Calif. Phone: 213-966-1763.)

Mrs. Sybil Collins, Dixon's mother, designed the interior. (Color scheme in each of the 20 rooms is different.) She plans to do the buying and to supervise a boutique, which will sell silver by Spratling, gold ornaments by Hunderto Arillano and custom jewelry from Frank Lowenstein of Mexico City.

It's obvious that the Collins family has had little time to spare lately. In one year, Dixon logged over 1,000 hours shuttling back and forth to Chivato in a Cessna 206 or a *Skymaster*. When work was begun, laborers hacked out an 800-foot temporary strip where much of the critical material was landed. Stone and heavy items were brought by boat.

Chivato is 300 statute air miles from Nogales, 470 from Ciudad Juarez and El Paso and 150 miles from Hermosillo, all-Mexican airports of entry. It's 495 miles down the picturesque eastern coast line of the peninsula from Mexicali, perhaps the best route for single-engine aircraft. Another 230 miles south puts you at La Paz.

As Collins and I cruised down the peninsula, he explained: "Baja is no place to practice flying. I believe that any flight strip shorter than 2,500 feet should be approached with the greatest suspicion. Sure, many pilots can handle these shorter strips, but there is little margin for error. At Punta Chivato, we now have a 3,500 north-south strip and will have a converging 4,000-foot east-west strip completed in not more than two or three weeks. Eventually, this will be extended to 5,000 feet. We've already purchased a small supply of jet fuel.

"The runways are all made with *calechi,* a native soil that turns almost as hard as concrete when it is soaked with salt water. We're working on the long runway right now, so we land on the 3,500-foot strip."

(Collins was contacted at press time and reported that the final portions of the two runways were being connected. This will produce a 4,200-foot east-west runway with a 3,500-foot high-speed turnoff to the north. He also reported his fuel "island" was complete and two 2,000-gallon storage tanks had been installed. Pumps capable of 40 gallons per minute are being installed and "we can get you off the ground in 15 minutes if you're in a hurry. Billing can be accomplished directly at the 'island.' " One hundred octane fuel is shipped by boat from Guaymas, 92 miles across the Gulf, in new Pemex drums and sells for 74¢ per U.S. gallon.)

Punta Chivato has a powerful Unicom on 122.8 at the bar, and an LF homing beacon has just been placed in operation on a temporary frequency (408 kc) with no identification coding. The runways have wiring and lights installed, but not yet hooked up. Smoke

Cy Schneider spent a couple of hours spear fishing at a depth of about 20 feet. He came back with a "full catch" of bococo, one of which he shows here.

How about that for a little water fun? (Almost like a 007 movie.) This is one of the two cabin cruisers, owned by Punta Chivato, that rent for $60 per day. That fee includes the necessary captain and mate.

pots are used for standby runway marking, and a rotating beacon is in transit to the area. However, flight in single-engine aircraft over Mexico at night is prohibited and pilots of twins should be extremely familiar with both the terrain and facilities before attempting a night flight in the area.

The resort has a 28-volt APU (auxiliary power unit), spare tires and tubes in popular sizes and a portable air compressor. Francisco Muñoz' Baja Airlines makes a regular three-times-a-week stop and will make unscheduled landings by Unicom request. "If we don't happen to have a mechanic on the field in case of a malfunction, we can always have Senor Muñoz bring in one of his men from Tijuana," Collins said.

Daily radio communication is maintained with KMI at Oakland, Calif., and guests may place direct telephone calls to the States.

During our visit, 10 (now 15) of the 20 units had been completed and filled. Another five units needed only floor tile, and foundations had been dug for five more units. Rooms have two double beds, and a couch or extra single bed can be added without crowding. Rates (American plan) are $35 per night per couple and include everything except boat rentals and the bar. Children under 12 in the same room are $10; over 12, $12.50. Single occupancy for the same room is $20.

The resort has two large cabin cruisers that rent for $60 per day (including captain and mate as required by Mexican law). Seventeen-foot brand-new Boston Whalers with 55-h.p. outboards rent for $35 per day including a boatman, while a 13-foot whaler costs $28. Half-day rates are available.

"There are people who like to fish, and there are fishermen," Collins explained. "We have enough fish within a few miles of Chivato to delight both types. Actually, the main reason we picked the location at Chivato was because of the excellent fishing; snug harbor; and beautiful, isolated surroundings. Anglers have caught just about

every kind of fish from our boats: dolphin, rooster, yellowtail, tuna and occasional sailfish and marlin during the summer months. We find good turtles, lobster and clams; and there's even an oyster bed with pearls."

A Los Angeles skin diver, Cy Schneider, came in from a boat trip of a couple of hours with a full catch that included a large bococo, a variety of snapper. He made his entire catch with a spear gun in 20 feet of water just off the tip of the point. "This is a paradise for spear fishing," he said.

The resort keeps a complete supply of fishing gear and lures as well as skin-diving equipment and 15 air tanks.

Shell collectors can have a field day along the beaches, therefore, pilots should be cautioned to make sure their guests don't suddenly come up with an extra hundred pounds of baggage. One enterprising commercial shell collector took 15 tons of local shells and shipped them out by boat. They were sold — as local products — in Florida!

A dry dock capable of handling 100-foot boats was partially completed when we were there. It utilizes seven-ton winches that came from the old U.S.S. Missouri. Once the fly-in facilities have been completed, a marina will be built in the natural harbor with complete power, fresh water, fuel and dry dock facilities.

There are other activities, for those who tire of fishing. A recreation room adjoins the dining room and has Ping-Pong, pool and game tables. One of the Grasshopper sand buggies designed for Earl Stanley Gardner is destined for Punta Chivato. Similar touring vehicles will follow. Duck and quail are available nearby during the season, and the resort operates a temporary camp for hunters who wish to shoot brant (a type of goose) on the west coast of the peninsula, just 30 minutes flying time from Chivato. There is a full-time guide (with boat) living near a 30,000-foot dry lake that is used as an airport. Supplies, sleeping bags and outboard motor are ferried across by air.

It takes two hours to drive to Mulege and three to Santa Rosalia. Once is enough! The trips by boat take 25 and 40 minutes, respectively. If you're flying, either town is just out of the traffic pattern. Tours of both towns are available, and many visitors take a boat to the clam beds of Concepción Bay.

Kaiser Gypsum has a large mine at San Marcos Island — 15 minutes by boat — with good hospital facilities, and the thriving copper mine at Santa Rosalia has a 24-hour-a-day hospital.

Future plans call for 10 hangars adjoining the resort. The design will be of stone and mortar with asbestos roofs to fit in with the carefully preserved styling of old Mexico that is maintained throughout the resort.

"Within the next year, we expect to build at least 20 rock and adobe homes and cabañas with wood-beam ceilings — similar to the present resort — for private owners. A long-term lease or purchase arrangement will be guaranteed," Collins explained.

During the Korean conflict, Collins flew as radar operator and copilot in AD5-W's from the carrier Bonhomme Richard. He became interested in Baja California after several visits to Mulege where he developed a friendship with Louis Frederico, former manager of Club Aero de Mulege (Hotel Mulege now). Frederico believed that the best fishing in the world was to be had at Punta Chivato. Both Frederico and Don Johnson, former assistant manager at Club Aero, are participating partners in the resort and live on the property.

The chef is Juan Valardi, who spent 23 years as cook for the Playa de Cortez Hotel in Guaymas, and there is an English-speaking bartender. There are 16 full-time employees at the resort, not counting the construction crews.

While special Mexican wines are featured, Punta Chivato follows the custom of almost all resorts in Baja California. Each visitor is greeted after landing with a margarita on-the-house. ◆

The first two planes to the left in this temporary parking area at Punta Chivato, a Cessna Super Skymaster and a Cessna 206, are ones in which Dixon Collins reportedly logged about 1,000 hours in one year while setting up operation of the resort.

Headed for some relaxation on the beach is Mrs. Lilly Powsner of Malibu Beach, Calif. At the top of the steps is one section of the accommodations available at Punta Chivato.

ISLA MUJERES

By ANNE BREMICKER

The hardest part of flying to Isla Mujeres was saying "yes" when my husband urged me to try a flying vacation for the first time. Where's Isla Mujeres? Well, it lies a short way off the east coast of the Yucatan Peninsula in the Yucatan Channel.

If you are wondering why we chose a tiny island six miles long and one mile wide (that's a generous measurement), then I must tell you that I am an inveterate reader of places to go in Mexico. I had read one short sentence about the island in a travel book and it had appealed to me. The second reason, and by far the sounder one, happened to be that it suited our purposes for our first international flight. There would be few mountains to contend with on our route down the eastern coast of Mexico; and, flying over a sandy beach, we would have one long landing field in case of trouble. In the back of my novice copilot's head, I must admit I felt more at ease because I could see you couldn't become lost, and, if you did have to ditch, the Mexican version of the CAP would have no trouble finding you. My husband shook his head at this feminine logic, but it did soothe me.

Once having said "let's do it," we began our preparations. Our first step was to write for a RAMSA card, which will save you much trouble, red tape and expense. It entitles you to free weather information. (A 60-day card will cost you $8.) At the same time, we sent for a set of Jeppesen charts.

As we studied our maps and planned our route, we were slowly gathering articles for our survival kit, too. We started by digging out of our camping equipment our pots and pans and a small portable stove. We added two blankets, a large can of insect spray, water, salt tablets, water-purifying tablets, a knife, a hatchet, hats with some fetchingly draped mosquito netting and various easy-to-pack food, like chocolate bars and canned corn beef.

Some of the airports at which we had scheduled stops were labeled as "Spanish-speaking" only, so I intensified my study of the language, and my Spanish teacher very kindly filled me in with some of the technical terms that all pilots use, for at these airports my husband wanted me to handle the radio. But don't let me unnerve you. As a general rule, we have discovered that at a busy air-port there is an English-speaking tower operator and that at the smaller airports, where only Spanish is spoken, there is so little traffic it doesn't matter.

Then one bright morning we were off, in our blue and white Cessna 205 — place of departure: St. Paul, Minn. In addition to our bags and our survival kit, we carried underwater diving equipment and a spare tire and spark plugs for the plane. We spent the first night at Dallas visiting relatives, and we were airborne early the next morning. We sat down at San Antonio for breakfast and, by shortly after noon, we had cleared Customs at Matamoros. Now we were really on our way!

We had removed three of the six seats in our plane for ease in stowing luggage, and it was here in Matamoros that we were able to do a favor for the Mexican Customs office. We were asked if we would mind taking along the *jefe* (chief) whose home was at Tampico, and of course we were delighted to do it. He was a very courtly gentleman in a beautiful uniform who spoke no English, and I must say this — we were waved through Customs in jig time.

It was at Matamoros that we had our first experience in filing a flight plan, a necessity while flying in Mexico (this is emphasized with a penalty and fine for failure to do so). You are asked your name, identification, passengers, color of plane, serial number, gas on board, speed, destination and ETA — and they are looking for you when you get there!

It was a beautiful flight down the coast over the sandy beach and the palm trees. There were mountaintops to our right touched with sun, but their great bulk was hidden in the clouds that develop around them in the afternoons.

At Tampico, we decided to push on, knowing that Tampico had little to offer in the way of an overnight stop. We had plenty of time to make Vera Cruz, and, somehow, that seemed more authentic for our first night in Mexico. We stayed two days there — in the beginning by intent, because we had spent two long days in flying and wanted to stop and rest a bit, and then from necessity because one of their "norther" storms blew in at an off-season time. Vera Cruz, usually hot, was cold; I wore my coat.

You will find at Vera Cruz a good paved strip and even a good terminal. Here, as at all other airports, we were treated with utmost courtesy, even real friendliness. There is a landing fee at all airports, which never exceeded more than $1.50, but this is more than balanced by the fact there is no tiedown charge — stay as long as you like. Moreover, I want to be sure to add that we had no difficulty obtaining a good grade of 100-octane gas, usually given to us directly from Mexicana Airlines' supply. It was almost too easy. Everybody had warned us of the poor quality of Mexican gas that had to be siphoned through a chamois, so we had tucked one of these into our plane, too. [Now available at the airport are 90/96 and 100/130 octane gas. — Ed.]

Our next stop was Campeche, a lovely, old, walled town (a remnant of former days when pirates roamed the coast) that now boasts two of the most amazingly modern buildings down on the waterfront. One is the governor's palace and the other the Hotel Baluartes, which would probably be the best place to eat and spend the night. For the really adventuresome, you might peek into the Castelmar-by-the-Sea, if you're fond of old colonial places. Campeche's economy, like that of the whole length of the coast, is based on shrimp and coconut, but it is also gaining a reputation for jungle hunting expeditions. We ran into three men from Atlanta who had just returned from the jungle with a bag of jaguar, royal pheasant and boar, and many tall tales. Campeche also has an expansive paved airport, thanks to the governor and his Cessna *Skyknight*.

Mérida, in Yucatan, is an international airport, of course; but even here, where traffic is heavy, we were treated with great courtesy by everybody, and especially by those nice persons who would listen to me state my wants in my halting Spanish.

Mérida is a busy town, predating Mexico City, a kaleidoscope of windmills, lovely old architecture, horse-pulled carriages, shiny mango trees, and Mayan-featured women in brightly embroidered white *huipils*, with ribbons in their hair and white, white petticoats ruffled at their ankles. I would recommend here, without any hesitation, the Hotel Montejo, a small hotel, family owned for some

Mrs. Bremicker on the grounds of the hotel Posada del Mar at Isla Mujeres. When lobster was served there, which was often, it was something to write home about.

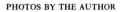

PHOTOS BY THE AUTHOR

An old dugout canoe, a relic from the past, and some of the native fishing boats on Isla Mujeres. Most of the native population spends its time fishing.

250 years, lovely, comfortable and cool. From Mérida you can easily reach the ruins of Chichen Itzá and Uxmal if you enjoy archaeological sites. If you do wish to see them, by all means use the public bus system. Buses leave in the morning and will bring you home in the late afternoon, all for about $1.50 per person. What's more, the buses are air-conditioned — hardly a luxury in the heat of Yucatan.

After four days in Mérida, we were airborne again, this time bound for Isla Mujeres, our southernmost destination. We flew over endless flocks of ducks wintering there. One huge pink flock, particularly, interested us; we decided that what we were seeing were flamingos. We would never make this trip again without binoculars.

Soon the water became very colorful in patterns of deep blue, turquoise and aquamarine and so clear you could easily see the reefs and, it seemed, even the shells on the bottom of the sea. Isla Mujeres lies only about five miles off the coast, but flying over water spooks me. We headed over open water with generous altitude so even I could see we could easily glide back to land in either direction in the event the trusty motor failed me.

Isla Mujeres has a northwest, southeast landing strip, 4,757 feet long and paved. When we were there, it was an adequate dirt field alive with workers of some sort, and we made a pass over the strip to tell them to lie low.

Isla Mujeres is an idyllic retreat if you yearn for a sleepy tropical island with rustling palm trees, empty white sand beaches, a sea that even at the end of a week had us still gasping at its beauty, lovely sunny days, gentle nights and a population that pays you no heed at all. Most of the people are busy fishing. It's possible to walk everywhere you would want to go — or to take a boat. There are a few cars on the island, but they would be real collectors' items in our country.

Fishing of all kinds is available, from serious, well-equipped boats to lazy little dinghys that require only a hand line. Scuba diving is a great attraction, too. I still can't believe the things we saw in those coral reefs. A walk on the beach at sunset can certainly make the pressures of a busy world seem far away. Isla Mujeres seems to be one of those places that has stopped in time. The first day or so you wonder what you will do to keep busy, and, before you know it, the hours are not long enough to do all the delightful nothings you want to do. We even went so native as to retrieve our camping equipment from our survival kit and to cook many of our meals out on the beach.

There is a large hotel called the Zazil-Hà that was in the construction stage when we were there, and the manager was kind enough to give us a tour. Its beauty of site and view we can attest to, and it is civilized and luxurious — and very expensive by Mexican standards. I also can recommend the Posada del Mar, which is much smaller and less pretentious; the rooms were clean and attractive, and the food was adequate. When they served lobster, which was often, it was something to write home about.

When you leave the island, you must observe a ceremony with some Customs officials because this is a free port. Not even so much as glancing at our bags, they sealed them with some very flimsy paper tape.

We then took off for Ciudad del Carmen. This is a small town that is fast gaining a reputation among avid fishermen, especially for bonefish. Here, again, you will find a handsome airport. Ciudad del Carmen was the only town in which we experienced any difficulty in getting a hotel room. Although we were the only tourists in town, it seemed that the next president of Mexico was going to be in town the next day, and already his retinue had filled the available rooms.

We had traveled completely without reservations (another point at which our less adventuresome advisors had thrown up their hands), but we were adamant on this point,

because we wanted to feel under no pressure to fly to a certain town on a certain day because of an advance reservation and a deposit when in fact the weather might have been marginal. Carmen's economy is shrimp. It ships more than a million pounds of the crustaceans a month to this country and gets a premium price for them. We enjoyed going down to the waterfront to watch the shrimp fleet, but we enjoyed eating the shrimp even more.

One more long day of flying, with lunch at Vera Cruz, and we found ourselves late in the afternoon flying over our own country, and the first thing we did was to call an airfield tower and inquire how much daylight we had left. (Yucatan and environs has no twilight as we know it.) It was so nice to talk to someone again while in the air. We had learned to fly with great ease of mind on Mexican navigational systems, and, in truth, I had become very fond of ADF. However, there is no one to call if you have trouble or if you just want to get the latest weather reports. It was a cozy feeling to hear the operator's voice coming into our cabin.

If you have wondered why I have pitched this story to a somewhat elementary point of view, that of a woman who embarked on this trip with her heart in her mouth, it's because on this trip to Yucatan we met so many couples in which the husband was a pilot but his wife refused to make such a trip with him, so they had used the commercial airlines, as, indeed, we had done up to this year. Over and over we heard the question, "How did you talk her into it?"

All I can say to those wives is that when I find myself daydreaming about another vacation, I think of myself in the seat beside my husband in our 205, happily navigating and poring over stacks of maps. Perhaps next time we will try the west coast of Mexico, and then there's that little town of Ocotlán that I've read about. I'll bet we could reach it by flying into Oaxaca. They have an airport there. ◆

BEACHCOMBING IN THE

BAHAMAS

By GILBERT F. QUINBY | *AOPA 37841*

A whole week with no schedule or commitments, an Apache, and a pilot with the heart of an explorer, are responsible for some interesting discoveries. The pilot returns home with seashells from 13 beaches

A short boat ride from South Caicos puts you on an island all your own, with no one else within miles. You have your own beaches, swim as you please, fish, go snorkeling and skin-diving, or just loaf, without interference. Admiral's Arms, a few miles away on South Caicos, can be seen from the island across crystal-clear water.

The Bahamas! For years I had devoured their beauty in books and magazines. I had nibbled around their lovely edges on a dozen busy flights. I had seen the fabulous "out-islands" as smudges on a horizon from 9,000 feet on a ferry flight, and I had buzzed at 500 feet down fantastically beautiful strings of jewel-like cays. I had stayed at two or three of their more popular resorts, enough to make me want to see and know more of the islands and the people beyond the "tourist traps."

Finally I was to have my chance. For one whole week I had no schedule, no meetings, no commitments; just one *Apache*, one set of skin diving gear, and The Bahamas.

It really started at West End, Grand Bahama, where Jack Tar's opulent establishment hosted an adventurous trade meeting, 60 nautical miles from the United States. "Big deal," I thought, quietly. But the palms, the coral, the beaches, the boats and the bars were all good at Jack Tar, and it was a good conditioning stop. Even on Friday, after the meetings when relaxation was the order, I was itching to get on with it.

So Saturday the less fortunate supercargo was delivered to various places in Florida, and the trip really began at West Palm Beach International with a spectacular 20-minute "international fuel stop." That's 20 minutes from actual time on, to actual take-off including taxiing, fueling, filing DVFR, getting general declarations, checking weather, etc., etc. Thanks to Tilford's excellent service, I was airborne and southeast-bound at 1953 Zebra.

Damn Zebra! When I reached cruising altitude of 9,500 feet and cleared the ADIZ and "Bimini omni" I started to sort out my times. The sun doesn't set on Zebra time, and I was flight planned to South Caicos Island, a nonstop estimate of 3:35 for 574 nautical miles. It would be dark. And, Caicos had a good coral strip, two or three flarepots, an excellent ADF beacon, and possible livestock on the runway.

So, I watched a spectacular orange sunset over Acklins Island as I glued the *Apache* to Yankee route. Mayaguana's cheerfully lighted strip was a mockery — USAF Auxiliary, landing with prior permission only. The black shadow of the northern Caicos group showed against the dark sea just about the time I saw lightning flash far ahead and to the right. Must be the usual evening thunderstorm over the central ridge of Hispaniola, I told myself uneasily. Raised Grand Turk, where the Air Force tower is always ready to help (hope they never try the prior permission bit on communications), and got good weather at Turk. Spotted the lights of the beacon at South Caicos, in and out of invisible scud. Landed without buzzing for livestock.

The Admiral's Arms at Cockburn Harbor is a far cry from the Jack Tar at West End. Liam Maguire, the proprietor, has a theory that tropical resorts fall into two categories: hot water resorts and cold water resorts. The rugged, adventurous traveler will endure the hot water resort quite cheerfully. But don't put a hot water tourist in a cold water place like the Admiral's Arms. The precious water is caught in a catchment basin, held in a cistern, pumped to a roof-top tank, and warmed by a tropic sun only.

Skin diving Sunday was moderately productive, and the lobster salad that resulted

Randy Quinby (left), son of the author, displays a good afternoon's catch of lobster on the porch of the Cutlass Bay Club, Cat Island. Club staff members share Randy's pride.

Late afternoon at South Caicos, looking west from the patio of Admiral's Arms. Early morning and later afternoon offer color photographers some of the best chances for startling pictures.

was guaranteed fresh. A couple of Snow ag-planes left to continue their ferry to Venezuela, hoppers sloshing with 300 gallons of gas each. The Anglican vicar and his family were visiting the parish, and as penance for missing church I offered them a lift to Grand Turk Monday morning. They accepted before I could think second thoughts about the reputation of the strip at Grand Turk Town, which was said to be marginal.

Dragging the Grand Turk Town strip next day, I had reason to reflect again on the "prior permission" syndrome. Grand Turk boasts a mile of hard-surface runway known as an "Aux AFB." Casual transients with

private airplanes are actively discouraged. At the other end of the island, between the town and the salt ponds, is a wide spot in the road that leads to the cemetery. Fortunately, the *Apache* just fit.

The vicar and his family duly delivered, I headed for the Bahamas. (Caicos is not exactly Bahamas politically, although the geography is similar.) I buzzed Cockburn Harbor and Unicomed that the vicar was delivered intact then took off on a dead-reckoned course to Great Inagua, land of salt, flamingos, and mosquitoes. Their ADF beacon was a good solid help soon after leaving the Caicos group, and landfall was on schedule in spite of the anxiety typical of the last five minutes of any overwater flight. Cutting across the deserted beaches of Inagua's eastern shore, I made for the northern coast line of the main part of the island. Saltwater ponds and lagoons held coveys of pink flamingos, and the island, like Mayaguana, is posted against flight below 2,000 feet except on takeoff and landing, to protect these nervous fowl.

The salt ponds and piles are visible before you can sort out Matthew Town and the only airstrip on the Inaguas. A Bahamas Airways DC-3 was on the ground as I circled, so there was activity, and I rode its wake. Customs cleared me into the Bahamas and the salt company man topped the tanks. I even got an excellent lunch at the company guest house in the charming village, one of the liveliest in all the Bahamas. But practically no tourist facilities, and through the heavy scent of bougainvillea, the pervading hum of mosquitoes. Bring DDT.

After takeoff, I tracked the Great Inagua homer outbound after a fashion, until I spotted the remote reefs of Northwest Cay barely awash in the trackless ocean. There would be a skindiver's paradise, I thought, as I coveted a boat to do this trip in. But could I do what I had already done in less than a month?

The south tip of Acklins was beautiful seacoast, but showed no landing area for mile after mile of beach and cove and tiny village until a wide spot in a road on the northeast tip. Elected not to land, and continued across the complex water-swamp-island strait between Acklins and Crooked Island. There on Crooked Island I found a typical DC-3 strip hard by a perfect semicircular bay that was too beautiful to resist. I landed, and had time to stroll down to the beach before the inevitable man drove up to stamp my cruising permit, extend his hospitality, and trade small talk. I found that I was at Colonel Hill, and it was alleged that accommodations could be had at the village on the ridge some miles from the strip. I declined with thanks and beachcombed for 45 minutes before takeoff for nowhere in particular. I was really getting the feel of island hopping.

Out to the north tip of Crooked Island, and due west across the channel, I was over the south tip of Long Island in 15 minutes. Here was an abandoned airstrip that I was curious about — it showed on some maps and was well off the beaten track.

It is still abandoned, overgrown with brush, and with only a Jeep track down the middle for access to the marine beacon light on the adjacent hill. The story goes that a hapless C-46 bellied in here years ago, and a crew cleared the strip, repaired and lightened the airplane, and flew it out. The way things are going in the Bahamas, that strip will be cleared again someday.

Strolling at 165 knots up the narrow length of Long Island, I poked into coves and examined beaches; flew over bay shallows, and along limestone cliffs. Passed a good airport at Hard Bargain almost entirely surrounded by salt pans and signs of the salt industry. Passed the "main" airport at Deadman's Cay where Bahamas Airways lands most every day. Up near the north end of the island I found a good strip, a tracery of freshly-bulldozed roads on the seaward ridge, and a cluster of new buildings with a sign painted on the roof of the largest saying

"hotel." That did it, and in no time I was bouncing up the road from the airport in a small European station wagon driven by Jörg Friese, a personable German who also managed the hotel. I was shown to an immaculate cottage, given very reasonable rates, and warned against skin diving on the windward coast. Dinner would be ready when I was.

After exploring the adjacent coast and finding it spectacular, I joined a modest group of Germans and natives at the bar and found I was at Stella Maris, a gung-ho operation — eager to teach, and eager to learn. They taught that developing land in the out-islands is a job requiring a million or two in capital to start. They taught that a good lot of three-quarters of an acre on a beach would sell fast at $7,500 per. They taught that a very decent home could be built on such a lot for $16,000 to $18,000.

They learned that you can't run an airport in the Bahamas without Unicom, and wisely bought one of the best. [One hundred octane fuel is available. — Ed.]

During the night I was awakened from a most comfortable sleep by the slashing sound of heavy rain, the crash of thunder, and the brilliant flash of tropical lightning counterpointing the monotonous drone of the air-conditioner. Exactly the right time of day for a frontal passage.

And in the damp and dripping dawn I combed the beaches again before an excellent breakfast and takeoff into cloudy postfrontal winds, nonstop five minutes to Cape Santa Maria.

This airport suggested a low pass before committing the *Apache* to the scrub-bordered sand, partly because of the possibility of ruts or soft spots, partly because the wind was cross and gusty. But one pass was enough to convince me that it was quite serviceable, and the roll-out was serene. I stripped to swim trunks in the airplane on the deserted strip by a deserted road that led to a deserted beach. A Jeep spoiled the solitude slightly — we met halfway from the strip to the beach. An elderly, friendly couple wanted to know if they could help. They were on their way back to Stella Maris Strip; this was the day the Bahamas Airways DC-3 came in. Shades of the small town railroad station of yesteryear!

The bay and beach at Cape Santa Maria are both beautiful and productive. A fine variety of seashells and crystal-clear water grace this perfect crescent of sand. And after an hour or so I looked up to see a shock-headed man in faded khaki shorts eyeing me silently. I remembered a remark in the lounge of Stella Maris the night before, and tried a long shot.

"You must be Walt Shubert," I said. "Harry Holman told me to look you up."

He smiled, we chatted, and he urged me to visit his home down the beach. Walt and his wife, Jo, are carving a splendid beach home out of the wilderness. Although their finishing and fitting were in process, they set a welcome cup of coffee before me. Daughter Bonnie provided a sugar apple from the nearby bush, and contributed a few excellent shells to my collection. I was driven back to the strip and waved off by Walt and Bonnie, with their sincere hope that I return ringing in my mind. I shall.

At 1,500 feet under broken to overcast skies I ambled aimlessly out over the north-

ern tip of Long Island debating which way to go. West was Great Exuma with gas and a taxi man at George Town who could take me to the hospitality of one of the three excellent hotels on the straits across from Stocking Island — but, I had been there, and I had plenty of gas. East was San Salvador with its "Aux AFB" where I could declare an emergency and comb beaches while they argued with the Pentagon about whether to impound the *Apache* for landing on a base I pay taxes to support on soil we don't own. I had never been to San Sal, but my mood was not one of catering to bureaucracy. So I went north past scattered showers to Cat Island, whatever that was.

It was another Bahama. Large, varying from swamp to "highlands" of 200 feet above the fantastic sea level. The sparse habitation and seldom roads had me digging for a detail map when I spotted the raw scar of an airstrip on the south coast. I circled and observed a few people and an interesting building on the bay near the strip. In pure pleasure, I landed, got out, walked over to a native working on a car and asked him where I was.

"Cutlass Bay," he said, with no noticeable concern at my confusion.

"Any chance I could get some lunch around here?" I asked.

"Sure. Clancy!" and a diminutive boy with an eager smile on his black face came up. He was 13, and my chauffer down the quarter mile of road to the Cutlass Bay Club, a building on a hill overlooking one of the most beautiful bays I ever saw.

Max Bates, part owner and chargé d'affaires at the club welcomed me. He walked out on this knoll less than two years ago, cutting through the brush with a ma-

A coral island which is a short boat ride off the town of Cockburn Harbor.

chete, and has created a marvel of tropical comfort. Eva giggled around the kitchen and produced ham and eggs which I suspect were some sacrifice. Max salted the luncheon conversation with stories of his trials in getting the material and labor in to build this place, and after lunch turned me loose on the near bay beach to prowl while he tended chores. His place was not quite ready for opening.

There was no gas at Cutlass Bay, so after takeoff I drove the *Apache* up to the main airport on Cat Island to circle with a keen eye for signs of refueling capabilitity. [Since Quinby's visit, 100-octane gas has been installed and the airstrip has been lengthened to 4,000 feet. — Ed.] None. But I didn't really need it. I had topped tanks at Great Inagua and was cruising economically. North past the fabled Hermitage, to Arthur's Town where there are hopeful signs that a muddy clearing near town will one day be a third airport on Cat Island, and across Little San Salvador to the southern tip of Eleuthera Island.

Now I was getting in to built-up country — gracious homes and modest clusters of development studded the coast up to Rock Sound, where a jet strip welcomes a couple of 707's a week. You can't stop progress, but the *Apache* and I looked down our noses and scornfully passed Rock Sound.

Eleuthera is a narrow, beautiful island with frequent habitation and infrequent airports. After Rock Sound, the airborne transient may drool at the beaches surrounding another Aux AFB halfway to Northern Eleuthera. Prior permission . . . and, near the bulgy Northern End, the island necks down to a causeway over surging surf and ragged cliffs before it opens onto the flat plains and thick vegetation of Northern Eleuthera. Little islands with popular resorts ring the main island, and I Unicomed one of the most famous. Yes, The Lloyds on Spanish Wells had one room left and they would save it for me. The car would meet me at the airport.

I landed and parked beside a Cessna 182 from somewhere in the western United States. Four determined tourists were spreading their sleeping bags on the wings and horizontal stabilizers to dry; they had camped out by a Bahamas airport the night before. I thought of the frontal storm and sympathized. And clearing Customs I found there was no gas at North Eleuthera either.

This was getting to be a minor annoyance. There has been great reduction in red tape, a welcome opening of many ports of entry, a virtual disappearance of the old Customs bite, but very few places to refuel your airplane. A number of these airports are "going to have gas in about six months" but though tempted, I really couldn't wait. One gets the subconscious impression that anything designated officially as an "airport of entry" and attended by a Customs officer would surely be equipped to pump a little fuel into an airplane. Not so. Watch it.

A new car is seldom seen in the out-islands, and the one that stopped for me and my gear at North Eleuthera Airport was only serviceable. A longish ride through the dry jungle growth of this interesting island gave me time to learn that they have a peculiar but productive agriculture. Citrus, papaya, avocado, and other fruit were growing in "orchards" which were hard to distinguish from the jungle. Cabbage grew lush

and full (in late November), one or a dozen to each irregular pot-hole of barely cleared but tremendously rich soil among limestone outcroppings. And all this was apologized for by the driver, since the recent visit of a hurricane had messed them up badly.

By boat to the quay at picturesque Spanish Wells, where all is pastel, compact, and vaguely cockney. The people are mostly white descendants of the English who fled here for refuge from the American Revolution, and the families and speech are preserved.

Peter Lloyd lived up to the legend he has become. Polished publican, gregarious bon vivant, his generosity as a host is adequately compensated by the prices he sets on his hospitality. Although one whole wing of his beach-front establishment was wiped off the island by Hurricane Betsy, it has been completed; and he gave the optimistic impression that the whole thing was somehow a blessing. For skin and scuba divers, the Lloyds is a mecca, and Peter a diver's diver. Certification of scuba skill from him assures worldwide recognition. But don't try to rent his gear without expecting to prove your competence. One of the many specialties in which he is seriously expert is sharks. Another is flying, and he would be lost without his Riley/Cessna 310.

After a memorable evening in the bar, and an even more memorable morning on the coral reefs, I reluctantly ran out of

Quinby found this airport, on Crooked Island, hard by a perfect semicircular bay, irresistible. He beachcombed here for 45 minutes before taking off for "nowhere in particular."

Quinby landed at this strip on a small island called Spanish Cay, but he didn't get to do any beachcombing there. He was ordered off the island by three men who drove up in a Jeep as the Apache landed.

money and had to depart in search of more. If there had been gas I could have gone direct to the United States from Northern Eleuthera. But I was assured that gas could be had at Marsh Harbor, a half-hour hop northwest.

Could be, but the Customs man said gas was vaguely "in town." No phone, no car, made it completely academic whether it really was there or not. There was no choice but to plot a "best economy" flight to Freeport or equidistant Nassau. So Freeport it was in just over 35 minutes, where the thirsty *Apache* got its fill of 100 octane (cheaper than 80) at a very busy transient ramp. A bongo band greeted DC-6's full of arriving pleasure seekers and gamblers, and Customs was cheerful and informal as they cleared me "outbound" to the United States. I filed DVFR and reported penetration of the ADIZ on a very crowded Miami Center frequency. I wondered if this ADIZ business was really necessary; thought about Castro and his aggressive antagonists; and guessed it was, unfortunately.

And the idyl was only half experienced. In Orlando, with the fine cooperation of the Showalter crew, I remained overnight, shopped a little, cashed a check, slept and endured a predawn takeoff with a stalwart son at 0530 on Thanksgiving morning. No longer solo, I topped the coastal clouds to Bimini en route to Nassau with quiet companionship. For all his eagerness and early morning energy, stalwart son slept as we climbed out over the cumulus at sunrise.

Nassau was mopping the terminal building floors as we checked in, left the bird to be gassed, and headed for Customs and breakfast in that order. They were dispatched, and I got a dividend to boot — a chat with Bobbie Hall, the personable director of air traffic control for the Bahamas. He is one of the dedicated ones, and devoted to opening the islands he loves to general aviation. Over coffee and clammy pastry, he enthused over my flight experience to date and offered guidance on my forthcoming days.

Thence to Norman's Cay — or key if you wish; they are interchangeable. On a dozen flights this enigmatic strip, marked **PVT** on

Outbound for snorkeling at South Caicos on another trip to the Bahamas is Author Gil Quinby at the far right. His stalwart son, Randy, is second from the left.

the chart, had challenged me. The island in the Exuma Cays was exquisitely beautiful, but the runway had big "X's" on it. So I had decided to land there and ask permission.

We were met with cheerful courtesy. Ken Laden and two youngish daughters welcomed us and made us at home, combing and snorkling the beach adjacent to the strip. The X's were for protection from liability, and the daughters quickly passed the word to an older sister at home; could stalwart son be an asset here?

We offered to carry out the mail but it was decided that Bahamas mail boat would get the job done just as well, since I was outbound. Traded gossip; a Haitian ship had run aground somewhere about 75 miles southwest down the Exuma Cays and the "government" boats and planes were converging.

Then off again to search the chain of

Exuma Islets for a suitable landing area. I had seen a raw new strip on my Palm Beach-South Caicos nonstop, and headed for it now. It was called Rudder Cut and it is also PVT, and consists of a dredged west half and an eastern half blasted out of the limestone ridge of the island chain. By this time there was a considerable breeze blowing the ocean against the eastward facing cliffs, and the windward, higher end of the Rudder Cut strip was interestingly drenched with periodic ocean spray for all its 25-foot height above "mean" (*really* mean) sea level. But the strip is most practical for *Apaches,* and the landing was followed by a visit from a Jeep full of delightful native family who made us most welcome and livened the proceedings by pursuing a shore bird which chose to sit on the runway against the vicious wind. Beachcombing was adventurous if not greatly productive, and

Airport on Gorda Cay, off southern Abaco, shot from the air by the author. Quinby reported it was a fine strip on a lovely private island, but the welcome wasn't so good.

snorkeling was out of the question.

So the *Apache* was run downwind to the bay end and it took off into the cliff spray. It reminded me a little of a carrier deck takeoff. And now it was a question of finding Cutlass Bay again, and this involved finding Cat Island, and this involved dead reckoning, and I lacked one basic ingredient. I was not sure where I had started from, since Rudder Cut is not on the map. So I took a heading that would over allow for the strong head wind, and would avoid all chance of missing Cat Island to the south. This "known error" worked, and landfall on Cat Island was made from a position well north of the south coast.

Max Bates, Clancy, Eva, and the Cutlass Bay gang welcomed us like old friends. And we quickly abandoned all thoughts of further island hopping at least for a couple of days. The food, the company, and the quarters were excellent. The bugs tolerable if repellent was used copiously, and the diving was terrific. With stalwart son as a diving buddy, we combed the coral heads — he for fish and lobster, me for rarer shells.

During one lazy afternoon I drove a party around the island on an inspection tour in the *Apache*. One passenger was a British agronomist who was stationed there by Her Majesty to improve the agricultural self-sufficiency of the island. He had Land-Rovered the place thoroughly, but it was a pleasure to enjoy the terrain and flora through his expert eyes from this new airborne point of view. Another passenger was Clancy, whose grin of pleasure at his first flight was simply blinding.

The Cutlass Bay sojourn was climaxed by a rip-roaring visit to "The Galleon," a garish pub run by Mr. Bains on the outskirts of Bainstown, population 37. There was jukebox dancing and hymn singing and foot stomping and hand clapping and great friendships made to the roar of the generator and the fade and flicker of the naked 40-watt bulbs. Mr. Bains was a proud and proper host in his narrow brimmed hat and bare feet. He was especially gracious to me — Clancy is his oldest son. My stalwart son cut quite a figure dancing with the native gals on the clean sand floor of this social center. Mr. Bains and I sensed each others' pride.

One of the natives had a bad toothache. There is no dentist on Cat Island, and he was stoically waiting for four days until the mail boat could take him on an all-day run to Nassau. So Sunday morning we took off to start the trip home with a full load; the toothache case was delivered into ministering hands at Nassau Airport in an hour. Max Bates accompanied us on an afternoon of island hopping that was a fitting finale to a wonderful week.

Out of Nassau, we landed first at Gorda Cay, west of Abaco. A fine strip and a lovely private island, tended by an old native who tried to extract £5 ($14) for our landing. We humored him up to but not including payment, and took off again with the beach uncombed. This was the first unwelcome mat in all our invasions of island privacy.

A small airport was reported to exist on the swampy east end of Grand Bahama at Riding Rocks, so we headed direct from Gorda to that area. Small it was, but hard and with good approaches. It was sort of sod-on-sand, and the *Apache* fit it well with a minimum of short-field technique required. A short walk through a mangrove brought us on a middling good beach — we were spoiled by now from our experience on fantastically beautiful beaches — with a minimum of flotsam to comb for shells and stuff. We encountered a couple who had driven out from Freeport some 50 miles west up the coast. There is an interesting looking resort here with good harbor facilities and I would imagine the fishing to be excellent.

Back in the air at about 3:30 p.m. we decided to try one more island. Northeast past Little Abaco there was a strip on a little island called Spanish Cay. It, too, was marked "PVT," and this one really meant it. Three burly men of sincere determination and no sense of humor at all rolled up in a Jeep and requested that we leave. Immediately. No, we could not walk down to the beach. Just leave. We left, wondering what reason prompted their inhospitable attitude. Our imagination ran through all sorts of dark and romantic justifications for their conduct, but returned to the simple fact that it *was their* island, and we *were* trespassing. But it was an unfortunate end to our idyl — that was to have been our last beach, and now, after a swing over Green Turtle Cay and a bit of cu-dodging we headed for Freeport, West Palm, and home.

Loaded with shells from 13 beaches the *Apache* dragged me up to Washington National that night — a long way from Cutlass Bay — and into the office almost on time the next morning. We had covered over 6,000 miles in 33 hours, and had reveled in the beauty of the Bahamas as only the flyer can see them. In eight days we had touched 17 airports on 14 different islands. And the Bahamas lived up to our fondest expectations.

There are more airports, and more islands and I will see them too one day. And on the next trip the joy of further discovery will be heightened by the pleasure of revisiting old friends. For in spite of Spanish Cay, the beauty of the Bahamas is exceeded only by the gracious friendliness of the Bahamians. ◆

Color photos by: (1) the author, top page 37, page 39, bottom page 40; (2) by Max Karant, page 36, center page 37, page 38, top page 40, page 41.

This big loggerhead turtle was brought into South Caicos, one of the places later visited by the author. It had been sighted at sea by members of a snorkeling party and caught by hand by the man in the picture.

THE AUTHOR

Gil Quinby, author of "Beachcombing In The Bahamas," has a real affection for the islands of the Caribbean. He has made many flights to that area and expects to make many more to the enchanted islands. Gil is vice president of marketing planning of the Narco Avionics Division of the National Aeronautical Corporation, Fort Washington, Pa. Prior to his present assignment, Quinby was Narco sales manager for 15 years. He is vice president of the parent corporation. A long-time pilot with better than 3,500 hours flying time to his credit, Quinby is a graduate electrical engineer. He served a three-year tour of duty with the U.S. Navy as an electronics officer.

Leisurely flight through these islands may be the cure you are seeking. PILOT editor, who tries it, reports: 'It's the sort of adventure that even a yachtsman will envy'

ISLAND HOPPING
AROUND THE
CARIBBEAN

By MAX KARANT | AOPA 18

This is George Town, Great Exuma Island, in the Bahamas. The buildings in the foreground are Peace and Plenty, a well-known resort spot among pilots. The town is at the left in the background. Beyond the town, toward the top of the picture, is the George Town Airport. Both Peace and Plenty and the next-door Two Turtles Inn have Unicom and pilots call for rooms and transportation as they approach the place.

If you're suffering from an acute case of cobwebs in the belfry, there's an excellent cure awaiting you in the West Indies — go island hopping. Get to the east coast of Florida as soon as you can, but take it easy after that. With a private plane it's the sort of romantic adventure that even the yachtsman will envy.

There are some basic requirements, of course. You need some time off, say a week or preferably two. You need a plane with reasonably good performance (particularly range). You shouldn't have any deep-seated phobia about flying over water, and you should have some money along with you (but not a lot, if you aren't determined to search out the $40–$50-a-day tourist traps). Then you should have the determination to relax and enjoy hopping from island to island, flying low around the beautiful beaches, mountains or jungles on each island, and just generally fitting yourself into the native life at each place. All of it can be colorful, pleasant and fascinating — including, incidentally, the varying amounts of red tape you run into.

In 13 days of island-hopping in *Twin Comanche* N13K I covered a route from Washington to West Palm Beach, Fla., non-stop over the Bahamas to South Caicos, then on to Haiti, Puerto Rico, St. Maarten (half French, half Dutch), Martinique (French), St. Vincent, Grenada (both British), Tobago, back to St. Maarten, South Caicos, Ft. Lauderdale, then Washington. These are places we actually made a stop. We had to content ourselves with aerial sightseeing around such romantic-sounding Leeward and Windward islands as Saba, St. Eustatius, St. Kitts, Nevis, Montserrat, Guadeloupe, Dominica, the Grenadines and, of course, such better-known spots as St. Thomas and the British Virgin Islands.

There were three of us: Perry Boswell (AOPA 3831), Stuart, Fla.; and Margareta

Sunset at St. Martin. This shot was taken on the Dutch side of the island (the spelling there is "St. Maarten"). This charming little island is a free port, where there are no Customs requirements; it has a modern airport with jet schedules.

Lamentin Airport at Fort de France, Martinique, as seen by the author as he taxied in after landing. N13K received very little attention here. The pilot had to pick a parking place — between the French Cessna 172 on the left and the Snow agplane on the right — get a baggage cart himself and empty the plane, then hunt up an attendant in order to get fuel. The airport has long runways and gets a lot of traffic, including jets, from the West Indies and Europe.

Ljunggren, a friend of Perry's, who speaks five languages and acted as interpreter whenever we needed it. She had arrived in the United States from Sweden just a couple of days before we left Florida.

After a brief stop at West Palm Beach to get fuel and rent survival equipment from Jim Tilford's (AOPA 8923), our next leg was nonstop to South Caicos, overflying the Bahamas entirely because of a lack of time, plus the fact that we've been there a number of times, and wanted to spend as much time as possible down in the other islands.

SOUTH CAICOS is an excellent place to "get away from it all," if you don't mind roughing it a bit. It's 573 nautical miles from West Palm Beach, has one hotel (more like a hostel), 16 beds, a 6,000-foot coral airstrip that's hard on low-hanging props because it hasn't been rolled regularly (a responsibility of the U.S. Coast Guard, which has a Loran station there), and a powerful homing beacon that I got clearly on my ADF-31 380 nautical miles away. If you're not the Miami Beach coat-and-tie-for-dinner type, South Caicos is a wonderful hideaway. They have Unicom, 100-octane, and six smoke pots if you must land at night (try not to; the runway's often populated by donkeys).

CAP HAITIEN on the north coast of Haiti is less than an hour's flight from South Caicos, has a good airport, and local people swarming all over the place with their hands out the moment they spot a tourist. My plane, the only one on the field, was met by 11 men. Margareta spoke French, the national language, and quickly helped us sepa-

This is the harbor of St. Georges, Grenada, taken from a fort overlooking the entrance to the harbor. That's one of the ancient cannons that was in the original fort.

RIGHT: An unusual view of the harbor of Grenada. "The most beautiful harbor I saw on this trip," the author says. The picture, incidentally, was taken from the window of his hotel room. Grenada, a British colony, is 21 miles long and 12 miles wide.

COLOR PHOTOS BY THE AUTHOR

Island hopping in the Caribbean always is a fascinating journey. This is what the aerial island-hopper sees for hundreds of miles on such a flight: little coral islands strung out in the spectacularly beautiful Caribbean, with the ever-present cumulus clouds marking the land areas.

Sans-Souci Palace at Milot near Cap Haitien on Haiti's north coast, where King Christophe resided until his death. The King committed suicide there on Oct. 8, 1820, after a revolt of his officers.

rate the essentials from the spur-of-the-moment inventions. Even so, it took 28 minutes before we could get into a cab (which promptly collided head-on with a truck) and head for the Roi Christophe Hotel. Highlight was a horseback ride up one of the country's highest mountains to La Citadelle, an incredible fortress then-King Christophe ordered built right on top of this remote peak. It took 13 years and 200,000 men to do it. We rode up single-file on horseback, easily the most nerve-tingling (and that's not all) adventure of the whole trip.

PUERTO RICO. I should say San Juan, because we spent our time holed up in purse-shattering hotels. I'd planned to overfly the country entirely, because it was the height of the winter season, we didn't have hotel reservations, and the place was swarming with tourists. But my transmitter selector switch shorted out, and the only radio shop in that entire area is at San Juan. Though a radio man "fixed" the trouble within a couple of hours after I landed, I'd made the mistake of going to a hotel without checking the finished work. That was Saturday afternoon. Sunday morning we arrived ready to go, but one quick check showed the radio man hadn't fixed it at all. We spent all day on the phone but couldn't find him, so had to wait until Monday.

ST. MAARTEN is the way you write the Dutch half of this island; the French half is written St. Martin. This charming, plain and picturesque little island is 167 nautical miles east of San Juan, has no Customs requirements, is a free port, and has a big modern airport with jet schedules (which regularly swamp the place with just one planeload). With no reservations here either (we had none anywhere), it was again potluck. I got a single room in one of the best hotels in Philipsburg, the Dutch town, for $16, including meals. We stopped here on the return trip and ended up in rooms above stores in town. We drove up to the French side of the island in a cab. The only way you can tell the difference is a small sign, and the road surface changes from concrete to macadam. On the way to St. Maarten we flew over St. Thomas and the British Virgin Islands, including the airstrip at Virgin Gorda, where they bar single-engine planes because one had an accident there sometime ago.

MARTINIQUE was the next overnight stop we'd chosen. The flight from St. Maarten took just over two hours, and it was spectacular. Sitting outside our hotel at St. Maarten the night before, watching the sunset over the sea, we could see a little island to the south, barely visible in the twilight. It reminded me of the fictional Bali Hai, so I was determined to fly around it the next day on the way to Martinique. It was even more spectacular up close. It's a tiny extinct volcano, sticks straight up out of the sea, and boats have a hard time getting ashore; you can only get there on a lighter, or in a Dornier Do 28 from St. Maarten, which lands on a strip hacked out of the side of the cliff. The island is Saba (SAY-bah); it's Dutch, is only five square miles in size and 2,900 feet high. Flying around it low and close was awesome.

From Saba we headed south a few miles over St. Eustatius (also Dutch), St. Kitts, Nevis (it's British, and pronounced NEE-viss), Montserrat (British), Guadeloupe (French), and Dominica (doe-min-EE-kah,

Twin-engine plane seen in the foreground is a Do 28, the type of airplane used to fly passengers to the little volcanic island of Saba, a few miles off-shore from St. Maarten. The picture was taken at Juliana Airport at St. Maarten (St. Martin).

N13K being refueled before takeoff from Grenada. Gasoline is being pumped out of a modern sunken pit, but that is not quite what it seems. Fuel is first pumped out of a barrel which is carried to the pit through an underground hose.

British). They are all spectacular from the air, and I'm going back to them some day. Many of these islands were discovered by Columbus in 1493. Dominica is a lush jungle that gets as much as 250 inches of rain annually, while other islands not far away must conserve their water.

Fort de France is a fairly large city, so we found rooms downtown quickly, with the help of girls from the tourist department. The airport is large and gets regular jet traffic. They seem to ignore general aviation, and we were on our own for everything but pumping gas. We had to carry our own bags, and the first greeting we got from anyone at the airport was that we would have to pay airport taxes immediately. A couple of restaurants in town made up for this; they were wonderful, in the inimitable French tradition. My room was air-conditioned,

had a bidet but no toilet, and cost $11.85 including breakfast. A taxi tour around much of the island was beautiful. Incidentally, almost everywhere we went in the West Indies the nicest, most helpful people proved to be the cab drivers and waiters and waitresses.

ST. VINCENT is British, and equally picturesque. It has an excellent airport just outside of Kingstown, the island's biggest community — but no gas. They'd let their last supply run out (a few drums) sometime ago, and just weren't interested in getting any more. But they were quick to collect a $4 landing fee, $1.20 stamp duty, $1.50 for parking, for a total of $6.70 "Beewee" (a British West Indies dollar is worth 60¢ U.S., so the total cost in U.S. money was $4). Like Martinique, this tiny island also demanded three general declarations forms on arrival,

and another three on departure.

The island itself is beautiful and we enjoyed our taxi ride over the hills, through the jungles and along the seacoast. We got rooms in one of the better downtown hotels. Mine had no screens on any windows, a triangular mosquito net hanging over the bed, a box of matches, and a supply of something called "Fish Mosquito Destroyer" made by the Blood Protection Company of Hong Kong. It's a long strip of some coiled material that you light when you go to bed, and the ensuing smoke is supposed to drive off all bugs, enabling you to "enjoy eight hours of peace, awake or asleep." The bed itself had nothing but a bare mattress and quilt. Result: quite an uncomfortable night, numerous bites, little sleep. Some of the worst food we had on the trip was here.

GRENADA has the most beautiful har-

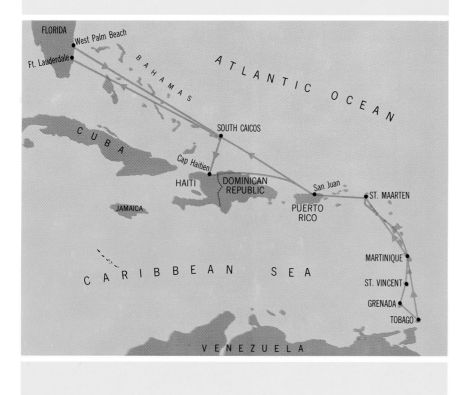

bor I saw on this trip. The island itself is as beautiful as can be, and we had to fly around it low, taking pictures. It's British, and pronounced gren-AY-dah. The flight from St. Vincent to Grenada is down a chain of tiny islands called The Grenadines, and weaving in and out along these beautiful little islands is in itself worth the trip. Then, as we flew low around the shore of Grenada, we flew around a little hill on the southwest corner of the island and found ourselves almost face to face with a big white ocean liner anchored in the harbor at St. Georges. As we circled the ship we could easily see the name "Shalom" on both bow and stern. She's the pride of Israel's merchant marine and had stopped at Grenada while on a 13-day Caribbean cruise out of New York. We ultimately wangled our way aboard, and found it to be a new, magnificent, fully air-conditioned liner. We tried to have dinner aboard (the food in some of the British islands is aimed at the stomach, not the palate), but she sailed that afternoon, and dinner was served at sea.

The paper work at Grenada was even worse than at previous islands — four lengthy general declaration forms on arrival, and four more on departure. The airport is excellent for general aviation, and has fuel available — but there's a trick to it. There's no gas in the modern gas pit. They hook another pump to a hose in another building, put that hose into gasoline drums stacked around the place, and then pump that out another hose into the pump out in the gas pit on the ramp. Then another hose pumps it into the plane. It took a half hour to get 24 gallons, and when I paid the bill an airline official "suggested" I give the gas man

a substantial tip before leaving the field.

The drive from the airport to St. Georges took an hour, was memorable and beautiful. The taxi driver was one of the best on the trip, and he made an educational sightseeing trip out of the ride. He took the mountain road to town, we climbed up alongside a crater lake shrouded in clouds, and to the island's highest point (1,910 feet). He stopped to pick samples for us of the cocoa, cinnamon, pigeon peas and nutmeg, which are the island's staple crops.

TOBAGO is one of the islands most recommended by Caribbean adventurers, and it's the one island I left in disgust without even going into town. We'd filed the required flight plan at Grenada, only to find that Customs hadn't been notified at Tobago. After locating the Customs officer on the phone he ordered us to stay at the airport until he arrived (over an hour later). Then they demanded a total of nine forms and $5, at which point we canceled our hotel reservations and flew back to the Dutch St. Maarten and spent another pleasant evening. After that, South Caicos, Ft. Lauderdale and home.

When time permits, I'm going back again, this time to visit places I had to miss. Saba, Nevis, St. Kitts, Antigua, Guadeloupe, St. Lucia and Dominica all look inviting, and I'm sure I'll find some others. All these lovely and romantic spots are near each other. Cap Haitien, for example, was just one hour from South Caicos — including local sightseeing. It was 0140 from San Juan to St. Maarten, 0046 from Martinique to St. Vincent, and also 0046 from St. Vincent to Grenada. The longest leg of any south of South Caicos was 0347, from Tobago to St. Maarten. ◆

Few people have ever heard of South Caicos. Most of those who have are pilots, and nearly all of them would be content to keep it the remote flyers' paradise it is. But not Liam Maguire, who started it all. As a young surveyor for the British government, who first saw the place in 1961 while on an assignment that included both the Cayman, and Turks and Caicos island groups, Maguire was unimpressed by all the sales talks he'd heard about the Caymans, but was fascinated by the Caicos islands, about which he'd heard nothing. He had worked first in the Caymans on his assignment, and while there met Brian Reid, III, of Illinois, who was interested in developing some land in the Caribbean.

From the Caymans, Maguire went to the Turks and Caicos groups and instantly fell in love with the remote little cluster of islands that is about 100 miles north of Haiti and the Dominican Republic, 415 northwest of San Juan, 460 southeast of Nassau and 590 southeast of Miami. In the Caicoses themselves (Grand Turk, a U.S. Air Force missile range base, is about 25 miles southeast of South Caicos) there are Grand Caicos, North Caicos, East Caicos, South Caicos and Providenciales; all of them combined have a population of just over 3,000 people. Only South Caicos had an old World War II coral airstrip and a powerful low-frequency homing beacon.

After finishing his assignment in the Turks and Caicos islands, Maguire headed for his next assignment, in North Borneo. To get to that distant Pacific island, Maguire headed across the United States. On the way, he stopped in Chicago to visit Reid and told him there was an old plantation house and

By MAX KARANT

AOPA 18

South Caicos was known to few pilots before Liam Maguire got there in 1962. He's changing all of that, though. Former 'hideaway' is becoming a favorite refueling stop for short-range aircraft and a vacation spot for those who really want something to write home about

CARIBBEAN
CROSSROAD

Members of the Flying Physicians Association relax at the small reception building on South Caicos Airport during a stopover in May 1966. The automobile is one of the several cars on the Island jokingly referred to as "solid wood Cadillacs" (they're not Cadillacs, incidentally) because wooden bodies replaced metal ones which have been eroded away by salt air.

Here is a close-up of Dr. Patricia Whiteside-Jones basking in the abundance of medicines brought to the island by Flying Physicians. She is seated on the doorstep of her "dispensary." Plenty of hard work was necessary, when the young doctor arrived, to make the place clean and sanitary. However, the author says it still doesn't look much like a dispensary.

Dr. Patricia Whiteside-Jones is the happy young lady in the center of the group back of the carton-laden wing. Dr. Whiteside-Jones is South Caicos' only physician, and those boxes contain much-needed drugs for treating the islanders. Flying Physicians, who brought the drugs, are pictured with Dr. Whiteside-Jones.

350 acres for sale in South Caicos rather cheaply. Reid not only bought the property, but asked Maguire if he'd be interested in settling at South Caicos if he (Reid) financed a small development company there to see what could be done with the land. Maguire immediately accepted, resigned his job with the British government, returned to England to settle his affairs there, then moved to South Caicos permanently in January 1962.

Though the airstrip was barely operable in those days, Maguire quickly saw its potential. Clearly it was an ideal refueling stop for short-range aircraft. And once pilots became accustomed to stopping there, anything else he could do to attract them would mean that much more to the island economy. Except for the airplane, the Caicos islands are far too remote for any other form of transportation. About 20 yachts a year stop there, usually on ferry trips to the Virgin Islands. There are no tourist boats.

The local Bahamas airline stopped there once every two weeks. Only other plane service was a Coast Guard supply plane (the Coast Guard operates a Loran station on the island), also once every two weeks. Only other planes that stopped by were usually those caught by excessive head winds, during ferry flights to South America. And when they stopped, they had to take the white marine fuel kept there in drums to operate the radio beacon.

Maguire went after the civil aviation business he knew was avoiding South Caicos. He put in aviation gas, and his first five drums lasted a month. By August of that year five pilots who had heard of the new look at South Caicos stopped by for fuel. One year later 45 planes refueled there, despite the fact that August is a bad month. In January 1966 he refueled 104 planes, and as soon as he can get the price down (100 octane costs 50¢ a gallon) Maguire expects business to boom. The high cost, incidentally, is due to the fact that he's had to pay prices that include shipping fuel by tanker from Aruba to Nassau (virtually passing right by South Caicos), transferring Maguire's comparatively small order to a smaller tanker which then works its way back south. But the volume of fuel being sold there now has reached the point where it's likely he'll be able to get a tanker to come directly from Aruba, Puerto Rico or the West Indies to South Caicos. When that happens, the price of aviation fuel should drop as much as 20¢ a gallon.

Having learned the size of U.S. general aviation, Maguire wrote letters to all the major fixed-base operators he could find in south Florida, asking their advice in connection with making South Caicos a refueling stop. His most encouragement, help and advice came from C. I. "Red" Gamber, Jr. (AOPA 257077), owner of famed Red Aircraft at Ft. Lauderdale. Gamber sent him a list of things to do, and how to go about it. Then Maguire solicited the oil companies, only to get turned down cold by all but Esso. Today, Maguire is the largest Esso distributor in the Bahamas outside of Nassau (though the Turks and Caicos islands are not actually in the Bahamas group).

Thanks to Maguire, the local government has become so air-minded that the island's economy and attitude toward the outside world are gradually changing. They have an airport program to provide three new strips

This is the runway of the South Caicos Airport, which is becoming familiar to more and more pilots visiting the Caribbean area. Liam Maguire has plans for paving and lighting the 6,000-foot runway. The airport program for the islands calls for three additional landing strips, but they will have runways not exceeding 3,000 feet in length.

Lynn and Liam Maguire at the official South Caicos "watering trough." It is the bar of the Admiral's Arms. Pilots leave their business cards on the bulletin boards back of the bar. The name "Liam," incidentally, is a contraction of "William" in the Irish style. Lynn is of French descent and comes from Sandusky, O.

A Customs officer inspects a shipment of fresh produce and other supplies imported by the author from Florida. Some supplies are hard to come by on the island. Margareta Ljunggren, who had recently arrived from Sweden via Florida, is seated back of the bag of supplies. Others on and around the "solid wood Cadillac" are (left to right): Liam and Lynn Maguire, Perry Boswell of Stuart, Fla., and an airport attendant.

throughout the islands, which will ultimately give the islands a total of five airports for about 3,000 people currently living there. David Lindsay, Jr. (AOPA 57465), publisher of the Sarasota, Fla., newspaper and owner of the company that makes high-performance general aviation *Cavaliers* out of *Mustang* fighters, also has discovered South Caicos and wants to participate in the careful development of the islands. As soon as the new airstrips are in, he wants to test a small local airline operation between the strips, with *Cherokee 6* combination passenger-cargo planes.

Unlike entrepreneurs elsewhere in the area, Maguire is determined to do everything possible to avoid turning the islands into a tourist trap. The 6,000-foot South Caicos strip will never be longer than 7,000 feet, but it will be paved and lighted. The other strips will be limited to about 3,000 feet. Hotels would be limited to 30 rooms each.

South Caicos presently is a true aerial crossroads. It's directly on the Great Circle course from the eastern United States to South America. It's within a 500-mile radius of Nassau, Montego Bay, Kingston, Santo Domingo, San Juan and the Virgin Islands, all of them within an easy two- to three-hour range of even the smallest general aviation types today. Almost every type of general aviation plane can be seen at the South Caicos strip at one time or another. There are oil prospectors, gold miners and diamond miners from Venezuela and Guyana (who often go north in rickety beat-up planes and return southbound sometime later in shiny new and expensive planes). There are ferry pilots and corporation presidents, doctors and accountants, plus quite a few wives and children. Smallest plane to go through was an ancient Cessna 140 (with an extra drum of gas on the right seat); largest outside the airline and Coast Guard ships are DC3's. The Rockwell-Standard (Aero Commander manufacturers) Grumman *Mallard* has gone through; the Rockwell family

spent the night at the Admiral's Arms.

One of the most powerful low-frequency homing beacons in the Caribbean sits a short distance from the end of the South Caicos runway; pilots report receiving it over 400 miles away. It's operated and maintained by Pan American Airways on its route between New York and San Juan. It was rumored slated for shutdown as no longer needed, but by then the air traffic over the route had grown to the point that FAA sent a plane down from Florida to look over the situation and make recommendations for keeping the beacon on the air. The whole installation has since been rejuvenated.

If the Caribe Hilton or Dorado Beach hotels are your idea of the ideal tropical holi-

day, then just land at South Caicos for gas and keep going. But if you like the Caribbean as it really is outside the tourist traps, South Caicos can be your destination — if there's room at the Admiral's Arms. The name of that hostelry is due largely to Maguire's wry wit. No matter how fancy it sounds, the Admiral's Arms is a rambling old wooden house with, as pilots everywhere know who have stayed there, sometimes embarrassingly thin walls. Originally, at its chummiest it held 16 people. Every so often somebody had to sleep on the couch on the porch; sometimes the lounging benches in the bar had to be used for an emergency bed. They have completed an additional eight rooms (with 16 beds) on the west end

The famous Admiral's Arms hotel may be seen in the background. The little blue house in the foreground has been rejuvenated for Liam and Lynn Maguire to live in. They had been living in the Admiral's Arms. Their move out of the hotel and the addition of eight rooms brought the capacity of hotel up to 32 guests.

This diver is holding up what is a delicacy to anyone from the States; to the natives it's a standard food. The lobster was speared by speargun in diver's right hand. Diver, incidentally, was guide for the author's group. Lobsters are easily seen in the crystal-clear water of the South Caicos area.

COLOR PHOTOS BY THE AUTHOR

of the old house. That's as far as Maguire intends to go with the Admiral's Arms; any further expansion will have to be another building somewhere else.

While South Caicos isn't plush, it's spectacular in its own way. The food is simple and good, there's always a breeze blowing in the windows at night (I found it cooler than Washington, D.C., in midsummer) and if you're interested in the breathtaking underwater beauty of the Caribbean, South Caicos is almost unsurpassed. Do you like lobster or conch? The ocean is teeming with them, and you quickly get all of these delicacies you can hold. All other types of fishing are virtually untouched, including a huge area of flats where the bone fishing is something they write home about.

The runway is soon to be improved, fenced and lighted. It's not wise to land there at night now because of the lack of lighting and the fact that the local wild donkeys seem to prefer sleeping on the dark runway at night (one man landed his Cessna 310 on top of one one night and it took a while to make repairs — to the plane, but not the donkey).

Liam's wife, Lynn, is a Yankee who happened to be a passenger in a plane that stopped over at South Caicos once. The two fell for each other so quickly that she sent a cablegram back to her boss almost immediately which just said "I quit, I quit, I quit." Though she's from Sandusky, O., she has taken to the native life just as though she was born there. She has learned to fly, and Liam is about to. Meanwhile, they have settled down to run their own little tropical paradise. ◆

This map shows how South Caicos fits in with some other of the better-known islands of the Bahamas. U.S. Air Force missile range base is about 25 miles away on Grand Turk Island.

CENTER: A picture of Cockburn Harbor, the town on South Caicos. This view is looking, generally, to the east. The single runway of the airport may be seen running from left to right across the far end of the land. In the foreground, just above the waterline and in the center of the picture, stands the Admiral's Arms. Salt evaporation ponds are at the far right.

RIGHT: This is a typical South Caicos refueling scene. The two Cessna 182's on the left are being ferried to Brazil. The author's Twin Comanche may be seen on the right. The automobile in the foreground is another one of those "solid wood Cadillacs" used to get about the island. Various models of automobiles are used for the conversion to the "solid wood" model.

53

By RICHARD OWENS, JR. | AOPA 46578

LATIN-AMERICAN BYWAYS

Little-visited areas of Mexico and Central America hold attractions for flying tourists, but some fields require planes with short-field landing characteristics

Every flying trip into Mexico and Central America for my wife, Peggy, and me has inspired additional desires to explore further beyond the relative confusion and commonplace of Acapulco and the like. After several trips down the west coast circuit of Mexico we struck out south and east of Acapulco and in a few years had pretty well covered the Yucatan Peninsula, including the Caribbean Islands of Cozumel and Mujeres, British Honduras, Guatemala, El Salvador and Honduras.

Our first trip to Cozumel was before it had really been "discovered" as it was with Isla Mujeres to the north. However, the next trip out there revealed the onslaught of progress with high-rise hotels beginning to obstruct the horizon and the tourists descending upon the little islands like the plague.

There seemed little left within the practical limitations of our aircraft — a *Cherokee 180* — which created any great incentive to fly until while in Tegucigalpa, Honduras, we had the good fortune of meeting a Mr. Bill Lady, a partner of the Aereo de Servicios, a flying charter service operating throughout Honduras. At this particular time we were headed for the Mayan ruins of Copán from Tegucigalpa. While inquiring concerning other places of interest in Honduras, Mr. Lady mentioned the Islas de la Bahía (Bay Islands) off the Caribbean coast and suggested that if we had the time and the inclination we should, by all means, make a special effort to visit them.

Who has even heard of the Islas de la Bahía? We hadn't until Mr. Lady had brought them to our attention, and even during a two-year interim before returning to visit them, we had little success obtaining any information concerning the Bay Islands. However, these islands and the ruins of Tikal

in the Guatemalan jungle were our destinations for this particular trip, with a flight farther south through Nicaragua and Costa Rica.

More specifically, our plans were to fly down the west coast of Mexico into Guatemala and visit the Mayan ruins of Tikal, across to the Caribbean and Honduras and then south through Nicaragua to Costa Rica and back home via the west coast of Central America and Mexico. We were to be joined by Wilmer (AOPA 84299) and Hilda Ulin from Forks, Wash., who were taking their *Bonanza* along and planned to travel with us to the Bay Islands then return home while we continued south to Costa Rica. After spending so much time flying alone over the desolation of Mexico and Central America, it was a comforting and interesting experience to have another aircraft along, especially over the more remote regions of the Guatemalan jungles and such.

We departed Port Angeles, Wash., separately on a Friday then rendezvoused the following day at Guaymas, Mexico, after taking separate paths through the United States. We hadn't planned on spending much time on the Mexican coast since we had a fairly full schedule on our itinerary in Central America, but we did want a day or two on the beaches to get a suntan under way prior to reaching the blistering heat of the Caribbean waters. So, consequently, we spent several days at the Hotel Malaque on Baja de Navidad, north of Manzanillo, acquiring our first painful coat of sunburn on their beautiful beach. After departing Malaque we refueled at Zihuatanejo, overflew Acapulco and headed inland to Oaxaca for the night. From Oaxaca we flew south back to the coast and landed at Tapachula to clear out of Mexico and file for Guatemala City.

Several years ago, entering Guatemala was a rather long, drawn-out, distasteful experience, but changes have been made and the formalities reduced to a minimum. Guatemala City is a beautiful, interesting city with much to offer from a tourist standpoint. We only stayed overnight and were up early the following morning making preparations to fly to the Mayan ruins of Tikal in the northern interior of Guatemala.

Navigating the some 200 miles north to Tikal was mostly a dead-reckoning affair for us since the only beacon functioning on this route was a 1,700 kc nondirectional beacon at Flores, 20 miles south of Tikal, which neither of us could work on our ADF's. There was also a 385 kc beacon at Flores which we could have utilized, but no amount of pleading with the officials could persuade them to make it operative for our flight. The direct route is practically nothing but tractless jungle with no check points of any consequence to assist navigation, so estimating the winds aloft from cloud shadows on the ground and making appropriate allowances, we came within 10 miles of beautiful Lake Flores just south of our destination. The lake in sight was a welcome relief after more than an hour of contemplating the dreadful consequences of a forced landing in the hostile environment of such a jungle. Sighting the ruins protruding above the jungle gave us a somewhat ominous thrill, almost as if we were discovering the long lost city for the first time. From the air there is little to indicate that it had been discovered yet since the jungle still enfolds the structures completely and only remnants of the highest temples break the monotony of the endless sea of jungle top from horizon to horizon.

The airstrip had been recently installed to

The Owens and Ulin planes on the strip at Tikal. The author flew the Cherokee 180 and the Ulins made the trip in the Bonanza.

One of the restored temples at Tikal, Guatemala, visited by the Owenses. The Mayan ruins of Tikal were one of the attractions that drew the flying tourists to Central America.

Typical of the receptions received by the visitors to Central America was the one on the Island of Utila. The inhabitants, who seldom saw a plane on the ground, crowded around the Owens Cherokee.

facilitate further study, excavation and restoration of the ruins. It was completely surrounded by the jungle in a fantastic setting. The adjacent thatched-roof buildings, strange vegetation and jungle noises reminded us more of scenes we had seen of Africa than Central America, and we were completely obsessed with it all.

Tikal (300 A.D.–870 A.D.) is one of the largest Mayan ceremonial centers and oldest Mayan cities now known. Its excavation was initiated only a few years ago; and since relatively little of its complex of structures has been uncovered at all, it still holds much appeal to those who desire visiting such a site in its more or less natural state. This feature, along with the spectacular setting and colorful past, makes it by far the most interesting Mayan ruin yet discovered. Accommodations are in thatched-roof cottages scattered around the "Jungle Lodge" and certainly are in keeping with the rustic theme.

Roads have been carved out of the jungle and an all-day cruise in an English Land-Rover covers most of the visible highlights of the ruins. The actual site of Tikal extends for approximately three miles in all directions from the center of the complex. It is so extensive and involved that it would take countless years to undo the destruction that the slowly advancing jungle has accomplished since Tikal's mysterious desertion.

The following day after lunch, we flew to

Flores and hired a dugout canoe for a trip to the village itself, which is located on an island on the lake. This was a fascinating side trip and we highly recommend it to anyone who can take the time and is fortunate enough to have his own aircraft available for the round trip. All in all, it was a completely wonderful two days and actually much more than we had anticipated.

Strangely enough, a blanket of fog creeps in over the jungle at this time of the year (March) practically every night and the early morning of our departure was no exception. Consequently, our takeoff was delayed until nearly 10 o'clock which shortened our flying day more than we had planned. From here we flew to the Caribbean side and landed at Puerto Barrios to clear out of Guatemala. There had been much guerrilla activity in this area at the time and we were advised at Tikal to skip Puerto Barrios if at all possible. To continue on as suggested, skipping Puerto Barrios and returning to Guatemala City for clearance, would have presented innumerable problems so we chose Puerto Barrios in spite of this advice and encountered nothing more than a horde of hostile-looking soldiers at the field who milled around us and the planes.

From here we crossed the Honduran border and landed at San Pedro Sula for clearance into Honduras. After a quick bite to eat and topping our tanks we departed and

at last headed for our Islas de la Bahía, a hundred miles down the coast. The north coast line of Honduras is a beautiful sight from the air with its snow white beaches and typical turquoise waters of the Caribbean. Heading out across the water to the islands requires a bit of dead reckoning since they are not visible from the coast because of the ever-present haze over the ocean. Watching them loom up through this haze was a thrill, since they were really our destination and we had been contemplating them for such a long time. It is truly a magnificent chain of islands and in a setting that defies description. There are no waters more beautiful in color than this part of the Caribbean and the overall scene is much akin to the South Pacific with the coral reefs, white beaches and swaying coconut palms lining every shore line. Since there are, strangely enough, no tourist developments in these parts as yet, one should keep this in mind if contemplating a trip through this area. Anyone looking for such luxurious facilities as available on the west coast of Mexico would be bitterly disappointed out here. But if, like us, you desire the unknown and unspoiled virgin beauty, these islands will come close to fulfilling your wildest dreams.

The Bay Islands consist of four major islands, Utila, Roatan, Barbareta and Guanaja, plus numerous lesser islands and reefs spread out over a distance of 50 miles, 25 miles off the coast of Honduras; and according to those who have seen them, these are some of the most beautiful islands in the world. Also the privately owned smaller Cayos Cochinos group should probably be included with the Bay Islands and are halfway between the mainland and the islands proper. The WAC aeronautical charts show no airstrips on any of these islands but actually five islands are accessible by air. However, several of these strips are quite marginal since they were privately constructed for high performance aircraft such as Cessna 180's and are used ordinarily by very proficient professional pilots. For example, strips on both Cayos Cochinos and Guanaja are substantially less than 1,000 feet and the approach and runway on Guanaja are about as hair raising as you would find anywhere.

We had no real plans except to see all the islands. We decided to fly the whole chain and spend the first night on Guanaja, the easternmost island. Guanaja has only one village, Bonacca, of any consequence and to get to it involves some rather unique problems. The village itself is located on a small island in a protected harbor approximately a quarter-mile off-shore. There are two strips on Guanaja but the one ordinarily used is five miles to the northeast of Bonacca and 3,000 feet long. The other strip, privately constructed and owned by the Aereo de Servicios, is just on shore from the village, but is only 800 feet long with a miserable approach, a built-in crosswind and a roll on the runway that would terrify a cycle driver. Since this strip was out of the question for Wilmer's *Bonanza,* we worked out a plan utilizing both strips that solved some of our transportation problems. The obvious undesirable feature of the larger strip was the distance from Bonacca which necessitated a 1½-mile walk — Wilmer and Hilda found two horses — to the coast then a six-mile boat ride to Bonacca. We both landed together at this strip and, after packing their baggage, Peg and I headed back to the small strip adjacent to Bonacca.

Transportation to Bonacca from this strip is by dugout canoe, which is obtained by buzzing the village. After making sure our canoe was on its way, we maneuvered the *Cherokee* onto the little strip, then embarked upon a wild, wet canoe ride to the village on the choppy waters of the harbor. The Ulins arrived several hours later by boat from the other end of the island. We spent the remainder of the evening participating in some strange festival taking place in the village. After a tour of the interesting village in the morning we returned to our strip. Because of weight problems on the short field, I left Peg there while I ferried Wilmer and Hilda up the island to their *Bonanza.* I then returned and picked up Peg and the luggage and headed for the island of Roatan.

We could make no definite or specific plans because of the lack of accommodations in these parts, so we landed at the village of Coxen Hole on Roatan to look the situation over. The strip there is approximately 2,500 feet long, paralleling a beautiful beach and only a short walk from the village itself. There is little air traffic around these islands, other than the few charter services from the mainland, so consequently our landing always attracted a multitude of curious people, mostly children, who would flock around the planes 'til they were hardly visible. Approximately 75% of the people here are

One of the beauty spots visited on the tour was the small island group known as Cayos Cochinos, off the Honduran coast. Here is one of them as seen from the air.

On the return trip, the Owenses spent a short time on the beaches of Acapulco then flew up the coast to Puerto Vallarta, one of their favorite towns. An aerial view of that resort appears above.

colored and, strangely enough, practically everyone speaks English, a carryover from the days when Great Britain possessed the islands.

We couldn't have landed here on Roatan at a more appropriate time. A combination of timing and other circumstances enabled us to meet some wonderful people. We were preparing to walk into the village when a truly gracious native woman, who was at the field greeting friends on a charter flight from the mainland, offered her assistance and walked us into the village. She invited us into her home for a cool drink and to meet the rest of the family. One thing led to another, and what was intended to be a quick stop and tour of the village ended in a five-day stay with our newly found friends on one of the most beautiful islands we had ever seen. Our hosts, John and Catherine Wood and their 10-year-old daughter, Daine,

own and operate the general store in the village.

The few days spent there were some of the most wonderful we can recall and left us with memories we will treasure forever.

After two days at Roatan, Wilmer and Hilda departed for the long trip home. Their vacation allowed only two weeks away from home. We suddenly felt all alone as we watched them disappear into the haze as they headed for the mainland.

Besides the people, we had, of course, the islands to enjoy; and every day was a new and thrilling experience for us. In addition to seeing much of Roatan, we made several trips to the islands of Utila and Cayos Cochinos and to La Ceiba on the mainland. We visited a stretch of beach on the west end of Roatan. It surely must be as beautiful as any in the world. Getting used to constantly flying over water was a bit difficult

The author and his wife, Peggy, found time to relax on Mexico's west coast on their way home. This photograph of Peggy water skiing was taken at Acapulco.

at first but after a few days of this our anxiety faded and we were actually enjoying it.

An excellent radio network installed by the Aereo de Servicios between the islands keeps the people well informed and they also were keeping track of our flights in the area. Consequently, every place we landed we were loaded up with mail and freight, if our subsequent destinations coincided with those of the addresses.

Cayos Cochinos is a small group of islands between the Islas de la Bahía and the mainland and the largest of these is privately owned by Bill Lady and his partner, Horton Kivett, of the Aereo de Servicios. Kivett was vacationing in Cochinos at the time and while talking to him, by radio from Roatan, he invited us over for a few days when we left Roatan. Here are two people who have made a popular daydream come true: they actually possess their own tropical paradise of an island and it is indeed that.

It is a small island, approximately three miles across, surrounded by a number of smaller reefs and islands barely protruding above the water with the ever-present coconut palms lining the beaches regardless how small the islands are. The terrain of Cochinos is anything but conducive to accommodating an airstrip but they have managed to carve out about 800 feet of usable runway, adjacent to the beach. For commuting they use a Cessna 180, which of course is an excellent short-field aircraft. It is quite a fantastic setting with the high swaying coconut palms, white sand beach and surf all within a few feet of the runway. The winter trade winds blow constantly at about 75° from the runway so this, along with its abbreviated length, contributes to a "busy" landing and takeoff, somewhat similar to

situation that exists at their strip on Guanaja.

They have developed their Shangri-la into something quite comfortable, complete with a large pier, a beautiful home and crew accommodations. Usually they have five or six men there to maintain it and harvest the coconuts and to fish commercially to help support the place. The water and marine life are probably no more suitable anywhere than here for skin diving. They do a considerable amount of diving and had a complete set of gear including a compressor for their aqua lungs which we were fortunate enough to also utilize.

One day we took their 18-foot outboard for a cruise around the islands of this group and made it a combined diving and fishing expedition. We stopped at several inviting looking coves on the islands to try some spear fishing and the underwater scenery was fantastic. The barracuda were plentiful and a bit distracting but we had learned previously not to panic at the sight of them despite the potential danger involved. However, a wounded barracuda is something again to reckon with so we settled for grouper, parrot fish, and the like, for our spearfishing endeavors. Later, trolling with a hand line, we did catch a five-foot barracuda; and I have its full set of teeth in my office to back up my "fish story."

The time finally came to leave "our" islands. We had already violated our tentative schedule by overstaying on the Bay Islands so we had only a week left to see El Salvador, Nicaragua, Costa Rica and fly both the complete west coast of Mexico and the United States to arrive home on time.

From Cochinos we flew directly to Tegucigalpa, Honduras. A sick ADF made it quite a struggle to "dead reckon" across the monotonous hilly country with any degree

of accuracy. Luckily we blundered upon Tegucigalpa about the time we had nearly given up. We checked out of Honduras then flew to San Salvador for the night. After obtaining our Costa Rican visas, we departed for San José with the idea of stopping in Nicaragua on the return flight if time permitted.

It was a beautiful flight over Nicaragua and Costa Rica. San José has two airports, the El Coco International and a smaller field practically within the city limits. We cleared into the country at the beautiful El Coco Airport then flew to the other for the sake of convenience in commuting to the city. We spent two wonderful days seeing the city and countryside and cooling off. San José is nearly 4,000 feet in elevation and the temperature drops considerably at night which was rather pleasant after two weeks of the tropical heat we had been getting used to.

Time was running short so we decided to skip the overnight stop at Managua and settle for a gas stop there. From Managua we flew to the Pacific coast, over El Salvador and Guatemala, then crossed the Mexican border again at Tapachula.

From there we flew the coast to Acapulco and decided to spend that afternoon and another full day there just soaking up sunshine on the beach. We have no particular fondness for Acapulco anymore but the beaches and city looked so beautiful from the air we couldn't resist the temptation. From there we continued up the coast a ways to an old favorite, Puerto Vallarta, for the remainder of the day and the night. We said goodbye to Mexico the following day, cleared out at Hermosillo and into the United States at Tucson, Ariz., then flew on to Phoenix for the night with friends whom we hadn't seen for several years. ◆

Proper research in weather, navigation facilities, and airports will enable you to have a more enjoyable trip

PLANNING A FLIGHT TO

LATIN AMERICA

Today's light aircraft are mighty dependable. How far the family air machine strays from its home depends more on the vision, ability and wherewithal of its owner than on shortcomings of the plane. With modest addition to equipment already in my Cessna 180, a friend, Galen Sparks, and I flew throughout Central America, South America and the Caribbean one fall. Leaving from and returning to Warwick, N.Y., the entire journey — about 16,000 miles — took 3½ months. We flew as far south as Santiago, Chile, crossed the Andes and returned home via the east coast. Happily, it was a successful and a safe trip. I like to think good preparation and careful flying kept problems to a minimum, but I also know we had a share of that unknown commodity — luck.

I found it most difficult to get all the information I wanted to plan the trip, an intermittent task which took five months. I soaked up a good bit of knowledge from numerous sources, but what I really wanted and failed to get was the advice of someone who had made the entire circuit in a lightplane. Having done it now, I hope to shed some light on the subject.

I heartily recommend a flying visit to Latin America. It takes great amounts of perseverance and patience, but the rewards amply make up for the occasional frayed temper. Airborne over smoking volcanoes in Nicaragua; crossing the Panamanian Darien; morning sun glistening upon the Peruvian Desert; flying through "Paso Cristo" from Chile to Argentina in the shadows of Mt. Aconcagua; the storybook setting of Rio de Janeiro; and your heart in your mouth (single engine) over the jungles and waters of the Amazon and Orinoco Basins, are some of the experiences which are not soon to

fade from memory. Moreover, many North Americans are woefully ignorant about their neighbors to the south. It is a wonderful and interesting experience to meet them and to learn of their aspirations, progress and problems.

Placing the rewards of such a trip aside for the moment, I wish to discuss aspects of flying in Latin America which the pilot should be familiar with ahead of time. Included are weather; airport facilities; radio navigation and communications; aircraft documentation; oxygen and survival gear; and, lastly, the importance of taking it easy.

Generally speaking, weather in Latin America is more stable than in the northern hemisphere. Frontal activity is far less and so are rapid extremes in the weather. The daily characteristics of southern hemisphere weather adhere closely to the season of the year. The seasons, of course, are the reverse of those here. Summer is noted for high temperatures, little rain — hence the term, "dry season." Winter means slightly lower temperatures and more rain — a great deal, in fact, in the jungle areas of the east coast.

Central America and the South American Pacific Coast are largely mountainous. We flew in Central America in September — their spring. Nonetheless, by 1400 at the latest, stratus clouds would cover the slopes and rain would fall. On several occasions, we played it a little too tight for comfort and arrived at a mountain field minutes before IFR conditions. The solution is to get an earlier start or route the trip in shorter hops.

The towering Andes, which run the length of South America's Pacific or west coast, present similar problems yet have several unique problems. As in Central America, build-ups and rain by midday are usual during the winter. Bad weather, however, seems to have greater tenacity. Our activities halted for an entire week in Bogota, Colombia, because of continually foul sky conditions. Moreover, it is good to have the best possible weather when flying the rugged, high Andes.

Farther south in Peru and Chile, the peaks glistened in the spring sunshine of early October, but the narrow coastal shelf extending from the Pacific to the abruptly rising mountains was shrouded by low (800 to 1,500 foot), thick stratus. This condition, which prevails from June to the end of October, is caused, I am told, by air that is warmed offshore and blown over the land and cooled with the resulting sky condition trapped by the mountains. Occasionally, sky, sea, and land become almost one. I found it expeditious to make a 180 several times.

Lastly, let's not overlook the Inter-Tropical Convergence Zone, more easily called the ITC. The ITC, confined mainly to tropical regions, occurs along the equator during summer and may move as much as 25° north in the winter. Although weathermen are by no means united on all aspects of the subject, it is agreed the convergence of northeast and southwest trade winds (southeast in the summer) uplifts unstable air. Resulting are stratus, stratocumulus and,

By JAMES H. HAMERSLEY | *AOPA 216084*

Planes line the beach during a Brazilian surf-side aviation week celebration at Santos.

at worst, long lines of cumulonimbus and accompanying rain, thunderstorms and wind shifts.

We met the ITC in Panama in early September. We met it again in the Guianas in November when it was moving south for the summer. The ITC is usually responsible for Latin America's severest weather — especially the terrific rains in the Amazon area from January to June.

It is always helpful to know about facilities at a destination field. This is especially true south of the border where airports sometimes lack items such as fuel, towers, navigation aids, etc. Imagine your predicament if you routed yourself to what appeared on the map to be a large airport only to find, upon arrival, that no services were available.

The most accurate and complete information about facilities is found in the "USAF/USN Flight Information Publication: Enroute-Supplement Carribbean and South America" published every two months. The pretentious title may be reduced to FLIP En Route or simply Blue Book for that is the color of the document. It does for Latin America what the "Airman's Information Manual" does for the United States and is indispensable. Besides the low-down on services and facilities, it lists the frequencies, power, call letters and hours of operation of all en route and terminal navigation aids. It also contains cruising altitudes, towers and en route frequencies, and an altimeter conversion chart from millibars to inches, which is very necessary.

Accompanying the FLIP Enroute is the FLIP Terminal containing instrument approach charts. Even if your flying is strictly VFR, this manual is still very helpful because you can look at a field's layout ahead of time.

Word of mouth is another but less advisable way to learn about the environment. Latin airmen are among the friendliest and most helpful people to be found anywhere. Information received from them is usually accurate, but it is rare that you get enough of it to be thoroughly briefed. It was my practice to ask them to mark emergency fields along my route on the map.

Good communications and navigation are important south of the border because it is routine and often necessary to fly great dis-

The author was flying at 15,000 feet on the Chilean side of magnificent Paso Cristo when he photographed the 23,081-foot summit of Mt. Aconcagua, Argentina.

Hamersley's plane is being refueled in Tumaco, Colombia, a task that requires a great deal of care.

tances over sparsely populated country. My bird was equipped with Narco Mark II and 12 nav/coms, a venerable Lear 12D ADF and a SunAir T-10-D. The SunAir, a 10-channel, high-frequency transceiver, was reduced to a portable unit. The radio was placed in a pilot's briefcase and utilized an electrical outlet on the panel for power and a reel antenna which ran through a tube extending beneath the forward cabin.

For VFR in Latin America, and there is no other way in a single-engine plane, a good VHF nav/com (90 channels plenty) is recommended. Most towers talk on 118.1 or 118.3; 126.9 is the primary en route frequency with the exception of Brazil and it is often a party line on which you can chat with airliners and the military if necessary. Inbound to Guatemala City and unable to contact anyone until almost there, I obtained necessary weather information from Jet Clippers 501 and 503, also inbound.

Airways frequency in Brazil is 126.7 generally. Other frequencies — mostly below the 126 series — are needed to contact Latin approach and departure controls where available.

Omnis are not prevalent; however, most Latin capitals and many larger cities now have them. Brazil had 14 at last count and there are 11 in Argentina. Knowledge of ADF is mandatory. The primary navigation now and in the foreseeable future is the low-frequency radio beacon. I earnestly suggest that anyone planning a Latin trip become proficient at tracking. I found it important in reduced visibility and when winds aloft were substantial and unreported.

High-frequency equipment is essential to safety on long hauls. Terminal forecasts are often unavailable and sometimes inaccurate, to boot. The only timely way for a low-flying aircraft to receive destination weather is to maintain HF contact. My practice was to call our destination as soon as practical once airborne. The SunAir usually worked well in daytime up to 700 miles. Occasionally, atmospheric conditions reduced range, necessitating relay through other aircraft. I found these HF numbers best in the following areas — Central America: 5619, 6567; South American west coast: 6537, 6664.5, 8820, 8837; South American east coast: 5619, 5680, 6597, 6664.5, 8820 and 8837.

Latin countries require less documentation than in the past. I have an idea the trend will continue as the use of light aircraft increases. According to the "International Flight Information Manual," the following countries require advance notice of arrival: Argentina, Brazil, Guyana, Chile, Colombia, Honduras, Nicaragua, Panama, Paraguay and Peru. Though not necessary, confirmation of this notice seems to expedite arrival procedures.

Look out for changes in government because they sometimes affect entry procedure. We arrived in Brazil to find that, for the moment at least, advance notice of arrival was no longer sufficient. The military caretaker government required air force as well as civilian authorization. We literally pleaded and argued our way from Pôrto Alegre to Rio de Janeiro where we finally secured military blessings.

Bolivia, Canal Zone, Dominican Republic, Ecuador, Guatemala, Mexico (when making direct flights to other than airports of entry) and Venezuela require prior flight clearance or landing permit or both and without which

A typical market day in Guatemala. It is a busy time for farmers, artisans, and traders who gather in the town square.

you may spend your vacation in jail and have your plane impounded.

In rare instances, small-town officials may not know the latest regulations or may not admit to knowing them. During a weather stop at Manta, Ecuador, an "hombre" whose identity or authority was never established demanded to see our permit to overfly and/or land in Ecuador. Galen explained in Spanish that the IFIM and, indeed, the Ecuadorian Embassy at Washington had assured us that none was required. (As of press time, there is a requirement for such permit.) Whereupon, the gentleman exclaimed that he and the embassy didn't work for the same people! While he pondered his next move, I made mine — quite a good short-field take-off.

Choosing emergency equipment was not a task we took lightly. We carried much of the survival gear listed in the AOPA publication, "General Flight Guide: Latin America and the Caribbean Islands." (This publication is available to members upon request.) We also had plenty of cold and wet weather clothing. For flying the Andes, we used a bottle of oxygen and light plastic face masks. The oxygen was essential on occasion such as the flight at 15,500 over mountains and weather near Bogota, Colombia, and the flight through magnificent "Paso Cristo."

Sometimes weather or mechanical difficulties will force a landing at a remote field. Be prepared for this likelihood and carry tie-downs, rope and a chamois for straining fuel. The weather encouraged us to land on the rough grass strip at Tumaco, Colombia, a small coastal community. We found the above items necessary and were glad to have them.

Early in the trip I had a rude awakening to the absolute necessity of working without haste. We flew into Mexico City at 12,000

skirting build-ups and rain. Upon landing, I was told to hold on the active. Not wishing a confrontation with a DC-8 taxiing toward us, I moved onto the runway shoulder, which looked like hard dirt. It wasn't! The left wheel sank deeply in mud. Two fire trucks, an ambulance and a rescue squad rushed to our assistance. Luckily, the only damage was to my pride. Then and there, I decided to take it easy, follow instructions to the letter, and remember there were new factors to deal with including heavily accented English on the radio, strange airports and unfamiliar methods of operation.

Aviation throughout Latin America is less developed than in the United States. One can become frustrated easily because things cannot be done with the speed and ease Americans are accustomed to. However, on the basis of the go-slow philosophy formulated while the "180" and her crew looked mighty sad, the numerous flights ahead passed virtually without incident. Have a good trip! ◆

THE AUTHOR

James H. Hamersley (AOPA 216084), a pilot for six years, has attempted to become as proficient as possible in this hobby. He has obtained a commercial pilot license and instrument, land and sea ratings. At present, he is a stockbroker in Coral Gables, Fla. Previously, Hamersley had earned Army jump wings while serving in the 101st Airborne.

By LENA and GUNNAR BRUNE | AOPA 21661

AROUND
SOUTH AMERICA
ON ONE ENGINE

For many years we had planned "some day" to take a trip around South America in our own plane. One spring we decided to quit dreaming and act.

The preparations required six months. First we obtained a group passport (for both of us together). We wrote the Washington embassies of each country we planned to visit to obtain the addresses of the nearest consulates and then wrote each consulate to determine the requirements of each country in regard to visas or tourist cards.

We each had 12 passport-size photos made, got smallpox vaccinations, and had them recorded on our International Certificates of Vaccination. We obtained a police certificate of good conduct. The bank provided a letter stating that we were traveling by private airplane and had the means to return to the United States. This was used instead of a return airline ticket, which is required by some countries. Various of these papers were sent to the consulates of each country we intended to visit, to obtain tourist cards or passport visas.

AOPA made all the arrangements for entering and traversing the various countries by airplane, including advance notices of arrival and, in some cases, flight permits. This was a tremendous help. AOPA also furnished the necessary WAC, ONC, and Flight Information Publication (FLIP) charts and a supply of General Declaration forms, which were needed every time we crossed a border. We carried a stock of carbon paper and ball-point pens for filling out forms.

We purchased: (1) an International Driving License for $2 from AAA International Travel Department, 250 Park Ave., N.Y. (this is valid in nearly all Central and South American countries when driving rental cars); (2) a RAMSA card for flying through Mexico, which we believe paid for itself on our two flights; (3) a subscription to "Flight Information Publication (Terminal) Low Altitude Instrument Approach Procedures: Caribbean and South America" to aid in instrument approaches (annual subscription of six issues can be obtained from the Coast and Geodetic Survey, Washington Science Center, Rockville, Md. 20852 or the AOPA Chart Department for $7.40); (4) "New Horizons World Guide," a very handy source of information especially on border crossings and Customs charges, from Pan American Airways, Box PAA, Jamaica, N.Y., for $2.50; and (5) a supply of traveler's checks.

We took as few clothes as possible. This paid off, as we were able to get laundry and dry cleaning done on short notice nearly everywhere. Also, we wanted to purchase some clothing in South America.

We carried two two-man life rafts; life jackets; a survival kit including signaling equipment, first aid kit, food rations, a gallon of water, and a solar still for converting seawater to freshwater; an automatic pistol, for survival use, but placed it inside a life raft to avoid having it confiscated — some countries are touchy about bringing in guns; and a preparation called Pomelin, which is very effective in counteracting the diarrhea so common to U.S. tourists in Latin America.

Three books proved invaluable — a poc-

The Brunes finally make that trip they had planned for 'some day' around South America. It cost them $2,395 for six weeks they 'wouldn't trade for anything'

The Brune Bonanza was thoroughly checked by Will Smith's expert mechanics at Moron Airport, Buenos Aires, Argentina.

ket conversational guide in Spanish; an English-Spanish, Spanish-English dictionary; and a basic Spanish grammar book.

We crammed all of this gear into our faithful old *Bonanza J-35* and headed south. We spent a minimum of time in Mexico and Central America, but would like to tarry there on a later trip.

Although Mexican tourist cards are supposed to be free, this is not true if you are transiting Mexico en route to other countries. We had to buy two $3 tourist cards for the trip south. These were taken from us when we left Mexico. It was necessary to buy two more (in Panama) for the return trip through Mexico. The cards for the return trip could not be bought in the United States.

Guatemala City deserves mention. At the airport there is a guide who did everything from handling our luggage to filling out our papers. We could not have gotten through without hiring his services because the local officials will work only through him. His help cost about $2 inbound and $2 outbound.

The flight through Central America was beautiful. There were numerous active volcanoes, blue lakes in old craters, and banana and coffee plantations. These plantations all have their own airstrips, used chiefly for duster planes. Often we could see a dozen or more strips at one time. The FLIP, ONC, and WAC charts show only airstrips 3,000 feet or more in length. We saw 10 airports on the ground for every one shown on the charts.

Those living in the eastern United States may prefer to take the island route to South America, through the Bahamas and West Indies. We strongly recommend this, as some of the most beautiful spots in the world are to be found along this island chain. Since we published Private Plane Flight Guide, Caribbean and Bahamas (Holiday Flight,

4762 Kyle Ave., Ft. Worth, Tex. 76133; 1961; $2.95), many new and improved airport facilities have sprung up.

Once in South America, our schedule called for at least two nights at each overnight stop. This provided ample time for sightseeing and getting acquainted. We tried to limit our flying to four or five hours a day, because it usually came to twice this amount including the time required for paper work, gassing the airplane, and arranging for taxis.

We found that flying over the Canal Zone in Panama is prohibited. It was necessary to fly out over the ocean to the Taboga Island VOR and then back in to Tocumen Airport, to bypass the Canal Zone. We rented a car at a reasonable rate and explored the Canal and the ruins of Old Panama, where the Spaniards used to hoard gold stolen from the Incas. We stopped in at Gelabert Airport, the general aviation field, and found that this is the place for any necessary airplane maintenance. El Continental Hotel, where we stayed, is very close to Gelabert.

The flight to Cali, Colombia, was IFR on top. We made a rule, and stuck to it, never to fly IFR unless our destination had good weather. Some countries in South America prohibit IFR flying without two engines, a copilot, or high-frequency radio.

We learned in Cali of a colossal error on the ONC chart. A mountain just 20 miles west of Calipuerto Airport was shown as being 8,695 feet high, but is actually 13,300. Imagine what a mistake like that could do to an instrument approach!

We also began to realize the deadly importance of pinpoint navigation. We had had our ADF overhauled before leaving, so we knew it was in good shape. Even so, many of the radio beacons could not be picked up until we were within 30 miles of them. On a 300-mile run between beacons, it is easy to miss these low-powered beacons

entirely. In some cases also, they were not operating when we needed them. So we had to rely heavily on visual navigation and, in some cases, returned to our starting point when we were unsure of our position and unable to pick up a radio beacon. VOR's are relatively scarce in South America. We found the WAC and ONC charts to be accurate along the coast, but leave much to be desired inland.

The scenery around Quito, Ecuador, was magnificent. The city lies at 10,000 feet elevation and is surrounded by mountains, including the snow-capped volcano Cotopaxi. We visited the nearby Equatorial Monument and several beautiful churches. We were appalled by the terrible poverty of most of the Indians here.

Leaving Quito, we filed for Talara, Peru, and our flight plan was approved. In flight, however, we learned from en route radio that Talara was closed for repairs! We made an instrument approach at Guayaquil instead.

From there for 3,000 miles in western Peru and Chile we were to fly over desert. We followed the Pan American Highway most of the way down the west coast.

At Lima we encountered an airport guide — "leech" — whom we couldn't shake. Although he tried to be helpful, he caused our taxi fare into town to be doubled because he reserved a taxi long before we needed it. We were able to rent a car and drove up into the foothills of the Andes, stopping at El Bosque Country Club. Since it was Sunday, there was quite a crowd of people boating at this delightful resort.

Arequipa, a picturesque town at 8,500 feet elevation, was our next stop. In the shadow of the volcano, El Misti, this town reminded us very much of Santa Fe, N.M.

At Arica we encountered the first of only a few tower operators who could not speak English. We soon learned enough Spanish

The ruins of Old Panama, a Spanish city dating from 1524, where gold stolen from the Incas was hoarded.

to communicate with them, with the aid of light signals. The biggest single factor that helped us to remove the stigma of the "overbearing American tourist" was the ability to speak a little Spanish. A hearty "buenos dias" as soon as we stepped out of the airplane performed miracles in easing the way through all the paper work required.

Although Arica is an airport of entry for Chile, it is actually four miles inside Peru. It was necessary to take a taxi to the station where the highway crosses the border, and clear Customs and Immigration there.

After more desert and hundreds of nitrate and copper mines, we stopped at Antofagasta, Chile. The Hotel Turismo was the only modern hotel in town. It had a breathtaking view of the busy harbor. Near the airport we circled to view "La Portada," a "natural bridge" formation in the ocean.

At La Serena, Chile, we could buy only 80-octane fuel, although the FLIP Supplement showed 100-octane to be available. We bought only what we needed to reach Santiago, figuring that the mixture of 80-octane and the 100-octane in the tanks would equal 91-octane, which we require. This probably contributed to the engine trouble which we experienced later.

At Santiago we found that a taxi strike was in progress; neither could we rent a self-drive car. We resorted to the buses and found them quite cheap (5¢), comfortable,

and clean. We rode the cable railway up San Cristobal Hill, saw the beautiful gardens, and had lunch at a restaurant on top.

Here, as in most South American cities, we found that most of the stores are located in arcades within the buildings, rather than on the streets. This was a big advantage in rainy weather. The stores were all closed from 1:30 to 4 p.m. for siesta. We also found that no restaurants opened for dinner until 8:30 p.m. or later.

All through the mountainous west coast of South America we found that the major airports usually had two radio beacons. One, about 10 miles from the airport, would be powerful and could be picked up some distance out. The other would be a low-powered radio beacon at the airport. Instrument climbouts or letdowns are performed by flying a racetrack between these two beacons. This method works very well, but it kept us busy retuning the ADF between the two beacons, as we had only one ADF.

Puerto Montt, Chile, was our farthest stop south. It rains nearly all the time there. Because the engine was running rough, we took the airplane to the nearby Chilean Air Force Base, La Chamiza, for some very capable repair work on the spark plugs and magnetos.

The airport director at Puerto Montt was under the erroneous impression that we needed a permit to leave the country. After

waiting two days for such a permit to arrive from Santiago, we gave up, returned to Santiago, and left the country there. No permit was needed.

This mix-up caused us to miss the Argentine Lakes area around Bariloche. It also caused us to go through some very formidable mountains. We went through Christ of the Andes Pass east of Santiago at 14,000 feet, with 23,000-foot Mt. Aconcagua, Argentina, highest peak in the western hemisphere, a few miles to our left. It was a little bumpy. We would advise making this crossing in calm weather, preferably in the morning, as it can get *very* rough.

Upon arriving at Mendoza, Argentina, we found that there were no charges for landing, parking, communications, or flight plans. This was also true in Brazil and Venezuela.

Because it was spring in the southern hemisphere, we began to run into a series of fronts. Usually there was very little advance information about these fronts. We spent an extra night at Río Cuarto, Argentina, because of poor weather. The Argentine Air Force kindly put our plane in their hangar while a severe front passed through. (Tiedowns are practically nonexistent in South America.)

This was cattle country, very similar to west Texas. We had some 70¢ steaks that were the most delicious we have ever eaten.

Weather reports differ from those in the

The cable railway ("funicular"), which runs up San Cristobal Hill, and the public buses were means of transportation used by the authors while they were in Santiago, Chile.

States, but were not hard to read once we became familiar with the system. Visibility is given in kilometers, ceiling in meters, and portions of the sky covered in eighths.

In Buenos Aires we landed at Aeroparque, the downtown airport, but found that no overnight parking is allowed, even though there are vast expanses of grass suitable for parking. We went to Moron Airport where we had some maintenance done by the very reliable Beechcraft dealer, Will Smith.

In northern Argentina and southern Brazil we encountered a great deal of rain. Monte Caseros, Paso de los Libres, and Iguaçu Falls Airports were all unpaved, and the water and mud really flew when we landed!

Upon entering Brazil at Iguaçu Falls, we were somewhat worried about the requirement that our General Declaration should have been approved by a Brazilian Consul at our last stop before entering Brazil. There was no Brazilian Consul at the last stop. To our relief, no one asked for this. We were required to go downtown to clear Customs, Immigration, and police.

Iguaçu Falls, larger than Niagara, can be seen best from the air. The cloud of vapor rising from the falls can be seen 30 miles away.

Intense rain caught us again at Santos, Brazil. Although the Brazilian Naval Air Station there advised that their field was closed because of the weather, we told them

it was an emergency and landed. They treated us very well, put our airplane in a hangar, and put us on the naval ferry to Santos. Santos is a beach resort about 50 miles from Sao Paulo. We enjoyed this unscheduled stop very much.

The next day we followed the rugged, island-studded coast up to Rio de Janeiro. The view was stupendous, and we agreed immediately that this is the most beautiful city in the world. Rounding Sugarloaf Mountain, we landed at Santos-Dumont, downtown.

Rio was one of the more difficult places to buy gasoline. In Brazil, as in Chile and Argentina, there is a black market in U.S. dollars. Gasoline companies demanded payment in dollars and would not take traveler's checks; some were willing to put a fictitious local aircraft operator's name on the receipt, which permitted us to pay in local currency. At Rio, and at some other airports in Brazil, we were forced to go to a bank, turn a traveler's check into dollars (at a loss of 5%), and pay for the gasoline to the nearest dollar above the price. The gas men *never* had any change.

The Gloria Hotel at Rio was in a convenient location. The taxi fare from Santos-Dumont to the hotel was only 50¢. The cable-car trip up Sugarloaf was spectacular, as was the cog-railway trip to Corcovado Mountain with its huge statue of Christ the

Redeemer. We rode Rio's very convenient and numerous buses and took the ferry trip to beautiful Paqueta Island, where no automobiles are allowed.

At Brasilia, the capital of Brazil, we were astounded at what has been done in so few years: a complete city, shaped like an airplane in plan view and partially surrounded by a lake, has been built. All buildings are of simple, futuristic design. Here we saw mammoth ant hills, four-feet high.

From Brasilia to Carolina we followed the Toncantins River. From Carolina to Belém, where there was no river, we followed a then newly completed, very straight highway which had at least a gravel surface and was suitable for emergency landing. This 400-mile stretch of highway through solid jungle is a real godsend for the single-engine pilot. Here we reentered the tropics and were glad to escape the series of fronts we had been dodging.

Belém to Cayenne, French Guiana, was a rather long hop. We obtained special permission from Customs at Belém to stop for gas at Amapá, Brazil, if necessary. Going northwest we had a tail wind, however, and made it to Cayenne easily. It is desirable to make this flight in the morning, because a phenomenon known as the "Amapá front" starts building up at noon.

Marajó Island, in the Amazon River, which is larger than Massachusetts, is largely cleared pasture land. Much of French Guiana, however, is jungle right down to the ocean, with no beaches. A forced landing here would have meant ditching in the water, and sacrificing the airplane. We were equipped to survive for a considerable period in such circumstances.

Here and in Surinam we saw many jungle villages with thatched-roof buildings. About 10 miles off the coast of French Guiana we inspected Devils Island. This dreaded penitentiary, where France sent political prisoners for hundreds of years, was closed in 1945. The French seem ashamed of it and do not encourage tourists, but it is an interesting sight.

Zandery Field at Paramaribo, Surinam, appears as all Dutch airports — very neat, modern, and attractive and surrounded by a myriad of flowers. It is, however, 30 miles and a $10 taxi fare from town. We learned that there is a downtown airport called Zorg en Hoop. After clearing Customs we flew to it. It is an excellent airport with a 2,700-foot paved runway and a control tower, but it is not shown on any chart. Taxi fare was only $1 from Zorg en Hoop to the beautiful Torarica Hotel on the banks of the Surinam River.

Surinam uses square nickels, and has a beautiful flag with five different-colored stars which represent the five races which live together in harmony. Surinam impressed us as being the shining star of the Guianas, very progressive, with a great deal to offer the tourist. There is even a casino in the Torarica for those who can't resist the one-

armed bandits. Surinam and Guyana are the only two countries we found where one drives to the left. There are thousands of bicycles and motorbikes.

The flight from Georgetown to Maturín, Venezuela, was rather desolate. The Orinoco River delta consists of mud flats, jungle, and very few signs of life. We were, however, within sight of beautiful Trinidad, which we had visited previously, during much of the flight.

On arrival in Venezuela, we found that we did not have a flight permit and were therefore limited to the international airports. We were not allowed to fly to Margarita Island. We arrived on a Saturday afternoon. The aviation offices in the capital, Caracas, were closed for the weekend, and we could not teletype for the permit. Since we had been denied entrance into Venezuela (and Margarita) on a previous trip, we were determined to visit Margarita Island this time. We landed at Barcelona and took the ferry from nearby Puerto la Cruz to Margarita. It was a slow trip (five hours for 60 miles each way), but worth it; the island is beautiful. We would certainly recommend a stop there.

After a fuel stop at Caracas, we proceeded to Maracaibo, where we circled the Lake Maracaibo Bridge, one of the architectural wonders of the modern world. Quite naturally, in the center of the world's largest oil field, gasoline prices were the lowest, 17¢ per gallon. (Highest was San José, Costa Rica, at 63¢ per gallon.)

At Cartagena, Colombia, as in many South American cities, we were unable to

rent a self-drive car, but arranged a tour. There are dozens of points of interest in this very old Spanish city, including the city walls, forts, dungeons, Palace of the Inquisition, and La Popa Hill. Prices were very low, probably because of the scarcity of U.S. tourists.

During the night, an "aguacero," the most severe storm we had ever seen, went through Cartagena. A very strong wind bent the palm trees to the ground, there was a deluge of rain, and lightning struck very close every few seconds. Aguaceros occur from May to November.

The cost for the six-week trip, for two persons, broke down as follows:

Gasoline	$ 630
Hotels	530
Meals	440
Airplane maintenance	205
Ground transportation	240
Passport, tourist cards, fees	225
Gifts	125
Total	$2395

Airplane maintenance consisted chiefly of work done before we left to put the airplane and radios in the best possible shape. The gifts were not an essential expense. However, we took advantage of the opportunity to buy many unique and inexpensive Christmas gifts, such as Chilean woodwork, Ecuadorian skirts, Argentine sweaters, and Brazilian handbags.

Next time we will do it a little differently. We will leave the traveler's checks at home

The airport terminal at Arequipa, Peru, is a modern and attractive facility.

Lena Brune appears amazed at the view of Rio de Janeiro from the 2,300-foot-high Corcovado Mountain.

Iguaçu Falls, Brazil, are larger than Niagara Falls. The Hotel das Cataratas in Brazil is to the right of the falls, and Argentina's Cataratas del Iguazu Airport is in the background. **PHOTOS BY GUNNAR BRUNE**

Route taken by the Brunes on their trip around South America (broken line through Central America indicates return).

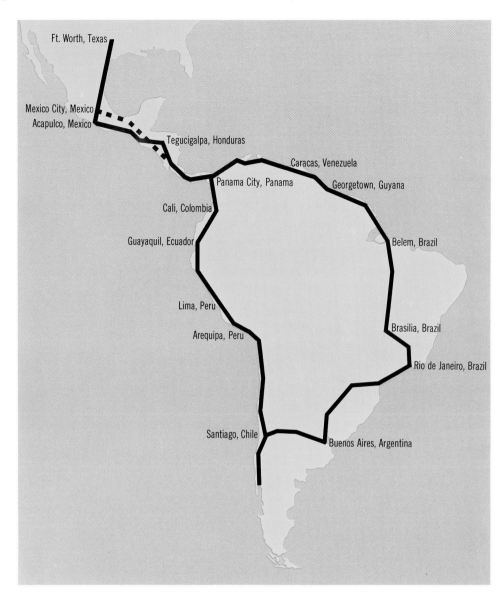

and take a money belt full of U.S. greenbacks, mostly in small denominations. We will take a full set of spare spark plugs and magneto points.

Most pilots will probably want to go to South America during the "down under" summer months, December to February, but it is pleasant any time of the year. The climate of the equatorial countries is controlled more by altitude than latitude. As an example, Quito, Ecuador, is always cool even though it is on the equator. The "dry" season varies considerably from one country to the next. Peru and most of Chile are always dry in the summer, but are apt to be damp and overcast in winter (May to October).

It is wise to find out immediately upon entering a country what the official and black market rates of currency exchange are. Otherwise the unwary traveler may be "taken" pretty badly. We tried to leave each country with as little of its currency as possible. The money could be exchanged at a bank in the next country visited, but always

at a loss; and no bank would accept foreign coins — only bills.

The amount of paper work was often overpowering, and the efficiency of the aviation departments is not quite up to U.S. standards. We were allowed to file a flight plan to an airport that was closed. In another case we were given an instrument flight altitude of 7,500 feet, although our destination airport was 8,500 feet. Fortunately, this airport (Arequipa, Peru) is in desert country and very seldom has instrument conditions.

Do not expect to get receipts everywhere. Many officials, especially Customs and Immigration officers, would not give them. Hotel bellboys offered to stamp and mail our postcards if we would give them the money, but we found it was better to buy the stamps and mail the cards ourselves. Otherwise they might not be mailed at all. Unless it was a meter taxi, it proved to be wise to agree with the driver beforehand on the price of a taxi ride.

There were some things that were hard to get used to: like the 220 volts which made

our shavers useless; the ever-present bidet, and the "C" on the water faucets which meant "caliente," not "cold."

But the trip was a really wonderful experience. We wouldn't trade it for anything. And we would wholeheartedly recommend it for anyone who has the time, as long as he goes adequately prepared and equipped. For us, single-engine flying in South America was a breeze. ◆

THE AUTHORS

Gunnar Brune (AOPA 21661) is a geologist for the Soil Conservation Service at Ft. Worth, Tex. He and his wife, Lena, travel extensively during their vacation time. They have written many articles about their journeys for The PILOT and compiled the very useful "Private Plane Flight Guide, Caribbean and Bahamas."

By RUTH and DON DOWNIE | AOPA 188441

FLY THE BYWAYS

RIGHT: Downie made this shot
of Piper's Cherokee Six from the
Cherokee 180C that he and his
family ferried back to California.
While in Florida, the author flew
this plane.

OPPOSITE PAGE: Lighthouse
in Palm Beach County, Fla.,
starting point for "will-of-the-
wisp, flip-of-the-coin, fancy-free-
type" trip.

*Turn back the clock by forgetting charts, radio
and navigational gadgets, and rediscover the
'fun flying' of the unbeaten path*

When was the last time you took a vacation flying trip with no specific plans, routes or destination in mind — a sort of will-'o-the-wisp, flip-of-the-coin, fancy-free-type trip, limited only by time available and weather? How many times have you overflown interesting places and thought that someday you'd like to land and look them over?

Next time the opportunity presents itself, and the weather is suitable, why not fold up the flight plans, leave the computer and radio airways charts in the "brain bag" and start off down the highway, railway or coast line? Then, when something interesting slides beneath your wings, chop the power and go

ball. The only assignment was to ferry a brand-new *Cherokee 180C*, N8233W, from Vero Beach, Fla., to Dan Bowles' (AOPA 140158) Pacific Piper Sales at Santa Monica, Calif. There was no rush and, since it was Easter vacation week, daughter Dana was out of school.

So we departed from the "home of the Cherokee Tribe" in Florida with no more idea of our immediate destination than to take a look at the launching pads at Cape Kennedy. Just to make sure that we didn't blunder into restricted areas, we called Melbourne Radio en route to be sure that no new Notams existed. Everything was clear, and we cruised up the Banana River at 2,500

Silver Springs Airport.

The operator thought that there was a good sod strip near the springs and a full-sized airport across town at Ocala. It seems that it depended upon the direction and the velocity of the wind as to which airport one used.

Thirty miles later, we were circling the Silver Springs resort and watching the ridiculous little glass-bottom boats making a jig-saw puzzle pattern down the river. The 3,200-foot Silver Springs Airport (elevation 75 feet) looked fine from the air with a covered hangar, gas pumps and what looked like both a landing area and taxiway.

One of the really "fun" things about such a "byway" trip is the number of really fine old-timers that you meet at these hideaway airports. John R. Henderson (AOPA 95555) and his wife were very good examples of this hardy breed who can make a living out of generally helping build aviation literally from the grass roots.

With a quick phone call, a motel station wagon picked us up and delivered us to the nearby motel. The manager said he'd be happy to drive us to the springs so we could catch the last jungle boat trip down the river before closing time.

You can read all about Silver Springs, its glass-bottom boats and the 650,000,000 gallons of water that come from its subterranean caves each day. Motion picture footage on the area dates back to six Tarzan films in the 1930's and also, according to the publicity background sheet, includes some Lay's Potato Chip commercials for TV. However, if you like things subterranean and jungle in the background, you'll enjoy the tour through Silver Springs.

Just off the other end of the Silver Springs Airport is "Six Gun Territory," including a steam train, gondola sky ride, the Can-Can girls of the Old West and other attractions.

Next morning we headed in a generally westerly direction and stopped for fuel at Perry-Foley Airport where the coast line swings west in Florida. Perhaps it was the hot, muggy day, but there seemed to be a minimum of activity at this off-airways stop. However, one family lived on the airport and fuel was available.

You can blame AOPA's travel section for our next stop. The November 1964 Pilot had two pages by Ben H. Ryan, Jr. (AOPA 82882), on Dog Island, Fla. So, when this six-mile-long resort showed up on the map some five miles offshore, we just had to take a look. It didn't take long for the 180C to circle the island, drag the 2,800-foot grass strip and turn in for a landing. On inquiry, the Tallahassee FSS advised, "There hasn't been much rain recently so the runway should be satisfactory." It was.

Without redoing Mr. Ryan's two pager, let's just say that Dog Island (actually called "Ile de Chien") is one of those places where you'd like to return. The one-woman cafe (a quonset hut) was due to close at 4 p.m. so that the operator, Doris Covington, could go "to town" on the one-hour, five-day-a-week ferry to Carrabelle, Fla. We thought that we'd like to spend the night in one of the eight guest rooms ($15 for the first night, $10 for each succeeding night) in a pagoda-shaped apartment house and do our own cooking, but that couldn't be arranged without approval of Owner Jeff Lewis who was out working and unavailable on the two-way

take a look. Perhaps it's a tiny airstrip that you've never heard of; it might be a resort town with a brand-new airport not yet on the charts, or even a little unattended border-town airport.

If you've never been there before, it's just that much more fun. The accustomed pressures of today's business schedules make such a trip unusual, and even more inviting. We had the opportunity to try it and had a

feet, ogling the launching pads and the new moonshot building in the distance, just like any other bunch of tourists.

Since Silver Springs' brochure advised that their field had "standby" petroleum service, we assumed that this meant hauling it out from town by truck. So we landed at Leesburg where Mooney Dealer Air South, Inc., topped our tanks efficiently. There were no under-the-cowling leaks, so we asked about radio. So, after a couple of hours of beach-combing, we climbed back into the air and headed westward. Perhaps some other time we will spend a night on Dog Island.

As we unfolded the Mobile Sectional, a number of interesting possibilities presented themselves. We flew down the coast line over Apalachicola, but there was still plenty of daylight. Panama City looked big and busy. Eglin AFB's control tower advised us to drop down to 1,000 feet to stay out of the path of the ILS, but only after two jets had whisked by our wing tips. Whew! We tossed a coin to decide about Pensacola, but considered this as "just another big town," and, since both daylight and fuel remained, we kept going.

The most interesting thing on the chart looked like Fort Morgan, a 2,500-foot flight strip on the sand spit at the mouth of Bon Secour Bay south of Mobile. When we asked Pensacola FSS if fuel was available, we received a "negative" from the FAA station, and a call from another plane in flight advised that the resort was open only in the summer.

It was either Mobile's big municipal airport (Bates Field) at dusk or something just a little closer. The chart showed a 3,200-foot, hard-surfaced strip at Fairhope, Ala., Municipal complete with lights and Unicom. A quick call on 122.8 brought an assurance that 100 octane was available and a question, "Did you want to go to the Grand Hotel?"

Since this was new country to us, we replied that we'd never heard of the place. We circled town for a quick look before landing, found the Grand Hotel was a very plushy resort with rates that started at $26 per day during the "off" season. After landing, taking on fuel and tying down for the night (no charge for one night's tiedown with fuel at 48¢ per gallon), airport manager Sam Witznadel drove us through the grounds of the Grand Hotel before dropping us, without charge, at an in-town motel. If your taste and pocketbook go for gracious living amid the finest of accommodations, put the Grand Hotel, Fairhope, Ala., on your list. A call on the Unicom will bring a car from the hotel.

Fairhope was a two-cab town. We met the cab company owner when she took us from the motel into the town's two main blocks. While talking over the cacophony of a water pump going out, she explained that this corner of the state is noted for pecans, azaleas and potatoes. School here has no Easter vacation but is closed one month early, in May, so that the potatoes can be harvested. Our "cabbiette" explained that Fairhope is an art center and also bases shrimp boats. It is also a gold mine for beachcombers to pick up unique shells, bits of petrified wood and Indian artifacts.

This last bit of information started a salvo of questions and answers which could very easily have kept us in Fairhope for a week. Ruth and Dana collect rocks, shells or driftwood on every trip, since I discouraged them away from gift shops (most of the time). Now I'm confronted with the problem known as gross weight for an aircraft versus costs in a gift shop, along with baggage space.

Next morning we rode to the airport with the same lady. This time the water pump was fixed, but the fan belt slipped. She must

have commiserated with the gals' disappointment not to have a day beachcombing with her, as she handed Dana an envelope. Written on the outside, "Pensacola incised rim shards of pre-Creek Indian pottery. — Estimated at 1200 to 1500 A.D. Late Mississippian Period"! A surprise present to Ruth was a piece of petrified wood. The lady cabbie took us on a "Cook's tour" of the town to see all the superb azalea bushes (more like trees) — at no extra charge — and then waited at the airport till we were airborne before going back to town. The 25-minute scenic cab ride cost only $1.75.

As we took off, we saw "our cabbie" wave to us, and, as we circled the field, we dipped our wings to her and continued west. From the back seat Dana commented, "Jeez she was nice to us. I'm beginning to get the idea of what you were talking about, Dad, you know, small airports and all that stuff. Can you imagine a cab driver in a big city, big airport, etc., doing all of that? Why can't we do this more often?"

Another day, another sectional. We'd planned breakfast on our first stop, so this meant an airport large enough for a cafe. We looked at Jackson and Gulfpark, flew around Keesler AFB at Biloxi and landed on the spacious field at Gulfport, Miss.

Part of our trio wanted to go north across Arkansas, Oklahoma and the "high route" through Albuquerque and Flagstaff. However, a check with weather showed scattered to broken thunderstorms, scattered tornadoes, rain and hail squalls in that area. So, naturally, we stayed with the clear, humid weather of the Gulf.

Everyone aboard had been in New Orleans before, so Dana asked from the back seat, "What's Baton Rouge look like? I'd like to see the Mississippi River and the State Capital."

So, we went to Baton Rouge. In our continuing effort to stay with the smaller airports, we landed at the older Downtown Airport and fueled with Louisiana Aircraft, Inc. Was there a rental car that we could use for an hour to look around town? No, but Jack M. Broussard, their parts manager, said, "Why don't you take that old Chevy of mine there on the end of the line. The keys are in it."

Having circled town prior to landing, we had a general idea of which direction to start driving. We passed the old State Capital building, which looks like a medieval castle. Driving along a levee, we saw freighters flying the flags of foreign countries, loading and unloading. After thinking of the Mississippi River in terms of barges and showboats, it was a bit of a jolt to see international shipping as a reality — probably the same kind of jolt some people get when they don't see cowboys or Indians at Los Angeles.

Dana developed a sudden hunger and thirst, and after several stops for ice cream, cokes and lemonade, it turned out she wasn't interested in the refreshments as such, but wanted to hear the people talk and to listen to their accents! It was explained carefully that this sort of thing could go on all night, so we circled on around town and returned to the airport.

When we returned, Mr. Broussard wouldn't accept a dime for the use of the wheels, and, since the car was already full of gas, we just had to believe him. Southern hospitality, you bet!

Undecided as usual, we headed westbound again and unrolled the sectionals. Here it should be noted that each leg of this no-flight-plan trip was made over either highways or railroads. Wherever the terrain required flying away from civilization, we filed

N8233W flies over a movie set at Bandera, Tex. Bandera has three airstrips, one of which is private. The Downies landed at the one at Flying L Ranch, then a grass-covered, oiled 2,600-foot strip. The strip is presently 2,700 feet and asphalt.

PHOTOS BY THE AUTHOR

an FAA flight plan, as we did later in the trip.

Shortly after takeoff, thumbing through some travel folders, Ruthie suddenly remembered a boat trip up a bayou to the island where Jean Laffite had his pirate hideaway.

Lake Charles, La., had been a radio checkpoint since World War II days, but we'd never landed there. The chart showed a fine municipal airport with a small private field, McFillen's, almost adjoining. So, why start at big airports now? We circled the 2,600-foot, oyster-shell (now sod), narrow strip and landed.

Service was quick and friendly. The McFillen Airpark has been an airport on the map since 1956 and a "back yard" airport for many years before that. Mrs. Nola Mae McFillen and her son, Marshall, operate a flight school there.

After a coke and a gas stop, we headed for Houston. No reason here to hit the Municipal Airport so we flew over the famed Houston Stadium and headed westbound to Dr. Hull's private enterprise where monthly tiedown still costs $10 and hangar sheds are $20. The doctor, an oral surgeon, lives in a two-story house adjoining the field and divides his interest between teeth and aircraft.

We have an old-time friend, Stan Mitchum, who hangars his construction company's *Twin-Bonanza* at nearby Andrea — so just leaving the pattern and taking up a heading of 20°, we were soon snugly tied down for a night of hangar flying.

Next morning, Stan drove us to Andrea in the only weather that we encountered on the trip — a slight drizzle from a prefrontal condition that petered out after 50 miles.

We "drove" down Highway 90 over the Eagle Lake omni. There's a nice-looking close-to-town airport that we'd like to see sometime. Then on down the road as the weather improved, right along with the midday turbulence. So where from here? Why not try a fly-in dude ranch? There are a number of them on the San Antonio chart.

The town of Bandera lists three strips. The paved, immaculate Purple Sage Ranch is marked "private." We landed anyhow, and it was. However, the caretaker was courteous and advised us that the strip and ranch layout were owned by the Continental Oil Company for corporate use only. He advised that the cafe at the nearby Flying L Ranch was open, so off we went.

Flying L owners have put retired veteran Eastern Airlines Captain (21,300 hours in 24 years) Steve Parker, in charge of their flight operation. The strip is 2,700 feet long and asphalt.

One of the Flying L fact sheets notes, among other things, that the ranch station wagon will make "county line liquor store trips at $2." Horseback rides are daily at 10 a.m. and 3 p.m., with a wrangler to accompany each ride. Rates begin at $15 per day.

The Flying L teams with the nearby Mayan Dude Ranch to supply that almost-real western motif for guests. They can handle 150 to 175 people on the two ranches that cover some 1,200–1,500 acres. Cowboy breakfasts, luaus, square dancing and a heated swimming pool are featured. Reservations should be made between June and August.

From Bandera, we skirted over the narrow, winding Texas highways for a restful fuel stop at Sonora. The airport adjoins both the town and golf course, and there really isn't so much transient traffic. Before we had departed late in the afternoon, at least one motel operator had called the city airport manager who lives in a trailer on the field to make sure that we didn't want a ride to town (no charge) to spend the night.

We were getting down on fuel when we landed at Sonora. N8233W took 39.1 gallons in her 50-gallon tanks, and the best words of the day were, "Of course, we have plenty of fuel. How much'll you have?" However, there were other towns on either side of Sonora with almost identical facilities: Junction and Ozona.

Westward again, this time into a wall of blowing dust. Midland and Odessa were down to three miles with the tops reported at 10,500 feet. We stayed with the road and discussed the possibility of landing at Ft. Stockton for the night. However, the name of Pecos, Tex., sounded just as interesting, and another few miles along the line. So we continued.

Carlsbad Caverns, N.M. The Downies took a 3½-hour conducted tour of the Caverns, and Don Downie's primary comment was: "It's hard for a pilot to talk about caverns. They make fine hangars for bats."

While at Silver Springs, Fla., the authors took time out for a cruise in this glass-bottom sightseeing boat.

73

One of the "hideaway" airports off the regularly plied airlanes visited by the Downies on their fly-for-fun venture was at Silver Springs, Fla. Shown in front of the Cherokee 180 the Downies ferried to California are (from left) airport operator, John Henderson, Don and Ruth Downie. PHOTO BY DANA DOWNIE

Manager Bob Gilmore helped tie us down at dusk, called the Ramada Inn for a gratis station wagon and we relaxed for the evening. At Pecos, you can buy a 36-ounce steak for $7.95. We didn't.

Somewhere during the evening, Dana came up with a folder on Carlsbad Caverns. Perhaps this note should be prefaced by a standing family joke about seeing Carlsbad Caverns. While ferrying a Navion from Brownsville to San Diego many, many years ago, Ruthie had expressed a desire to see the caverns. It was a typical rush "pilot's trip," so we circled the parking lot and let her peep down into the entrance. Thus, she had "seen" Carlsbad Caverns. The same thing happened on a J-3 *Cub* trip previously.

This time, the pilot didn't get away with it. The two gals decided that we were going to tour the caverns. Everyone was up ahead of time, and all the bags were packed and ready to go. So we flew the 75-mile hop to Carlsbad and landed at Jack White's (AOPA 216110) airport just on the edge of White City. His father had established the town in 1928.

This time we didn't even have to call for a car. Usually, when you circle town, someone comes the short mile to the airport, but a rental car was bringing a load of passengers out to a Cessna 206 just as we taxied in. We swapped stories on the better places to stop en route, and the Cessna crew departed while we headed for a 3½-hour conducted tour of the caverns. Rates on the rental car were $7 for the day and 20 miles on a Ford Falcon — more than enough to drive the seven miles up to the caverns and return. Mr. White advised us that there were enough motels in town to handle up to 1,200 people, "depending upon how well they're related. We have 62 rooms in our own motel alone."

It's hard for a pilot to talk about caverns. They make fine hangars for bats. They're damp, cool and far underground. National Park Rangers assigned there refer to the assignment as "the bottom of the barrel," but it is certainly worth seeing — once. After a three-mile, 3½-hour walk, a certain sameness becomes involved, but it is honestly worth the time and effort, even the sore leg muscles the next day.

Then the longest hop of the entire trip: two hours, even, to Columbus, N.M., where it is only three miles across the border to Las Palomas, Chihuahua, Mexico, for a quick shopping spree. We overflew El Paso and filed with the FSS to Columbus where we closed our flight plan down the lonely section of international fence line with Deming Radio.

"When you get on the ground, would you please advise us the condition of the airport," asked the Deming operator. "We haven't had any reports in the past couple of weeks."

So we dragged the field quite carefully and landed on the smooth hard-adobe surface without incident. However, one can sometimes expect puncture weed on the runway.

With fuel and sunlight getting down, we turned up the highway to Deming, N.M. There the FAA has an FSS. The huge airport was a World War II training base. It was here that I first learned the idiosyncrasies of instrument and twin-engine flight and the primary rudiments of military discipline that were required of service pilots. The foundations remain, but nearly all the buildings are gone.

Airport Manager Lee Odell topped our tanks and drove us in to the comfortable Plainsman Motel owned by an ex-AF pilot. A no-charge ride out to the airport was a regular part of his service.

The transcontinental highway was under

construction as we merrily passed long lines of slow-moving autos. We cruised at 500 feet to enjoy the sight and to keep below the forecast head winds. There are so many colorful names in this area of the Old West that it was hard to pick a landing spot. Lordsburg was too soon, so we settled for Cochise (named after the famous Indian chief) where the county maintains a fine strip just west of the town of Wilcox. Operators, the Glen Morris family, had moved into a trailer on the airport, finally, after driving out to the airport many a time for night refueling.

"Our Unicom's never turned off," said Morris with a friendly smile. "We don't have any rental cars yet, but we do have a few 'loaners' that pilots are free to take to town; and the motels in town will pick up visitors."

If you land at Cochise County during the forest fire season, look out for the borate bombers that are based there each year.

Despite the best efforts of FAA, there are still many off-airways spots where omni bearings are unreadable at the lower altitudes. Pilots, particularly beginners, planning a leisurely junket without flight plans should follow established highways or railroads and should carry a full set of large-scale sectional charts. If you're going to navigate by pilotage, you need all the information you can get.

Make it a habit to ask each local airport operator about the places of interest in the direction you're going. Chances are he'll know of a spot you've never heard of, and he'll be able to tell you the current condition of some off-airways dirt flight strip where you might plan to land.

Keep track of your weather whenever you can hear an FSS, and don't be hesitant to ask for an area forecast even though you may not be on flight plan. The FSS operator will give you a good picture of what the weather may be up ahead.

Service at the larger terminals has improved greatly within the past few years. However, an off-airways trip shows a somewhat different picture of aviation where people have the time to be friendly, to sit and "hangar-fly," to brew a cup of coffee on the house and make a phone call to get you both a motel and transportation.

There's always the problem of not being able to see everything. There must be a good bit of give and take in the cockpit in choosing destinations. Then, there's the advantage of making shorter hops, with more opportunity to stretch, talk and see new scenery from the ground rather than the usual 8,500-foot, best-altitude, full-throttle view.

As usual, we overflew the busy airports at Tucson and Phoenix and made our final fuel stop at Blythe, Calif. Prior to crossing the Colorado River, we circled low over the small town of Salome, Ariz., but erosion was visible on the dirt runways following a recent cloudburst.

You can take your choice of two airports at Blythe: the large former AF training base some seven miles west of town on the mesa or the much smaller Heron Field adjoining town to the east. The narrow oiled strip at Heron is 2,600 feet long, and there was a huge truck and trailer parked at the short end of the runway. However, N8233W was getting accustomed to these smaller fields by now. The main advantage of Heron Field

is its immediate proximity to both cafes and motels.

Unfortunately, a good thing can't go on forever. Pacific Piper needed their 180 to lease out to a flying club. The week of vacation was just about over, so we resisted the temptation to spend the night at one of the many interesting resorts near the Salton Sea and churned into a smoggy sunset toward Santa Monica.

The past 3,000 miles had been strictly flying for fun. We all agreed it had been the "funnest," most restful and leisurely trip we had taken. It's not only a grand way for teenagers to be introduced to new sections of the country — it's also a fine way for a pilot to sit back and enjoy his flying, rather than being a slave to his flight plan, computer and time schedule. Flip a coin and see if you don't agree. ◆

Flying over Silver Springs, Fla. The authors landed at the 3,200-foot Silver Springs Airport, operated by "old-timers" Mr. and Mrs. John Henderson.

Keeneland Race Course at Lexington, Ky., is within walking distance of an airfield. Pilots seeking an exciting weekend, convenience, and southern charm are invited to visit horse farms and witness horse sales also

THE BLUEGRASS STATE

By IRENE SULLIVAN

Until automobiles can fly or airplanes can take to the road, the private pilot will have one problem, namely, finding a vacation spot where he can anchor his plane for a weekend without having to pay a fortune in cab fares or car rental or without having to limit his sightseeing.

Pilots who, like us, look at a weekend vacation with one eye on convenience will love the Bluegrass country at Lexington, Ky. Set down at Blue Grass Field and you can enjoy a day or a weekend of horse racing — and this includes a motel, meals and a visit to a horse farm — without a single transportation worry.

Right across from the airport is Keeneland Race Course, a pretty little track most convenient to pilots. Just check with the tower, taxi onto the luscious bluegrass and park opposite the Keeneland entrance. Hop across the road and you'll have as short a walk to the grandstand as if you'd parked your car on the lot. Keeneland is so accessible to pilots that if you're a speedy handicapper, you can bet on the eighth race and be out to your plane and off the ground in time to see it from the air.

We didn't discover Keeneland until we had moved practically on top of it. If we had, remembering many weekend trips made out of Chicago, we would have been frequent visitors.

The Bluegrass State, named so for the deep color of the grass which overlies rich limestone, has been the center of horse breeding and an important part of horse racing for many years. In 1793, the Lexington town council had to prohibit horse racing on Main Street. The Keeneland site was granted to the Keene family by Patrick Henry, then governor of Virginia. Keene built the $1\frac{1}{16}$-mile track and original clubhouse as a place for his friends to come and watch their thoroughbreds race.

Keeneland is a public track now, but as you sit and watch the races in this colorful,

unhurried atmosphere, you feel more like a friend of John Keene, out to match your horse against your neighbor's. Remember the scene at the races in the movie My Fair Lady? Everything was old, plush and genteel. Well, that's Keeneland. Snack bars, restaurants and all the concessions that make a place seem commercial are discreetly located.

One of the most colorful ceremonies in horse racing takes place before each race in the walking ring behind the grandstand. Here you really appreciate Keeneland's smallness. Even on the busiest days, when the crowd hits 20,000, you can still get within patting distance of the horses and watch for the one that might wink at you. The pure spectacle of it all — the jockeys in their bright garbs, the grooms, the beautiful horses, the old stone grandstand, the blue, bluegrass and the trees in bloom — is terrific.

Keeneland is a nonprofit track (all profits go to Kentucky charities) and it is small, but the horses it attracts are the biggest. In addition to the best from the neighboring horse farms, Keeneland gets many of the country's biggest stakes winners in the fall. The spring meet is particularly exciting because the last 50 days of conditioning a Derby horse are supposedly the most vital, and Keeneland is the training ground for many Kentucky Derby winners.

Grandstand admission is $1.25. What you win or lose from there is up to you. Roast beef, ham and corned beef sandwiches; beer; hot dogs and popcorn are sold over the counter. There is also a small restaurant. Post time is 2 p.m. Exact dates of spring and fall meets may be obtained from the Department of Public Information, Frankfort, Ky.

Two famous Lexington inns, the Imperial House Inn and the Campbell House Inn, are located about three miles from the airport. The airport limousine stops at both. Double

Off and running or approaching the finish — the excitement of the "sport of kings" grips the crowd at beautifully kept Keeneland.

The Blue Grass Field at Lexington is a short distance from the Keeneland Race Course. This photograph of the airfield was taken from the course grounds.

rooms start at $16 at the Imperial House and are from $15 to $18 (children under 12 free) at the Campbell House. The dining rooms at both places are excellent. A warning, however — make your reservations early because both inns are very popular with horse owners, breeders and jockeys.

If your winnings are high, and you're in the mood to celebrate, Louisville and Cincinnati are both only one-half hour away by air. Louisville's Standiford Field has an excellent Polynesian restaurant.

Before you leave Lexington for good, however, don't miss out on a visit to a horse farm. We found this as fascinating as a day at Keeneland. Calumet Farm — picturesque, red and white, rolling — adjoins Keeneland and is within walking distance of the airport. This is one of the country's largest farms and is the home of Citation, the first horse to win over $1,000,000, now a top stallion there.

While Calumet has the advantage of convenience, there are other farms nearby. Among these are A. B. Hancock's Claiborne Farm, home to the 1965 top filly, Moccasin; Leslie Combs' Spendthrift Farm, where such master sires as Nashua, Gallant Man and Turn-To, each worth over $1,000,000, live like the kings they are; J. H. Whitney's Greentree Farm; John Galbreath's Darby Dan Farm; Lou Doherty's Stallion Station; and John Gaines' $3,600,000 syndicate of sires. The Bluegrass is, in fact, more noted for horse breeding than racing, since nearby Louisville's Churchill Downs steals the racing show. But the Bluegrass does both with distinction. Eighteen of the 20 leading sires in the U.S. (64 out of the top 75) are presently living on Bluegrass farms.

About 200,000 tourists visit these farms annually, probably because, as we found, there's no better way to end a Keeneland weekend than to visit one and see the luxurious way these horses are fed, bred and bedded down. It's like going backstage at the Met. There's no admission charge to see the farms, which are open 10 a.m.–4 p.m. (Calumet is closed on weekends.)

Flying to Lexington when Keeneland isn't open is a little like flying to New Orleans

after Mardi Gras. It's not as exciting, but there's still plenty to do, horse-wise.

Besides thoroughbred racing (a thoroughbred, by the way, is a horse which can be traced through all branches of its ancestry to horses recognized in a stud book kept in New York City), there are the standardbred races, the trots, at the Big Red Mile, about two miles from the airport. Lexington's Red Mile Clubhouse is a good spot for dinner.

If you've never been to a horse sale, that too is a treat. The fast-chanting auctioneers, high bidding, and beautiful horses are infectious; it's hard to resist the temptation to bid. (The fact that you came in an airplane *might* quiet you.) There is a fall thoroughbred yearling sale, standardbred yearling sale, saddlehorse sale, and the broodmare sale. The Department of Public Information also has the dates for the trot meets and sales.

If you stay overnight in the Bluegrass, a tiedown at Bohmer Aviation will cost you $1.50. Chuck Bohmer has quite a going op-

eration with complete facilities and repairs.

As you leave the Bluegrass, take a last aerial look at the rolling countryside, white fences and columned farmhouses. We hope you won't forget it. The Bluegrass is pretty good to pilots. ◆

THE AUTHOR

Irene Sullivan, a former editor for the Lexington Leader, began flying at Sally's Flying School (Wheeling, Ill.) in a J-3 Cub. Of that plane, she says: "I can think of no better for a beginner — and particularly a woman — to start off in." While she lived at Lexington with her doctor-husband, Donald C. Sullivan, Mrs. Sullivan flew in a Cessna 172, but she missed the J-3. The Sullivans now reside at Chicago.

Thirteen golf courses are within an eight-mile radius of Pinehurst-Southern Pines Airport, and a new one will be ready soon

GOLF IN North Carolina SANDHILLS

By PAGE SHAMBURGER | AOPA 22129

When a pilot's voice comes over the Pinehurst-Southern Pines Unicom in North Carolina saying, "I'm over the golf course. Where is the airport from here?" he really shouldn't criticize Marie McKenzie, who patiently asks "Which golf course?"

That pilot probably doesn't realize there are 13 complete golf courses within an eight-mile radius of that Unicom. Number 14 is under construction.

Well known as "the winter golf capital of the world," the Sandhills section of North Carolina is fast becoming the golf capital of the flyer's world. But let's start at the beginning.

South- or northbound on Victor 3–Victor 155, the needle points to SOP omni, a remote out of Fayetteville. An 89° FROM heading brings you over the airport, where a 4,500-foot, hard-surfaced runway offers clear approaches and lights on request. A

crosswind grass runway is over 3,000 feet long and quite good. The area prospers as a midsouth resort due to an unusual thermal belt and sandy soil. Those combined make good grass runways, too. The sod never gets soft or muddy — it simply drains and dries immediately.

L. C. "Buck" McKenzie is the airport manager and operator through his Resort Air Service. Maintenance, all octanes and jet fuel are available. So, when the fly-in golfer lands, his only problem is where to go.

Starting in the northern edge of the pattern, it's Whispering Pines. A telephone call brings courtesy transportation from the motel, located on U.S. Highway 1, just north of Southern Pines. The rooms run from $9

single off-season to $32 for the "deluxe golfer's suite" in season. A restaurant is on the premises; so are a lighted putting green and swimming pool. The motel is part of the 2,000-acre complex of Whispering Pines where groups can often have rental houses by the week.

For flyers in the motel or in a rental house, daily or weekly memberships are granted at the clubhouse on approval of the board of governors. A member of Eastern Air Lines Flying Golfer Club, the Whispering Pines par 72 18-hole golf course measures 7,151 yards with Pencross bent grass greens and full irrigation. The nine-hole West Course currently is being expanded to a full 18 holes.

*Whispering Pines, a 2,000-acre resort, has a par 72 18-hole golf course. The West Course of nine holes is par 36,
and additional nine holes are under construction.*   PHOTO BY EMERSON HUMPHREY, SOUTHERN PINES, N.C.

Heading south along U.S. 1, the next tees are at the Southern Pines Country Club, owned and operated by the Elks Home of Southern Pines, Inc. A golf shop, snack bar and dining room are in the clubhouse and are open to any Elk from any part of the country and to guests of Elks or of members. Andy Page is the professional. This 18-hole course is nearest the downtown section of Southern Pines and the closest course to many major motels along the highways.

Still a little farther south and west is the new Country Club of North Carolina. The first 18-hole course is open, but only to members and their guests. In this case, the members must accompany their guests.

On the double road between Southern Pines and Pinehurst and back in the direction of the airport are the Pine Needles Lodges and Country Club. Each chalet-type lodge has five bedrooms and baths wisely designed for privacy or for use as a group cottage, and even larger lodges accommodate as many as 36 people. The main dining room, golf shop, card room and recreation room are in the clubhouse. Designed by Donald Ross, this 18-hole course has Pencross grass greens and is open year around. Advance reservations are suggested. The Pine Needles gives pilots courtesy pickup and delivery service. Rates are from $18 a day per person, American plan, to $31 at the height of the season. A special golfer's package plan, off season, is $111 per week which includes room, three meals per day and greens fees.

The Pine Needles invites flyers to drop in early in the morning and play golf all day for either $6 or $10 greens fees, depending on the time of the year. Plenty of caddies, electric carts, and pull carts are available here, and the golf shop has all types of equipment and sportswear.

Pine Needles' owners, Warren and Peggy Bell, believe in informality and spend nearly all day in their club protecting the friendly atmosphere. Warren was a professional basketball player, but after getting the golf bug, he quickly brought that game down to a five handicap.

Peggy is a touring golf professional and was chosen Teaching Lady Professional of the Year in 1963. She is affiliated with A. G. Spaulding golf equipment company, and is a former Titleholders Champion, Eastern Open Champion and three-time Ohio Amateur Champion. She has been on two Curtiss Cup Teams and on the International Weathervane Team. Lee Kosten is the teaching professional at the Pine Needles, and Mrs. Kosten manages the golf shop. Warren has decided the flyers are good business. In addition, a close scrutiny of his books shows that general aviation planes give him a much larger radius for potential customers. The more planes, the better, is his attitude! In fact, the Sportsmen Pilots Association joined the Bells for a meeting.

Nearly across the road from the Pine Needles is the Mid-Pines Hotel and Country Club. Advance reservations are necessary at the Mid-Pines, and the charge for airport pickup is $2.

The Mid-Pines is open from late September until mid-May, and the hotel can accommodate 175 people. The adjoining Golfotel's 10 units overlook a lake and are beautifully furnished. Room rates are $30 to $50 per day, double, or $17 to $26, single, depending

The 4,500-foot, hard-surfaced runway at Pinehurst-Southern Pines Airport has sufficiently clear approaches for everything through small jets. It's not unusual to see several Gulfstreams, two or three JetStars, several Convairs and DC-3's alternating in the tiedown spaces with Comanches, Bonanzas, Cessnas and other single-engine planes. PHOTO BY JOHN G. HEMMER, PINEHURST, N.C.

The Pine Needles Lodges and Country Club bus meets flyers at Pinehurst-Southern Pines Airport. Pine Needles has an 18-hole, Donald Ross-designed course which is open year around. PHOTO BY EMERSON HUMPHREY

on the time of year. That rate includes meals and lodging but not greens fees.

The Mid-Pines has a special $99 package plan of seven days, six nights — room, meals, and greens fees — from late November until February 15 each year. For daily transient pilots, the Mid-Pines starter will try to work you into the schedule, but they do insist that this is nearly impossible on Saturdays from March 15 through April 15. Tournament winner Julius Boros is the touring professional at the Mid-Pines, and Ernie Boros is resident pro.

Golf is the predominant interest at the Mid-Pines, with an 18-hole Donald Ross course, practice tees, putting greens and golf shop. Modern convention facilities at this hotel can accommodate 300 people for meals and meetings.

On west along the double roads, and less than two miles from the airport, is Knollwood Fairways, the newest golf area in the Sandhills. If a transient prefers to stay in one of the many local motels, he might choose Knollwood Fairways for his game. Semiprivate, this club allows daily players with motel management introduction. The grounds include a nine-hole regulation course and a par three short nine with holes averaging 150 yards. Open all year except Sundays, greens fees of $5 permit playing both courses or any combination all day. For the par three course, greens fees are $1.25 during the day and $1.50 at night. That's right, the short nine is fully illuminated with 1,000-watt mercury vapor lights which actually make the grass greener and the ball whiter at night than during the day.

PGA Class A teaching pro at Knollwood Fairways is Doug Jetter. Complete clubhouse facilities, golf shop and practice tees with natural turf are all open all year.

In Pinehurst, all golf is centered at the Pinehurst Country Club. In this one spot, five Donald Ross 18-hole championship courses fan out like fingers on your hand. This is a private club, and starting times are available only to members, to guests of members, or to guests in the local hotels. Two of these hotels, the Carolina and the Holly Inn, are owned by Pinehurst, Inc. Three others, the Pine Crest, the Manor, and Magnolia have arranged golfing privileges with the club for their guests.

The big, yellow Carolina Hotel is open from October until May and has such things as fashionable shops in the lobby and horse-show rings and putting greens outside. Rates for the 255 rooms are all American plan, with singles from $17 to $25 daily and doubles from $32 to $46, depending on the season. The Pinehurst bus and a horse-drawn victoria run a regular schedule from the Carolina to the country club.

The Holly Inn is open year-around, and American plan singles are from $14 daily. It is in the center of the village and has a heated swimming pool plus an orchestra on Saturday nights. Both the Holly Inn and the Carolina offer special package plans from near the end of November until mid-February.

In Pinehurst if you tire of golf, you'll find tennis, lawn bowling, horseback riding and racing. The Pinehurst Gun Club has skeet facilities, and the Shooting Preserve offers quail and dove shooting. It is called Golftown, USA, though, and the center of Pinehurst is and probably always will be the country club. So, when you're over several golf courses, you're probably in the Pinehurst-Southern Pines area of North Carolina. And don't be upset when the Unicom asks you which golf course! ◆

INDIANS And SMOKIES Attract Tourists

By JANE M. DACUS

THE AUTHOR

Jane M. Dacus, author of "Indians And Smokies Attract Tourists," is a native of North Carolina who currently resides at Memphis, Tenn., with her husband, daughter and son. She said the family "all love flying!" The Dacus family has flown to the Bahamas twice in two years, both times via the Smokies.

Ancient crafts are practiced at the Oconaluftee Indian Village, Cherokee, N.C. The village, a full-size replica of an eighteenth century Cherokee community, has been described as a "Living Museum."
PHOTO BY LOU HARSHAW,
COURTESY OF ASHEVILLE CHAMBER OF COMMERCE

The Great Smoky Mountains in North Carolina have been called "a land of accessible isolation." This photograph of a rustic scene may emphasize the point.
PHOTO BY BOB LINDSEY,
COURTESY OF ASHEVILLE CHAMBER OF COMMERCE

"Unto These Hills" is being produced at 8 p.m. June 26 through Aug. 29, 1967 (excluding Mondays), at the Mountainside Theater, Cherokee, N.C. These are a few members of the cast, which numbers over 140 persons.

A clear blue sky above and majestic mountains visible as far as the eye can see are all yours when you go flying in the Great Smoky Mountains, a part of the Appalachian Mountain system. Pilots should find a trip to the North Carolina "Smokies" a treat.

Most of the year my husband, Dale Dacus (AOPA 278755), and I are "flat land" pilots in the Memphis, Tenn., area. When vacation time rolls around we head for North Carolina in our Cessna 172. In four hours, we can be in the heart of the mountains.

Every trip is a new adventure. From the air one can see the vastness of the mountains, many of which are unexplored. Visibility range will depend on the time of year you visit the area. The colors are pretty in any season, but in spring and fall they are most outstanding.

There are many airports on the fringe of the mountain area, but only a few in the center. We always land literally on top of a mountain at Sossamon Field, Bryson City, N.C. (Charlotte Sectional). This strip is 2,265 feet long and paved, and it has a turn-around area. Attendants are at the field during daylight, and pilots will find tiedown and hangar space and fuel available. A rental car service is based at the field, and pilots who carry "flying" motorbikes will be able to use them to good advantage in the area.

The man responsible for building this airport, Le Roy Sossamon, a North Carolina businessman, author and pilot, is always helpful and will give pilots advice on flying in the mountains. As we came in for the first time late in the afternoon, he kept in contact with us by Unicom. With his directions landing was a breeze.

Bryson City is approximately eight miles southwest of the center of the Cherokee Indian Reservation. We particularly like the drama, "Unto These Hills," and the Indian Museum; and we never miss the opportunity to buy native craft from the Indian shops.

Two miles west of Bryson City is the head of Fontana Lake, a haven for fishermen; and two miles north, in the Great Smoky Mountains National Park, is the Deep Creek campground. There are countless horseback and hiking trails there, and even an icy "swimming hole" near the camp for the more adventurous.

In every direction of the city there is a point of interest — a gorge, a high peak, a river, or a lake. Approximately 20 miles to the northwest is Clingmans Dome at an altitude of 6,643 feet. To the west is a wintertime paradise for hunters, who can bag bear, deer and wild boar.

Asheville, N.C., is 30 minutes in our Cessna to the east. It is most worthwhile to see the beautiful Biltmore Estate and attend summer plays at the theaters. Near Asheville is Mount Mitchell, the highest point east of the Mississippi River at an altitude of 6,684 feet.

The airport is 12 miles south of Asheville. Fuel, rent-a-cars, limousine, and taxi are available. Two-way radio is required. Another field, Asheville Airpark, is one mile northwest of the city. This is an 1,800-foot (800 paved and 1,000 turf) private strip, but "visitors are welcome at own risk."

For action, for beauty, the Smoky Mountains are unsurpassed. ◆

By GUNNAR BRUNE | AOPA 21661

A Report on Some Interesting

TEXAS VACATION SPOTS

Lakeway Inn visitors sunning at poolside and cottages are seen from the restaurant.

Fly-in resorts, some at lakeside, provide a mood of Texas cordiality for vacationers. One lodge even offers flight training.

West of Austin, the state capital of Texas, stretches the chain of Highland Lakes on the Colorado River. A large number of airports serve these lakes, many of them with resorts attached.

Fast becoming a favorite among flyers is Lakeway Airpark and its adjacent resort. The 3,200-foot paved strip lies 18 miles out on the Austin omni on a 254° radial. A call on 122.8 will bring the station wagon to the airport to pick you up.

The Lakeway Inn, which is open year-around, is situated on a beautiful point of Austin's chalk cliffs which jut out into Lake Travis. All rooms have a private balcony overlooking the lake, and many have fireplaces. Rates range from $16 to $27 for two, and there is no charge for children. Bicycles are provided free for transportation around the grounds. Each guest is given a basket of fruit and champagne. There is an excellent restaurant, an informal snack bar, and a private club. (In Texas you can obtain mixed drinks only in private clubs.)

Visitors may fish, sail, and rent speedboats at the marina. A large cruise boat, the Tony I, makes a Sundown Cruise each Saturday during the summer. Other pastimes include swimming, water skiing, shuffle board, tennis, golf, horseback riding, skeet shooting, and an outdoor theater.

Lakeway Estates, a residential development near the inn, is growing fast. Many beautiful homes are being built of the local limestone. A school and church are under construction.

For those who like more modest and rustic surroundings, there is the Bar K Guest Ranch. Lying 10 miles north, across the lake, it also has its own paved strip, 2,600 feet long. The Bar K has horseback riding, boating, and many other activities.

Seventy-five miles to the southwest, in the "hill country" around Bandera, are clustered some of the finest fly-in guest ranches in the country. Best known are the Flying L, Mayan, and Lost Valley, all with their own airstrips. Horseback riding, swimming, outdoor barbecues and steak roasts, hayrides, and night life are favorite diversions here.

The concept of learning to fly or working on a new rating while vacationing is being promoted by Chaz (AOPA 240642) and Chris Green at their Kickapoo Lodge on Texarkana Lake, Maud, Tex. Guests at the resort, which is located in the Piney Woods of east Texas, may take advantage of a variety of flight training courses offered by Flight Proficiency of Dallas and enjoy other recreations—boating, skiing, swimming, skeet, trap shooting, golf, and hunting.

The 2,250-foot paved and lighted airstrip is located 25 miles on the 212° radial of the Texarkana VOR. There is Unicom, and 80- and 100-octane fuel are available. Visitors may taxi very close to the lodge or call Chaz, who will put down the red carpet and provide a ride in the station wagon.

Rooms, in either the lodge or bungalows, are $8 single ($10 for four) and up; and there is a 20% discount for visitors who take flight training courses. Meals are served in the restaurant, and cars may be rented if a ride into town is desired. Since the Kickapoo Lodge is located near main airways, it is convenient as an overnight stop for flyers.

On your next flight through the Southwest, stop in at any of these spots and enjoy some real Texas hospitality! ◆

By ROBERT N. MOOREHEAD, JR. | AOPA 226811

Corporation pilot who flies Cessna for pleasure tells about
resort attractions in northeastern states and nearby Canada

Let's Go Flying—
NORTH

After living overseas and flying for foreign airlines for 11 years, I came home for a corporate job. Here, I found a new world in the lightplane, and I became an addict after a *Navion* trip to the West Coast and back. Like a fly caught in the swirling vortex of a draining sink, I found myself immersed with half ownership of a Cessna 195.

Shortly after acquiring this gem, Jean, my map reader-wife, and I started north. No plans — just ideas and curiosity. After flying "long enough for a day," we called Basin Harbor (Vt.) Unicom and asked if they had room for us. Sure 'nuff. When we taxied up, the station wagon was there. We learned during the check-in that we would have time for a get-acquainted saunter around the 600 acres — from the Lake Champlain water front, through the apple orchard to the well-manicured golf course — before a get-acquainted cocktail hour. The casual, friendly living is in cottages at Basin Harbor, and you partake of meals in the dining room, which has a very digestible view of the lake.

As much as I would've liked to spend the three days allotted, the horizon lured me on, so we left that charming place and hopped into Burlington for fuel and a weather check. The only direction to go was north so I cranked up and scooted out, under and ahead of a front that was giving the East Coast a dousing. We had tail winds I didn't count on and found ourselves over Sky Lodge at Moose River, Me., much sooner and much, much higher than expected. Now here is the place that I think all pilots dream about. You park your aircraft at the front door, literally. Jean and I had lunch then walked the two miles into Jackman and browsed around. We found a dealer in antique sleighs. He was almost apologetic for charging $25 for an item!

The next morning we chamoised some fuel into the 195, called Millinocket for the weather and filed a flight plan direct for Montreal, where we cleared Customs. Before the prop had stopped turning, a friendly lady opened the door and asked "where from," "going to," and "how long" (don't rush home atmosphere). She said, "Have a good time and with this paper you can check in the USA wherever convenient." That was a good relationship — I didn't even have

Author Moorehead beside the Cessna 195 in which he made this trip.

to get out of the airplane; no fees. Forty-five minutes later we were at St. Jovite.

This strip is a quarter mile from the lodge, but a call on Unicom will have the car waiting, with the driver to help you tie down.

Such a splash of color nature gives this country in the early fall! Lots of real estate in autumn color broken up here and there by a deep blue lake.

If you want a little more formal luxury than the lodge provides, you can go 'round the corner of the lake to the Gray Rocks Inn.

The next morning was bright so after calling Montreal on the drop line provided and finding the weather ideal for the flight south, we filed for Ogdensburg and Customs. This stop could have been painless, but the inspector had to spoil it by reminding us we should stay in the aircraft until he arrived. That would have been 20 minutes. I remarked that I love that 195 but there are some things it is just not equipped for! He made a polite "ha."

So it was still a beautiful morning and we rubber-necked up the St. Lawrence to the Thousand Island Club at Alexandria Bay and landed on what is represented as a runway but looked like a bad fairway (but that suited me fine) in the middle of the golf course. We were working up an appetite for

fruit salad on the veranda, but found the kitchen closed for some reason. It was a good try. That looked like a likely spot so we'll try it again in the future because it does have convenience, and I imagine the lapping sounds from the river make a delightful lullaby.

So we cranked up our vacation flyer and hopped over to Watertown for a hot dog at the terminal lunch counter, refueled and soared on down to Trenton, counting our blessings. ◆

THE AUTHOR

Bob Moorehead joined the Aircraft Division of U.S. Steel in 1956. He had just returned from overseas where he had flown for KLM and had helped form El Al Israel Airlines. He says, "Watching the formation of this new country, Israel, was a study in humanism." Bob's interest in flying began in 1932. He instructed for Major Moseley's RAF program and flew the Pacific with the Consairway Division of Consolidated Vultee.

A MAINE DISCOVERY

For the first time in our experience, a brochure not only lived up to its promises, it surpassed them. My wife, Eloise, and I have had much experience comparing promotional copy with reality, so we are not really surprised when the actuality is less impressive than the promise. However, in the case of Sky Lodge, we felt the brochure failed to adequately describe one of the freshest, most friendly spots in New England.

A weathercast initiated our voyage of discovery. One evening's forecast of a big, fat high of cool Canadian air over New England started us thinking of an overnight flying trip — just somewhere. Yet we wanted to do something just a little bit different.

For one reason or another, like fishing trips that never came off, we had never explored the Moosehead Lake region of Maine. After my decision to look over this area had been debated and finally ratified by wife and the one son at home (there was some muttering that a day at Martha's Vineyard would be nice), I remembered Sky Lodge and its promises.

A telephone call for reservations and information was answered by the friendly voice of the owner-manager, Ed Landgraf, who assured me that their sod strip was not the usual rollercoaster track pointed down-hill. There are pines on one end and there is a power line on the other, but Landgraf has cut the forest well back and has had the power line buried where it crosses the west end of the runway. There are 1,750 feet, not 1,700 as indicated on the Lewiston Sectional, that are fully usable.

With beds assured, my wife, the Number 3 son, Kent, and I lifted off from Nashua, N.H., and pointed *Cherokee* 7581W toward Moose River, Me., and Sky Lodge Airport 200-odd miles away.

The first sighting of our destination cannot be described. There were mountains and rivers and lakes everywhere, lighted by the soft rays of the late afternoon sun. Iridescent is the word that comes to mind, but it isn't enough.

In the midst of all this beauty, just north of the twin villages of Jackman and Moose River, stands one large, handsome log lodge on a hillside. That's Sky Lodge, and the American flag flying beside it is the wind sock.

The strip is exceptionally smooth and wide, and is manicured far better than many house lawns. For that reason, the field is not as readily visible from the air as perhaps one would like — it blends with the rest of the lodge grounds. For the benefit of those who may wish to discover for themselves this de-lightful spot in the North Woods, the runway is 9-27 and is immediately adjacent to and north of the main lodge. On the east end, from which landings are usually made — the wind is ordinarily out of the northwest — the forest is cut back several hundred feet to facilitate a short approach. This cut is a good marker for runway identification and determining the center line. On the west end, the power line is buried to eliminate hazard. Therefore both approaches are clear, but reasonable precaution against overshoot should be observed in all landings. If you have ever played ball in sneakers on wet grass, you have already discovered just how slippery rubber can be on wet grass. A short approach is always in order, particularly after a rain.

Only 80/87-octane fuel is available at Sky Lodge, but 100 octane can be bought at Greenville, 37 miles southeast by the compass at the southern tip of Moosehead Lake. A trip for gas is an experience in itself. Greenville boasts an excellent hard-surface field, but it's strictly self-service. You pump your own gas, make out the sales slip, and get your own change from the cash box.

There's no problem in getting acquainted on arrival at Sky Lodge. Other pilots seek you out immediately as well as do the interested earth-bound guests, which include

By KENNETH A. YOUNG | *AOPA 235848*

Good flying weather and advertising

promises prompt Massachusetts pilot and his family

to find a delightful vacation resort

Sky Lodge in the beautiful North Woods stands out on a hillside. The smooth, wide airstrip is immediately adjacent to the lodge. At the east end of the runway the forest is cut back several hundred feet to facilitate short approaches.

PHOTO BY LOEBEL, NEW YORK CITY

Kenneth and Eloise Young beside the Piper Cherokee.

most makes one wish for a rainy day. There are books, magazines, and games for all ages and in great abundance. The Landgrafs seem to have thought of everything.

The food is exceptionally well prepared, in variety, and reasonably priced. One touch that I particularly liked was having the same waiter for every meal.

After seeing the facilities and attractions, we were surprised also that room rates are the same as at almost any highway motel, $16 for double occupancy. Every room has a private bath and is unusually large and well furnished. In the lodge itself, many rooms have large, fieldstone fireplaces. For those who like the American plan, both daily and weekly rates are most reasonable.

Because of all the things to do and the talking to be done with new friends, the hours passed much too swiftly; but we had to get back to the rest of our family on the second day. Reluctantly, and several hours later than planned, we lifted off for the return trip to Nashua. All three of us enjoyed every minute of our brief stay at Sky Lodge. We ate well, slept well, and met interesting and congenial people — and the hangar flying was most enjoyable, too. We'll go back before long. ◆

almost everyone.

Shortly after our arrival, a Cessna 172 pilot and I, along with our wives, spent an hour or two dispelling some mistaken notions that nonflyers somehow acquire. Our gray hair and the fact that neither of us had taken a flying lesson much before the age of 50 appeared to convince the wife of an interested husband that she could approve his taking instruction. My wife puts the finishing touch on such discussions by casually remarking that she feels much safer flying than driving a car on a highway. This, by the way, is quite a change in a gal who didn't

speak to me for 24 hours after she discovered that I was taking flying lessons at the decrepit old age of 49.

While at the lodge, one can enjoy a dip in their private pool, engage in a vigorous game of badminton, or play their challenging nine-hole, mountainside golf course. Horseshoes, shuffleboard, target shooting, and archery are also available. All outdoors is right there — hiking, boating, canoe trips. Trout and salmon abound in the region, and fly fishing is in season from iceout until Sept. 30. For the hunter, the lodge is open through November. A browse through the library al-

THE AUTHOR

Author Young, who soloed in 1962, resides at Groton, Mass., with his wife, Eloise, and three sons. He is executive vice president of M. R. Lynch Associates, Inc., a firm specializing in writing and advertising agency services for technical/industrial clients.

THREE
EAST COAST
OCEAN BEACHES

Virginia Beach offers enjoyment to people of all ages and tastes. You can just sun on 28 miles of white shore line, or, if you are more energetic, there are boating, fishing and surfboarding.
PHOTOS BY VIRGINIA DEPARTMENT OF CONSERVATION AND ECONOMIC DEVELOPMENT

*Sunshine and cool breezes entice visitors
to Virginia Beach, Ocean City and Rehoboth.
Landing facilities in area
make all three attractive spots for flyers*

The boardwalk at Rehoboth Beach looking south. Amusements for just about all tastes can be found there.

Around July and August when it gets too hot for comfort throughout most of the United States, a flyer's thoughts might turn to the beach, where he (or she) can sun and cool off to suit the individual "thermostat." What better place to do this than an ocean beach, where you can cool off quickly by riding the waves and can enjoy cool evening breezes?

Virginia, Maryland and Delaware have some of the best beaches in the United States for the sun-and-surf seeker, with fly-in facilities that make them a natural for the vacationer with wings.

VIRGINIA BEACH

A spot well known throughout the East is Virginia Beach, Va. Four airports with complete facilities serve this area, South Norfolk at Chesapeake, Norfolk Municipal at Norfolk, Portsmouth and Suffolk Municipal. Details on facilities at these airports will be given at the end of this section.

For the primary attraction — beaching — Virginia Beach offers 28 miles of ocean shore line that run from the dunes of Cape Henry to Virginia's Outer Banks. The surf is said to be superb with long rollers for riding the waves, and a fine sand bottom extends way out, smooth and free of shells. The water temperature is reported to be refreshing in the hottest weather. There are 32 blocks of cement boardwalk along the oceanfront.

If you get tired of lying around on the beach or riding waves, there are plenty of other things to do around Virginia Beach. Golf courses, open the year around, may be used by guests of hotels belonging to the clubs. Both fresh and saltwater fishing are available — there are three fishing piers, bay and lake fishing, inshore and offshore game fishing. Back Bay, on the north-south flyway, has largemouth black bass fishing the

year around and deer hunting, goose and duck shooting in season. Among other diversions are a bay sightseeing cruise, jeep buggy trips down the Outer Banks, summer theater, biking on the boardwalk, miniature trains on the boardwalk and bowling.

If you want to range further in your sightseeing, here are a few high spots. You can see Norfolk's Azalea Gardens which are at their height in April when the International Azalea Festival is staged there, you can go to Mariner's Museum with its relics of the sea and seafaring lore — within an hour's drive — or you can visit the historic towns of Williamsburg, Jamestown and Yorktown, all within 60 miles of Virginia Beach.

Virginia Beach has almost innumerable accommodations of every type and price conceivable: hotels, motels and motor courts, apartments and efficiency cottages, inns, guest houses and lodges. A directory of places to stay and price ranges can be obtained from the Commonwealth of Virginia, Department of Conservation and Economic Development, Division of Public Relations and Advertising, State Office Building, Richmond, Va. 23219.

Here are some of the airport facilities within range of Virginia Beach:

Chesapeake — South Norfolk (Norfolk Sectional), four miles south of South Norfolk. There are two turf runways (3-21 is 3,250 feet long and 9-27 is 3,000 feet), 80/87 and 100/130 fuel, major repairs, hangars and tiedowns, weather information. Among other services are courtesy car, taxi and charter service. South Norfolk Airport is attended during daylight hours.

Norfolk — Norfolk Municipal (Norfolk Sectional), four miles northeast of downtown Norfolk. There are three paved runways (1-19 is 5,002 feet, 4-22 is 6,000 and 13-31 is 4,856 feet long). Available are 80/87, 100/130 and jet fuel as are major

and minor repairs, hangars and tiedowns, beacon and runway lights during darkness, weather information. Among other services are limousine and charter service. Norfolk Municipal is attended 24 hours a day.

Portsmouth (Chesapeake) — Portsmouth (Norfolk Sectional), seven miles west of Portsmouth. Runway 1-19 is 3,000 feet, and Runway 9-27 is 2,700 feet long; both are sod. Fuel in 80/87 and 100/130 octane is available, as are major and minor repairs, hangars and tiedowns, flarepots on request, Unicom, courtesy car, taxi and bus and charter service. Portsmouth Airport is attended during daylight.

Suffolk — Suffolk Municipal (Norfolk Sectional), four miles south of Suffolk. There are three 5,000-foot concrete runways. Among services available are 80/87 and 100/130 fuel, major repairs, hangars and tiedowns, weather information, Unicom, courtesy car and taxi and charter service. Suffolk is attended 24 hours a day.

OCEAN CITY, MD.

Ocean City, Md., is another well-known beach on the East Coast. Ocean City Airport, 2½ miles southwest of the city, has a 3,400-foot asphalt runway. Among services available are 80/87 and 100/130 fuel, tiedowns, beacon and runway lights during the summer and on request during the winter, weather information, Unicom, courtesy car and taxi. The Ocean City Information Center says that it provides jitney service to and from the airport for private flights.

Ocean City has a seven-mile expanse of beach and boardwalk, and it is claimed that the bather is safe from sudden dropoffs and water holes, as the constant movements of the waves quickly sweep sand into any holes that might appear on the ocean floor. There are innumerable accommodations of all types, many of them right on the beach. A promise is made that you will gain weight on the food, which ranges from Maryland oysters and fried chicken to Chesapeake Bay crab to a six-course Polynesian feast.

A feature of the boardwalk that the kids will love (and parents will enjoy too) is the eight-block amusement area, which features rides and penny arcades.

If you're a fisherman, you may get too involved in pursuing this hobby at Ocean City to make it to the beach. There's a lot of emphasis on white marlin fishing, and each September an open tournament is held for marlin fishermen with many prizes and trophies awarded. All that is needed to enter this tournament is a desire to challenge the sleek marlin. Ocean City has easier fishing, too; cruisers are available that take fishermen out into the ocean about 10 miles where they generally anchor over a sunken wreck. Fishermen can then expect to catch porgy, sea bass and blackfish. Other fish that can be caught are bluefish, sea trout, tautog early in the spring, rockfish, blues and kingfish by surfcasting, and tiny bass called Black Wills from any dock by hook and line.

Even if what you have in mind to do is just lie on the beach, eat and maybe do a little fishing, there's one bit of sightseeing that you really must do. Just a few miles west of Ocean City is Frontier Town, a 25-acre cowboy village, where you can pan for gold; ride a riverboat; see a western-type jail, "Boot Hill" and the Golden Nugget Saloon.

DELAWARE'S 'GOLD COAST'
By WILLIAM L. HILL, II
AOPA 237171

A very popular place to fly when it gets hot is the area of Rehoboth Beach, Del. Rehoboth Airport, operated by Aircrafters, Inc., has four grass runways: 3,300, 2,887, 2,475 and 1,900 feet. Eighty and 100 fuel are available, as are hangars and tiedowns, major and minor repairs, runway lights on request, Unicom and weather information. Among other services are courtesy car, taxi and car rentals and charter service. Rehoboth Airport is attended 7 a.m. to dark in the summer and 8 a.m. to 5 p.m. in the winter. As an added attraction, any maintenance can be performed while the pilot and "crew" enjoy the beach facilities.

Delaware enjoys over 80 miles of Atlantic coastal waters. Stretching from the upper waters of Delaware Bay to the semitropical Gulf stream, which threads its way north just offshore, every type of sport and seaside recreation may be found. The principal resort city is Rehoboth Beach. Rehoboth is unique among the Atlantic resorts in that it successfully combines family recreation facilities with the ultimate in healthful and interesting relaxation.

Extending the length of the town is a new boardwalk on which are found amusements for practically all tastes. On the east side of the boardwalk are miles of clean white beaches from the Henlopen Capes to the Chesapeake Bay. The city employs an extremely competent beach patrol which has an unblemished safety record. For the parents who favor quieter waters, there are several inland bays. In these waters are found clams, crabs and oysters in abundance. All beach and fishing supplies, including umbrellas, chairs, rafts, clam rakes, lines and bait, may be rented at any of the beach

For those who like to add a dash of athletics to their vacations, Virginia Beach offers horseback riding, tennis and golf at five courses open the year around.

Two gaily painted trolleys shuttle vacationers back and forth on the 36-block boardwalk at Ocean City, Md.

stands or bait stores in the area.

There are a wealth of accommodations in the Rehoboth Beach area — hotels and motels, apartments and cottages, inns and tourist homes. You can get a list of these, as well as much other information on facilities in the area, from the Rehoboth Beach Chamber of Commerce.

Only a couple of miles to the north of Rehoboth is Delaware Bay. Leaving from the town of Lewes are charter boats which catch every fish from marlin to blues in astonishing numbers. Lewes is also well worth visiting for its historical lore. Founded in the 1630's by the Dutch and raked by naval gunfire in the War of 1812, Lewes proudly displays many of the artifacts of these periods in the Zwaanendael Museum.

Bordering Rehoboth on the south is Dewey Beach, which offers speedboats for hire, skiing lessons and a sailing club which rents sailboats to the public. A little further to the south is Indian River which rivals Lewes in charter fishing, and stretching between them are miles of unspoiled beaches which provide solitude for the sun worshipper.

A supplement to the aquatic pastimes are a wealth of facilities. Adjacent to the town are golf courses. Rehoboth sponsors a concert on the mall beside the ocean every week which features many prominent orchestras. There are bicycles and motor bikes for rent, and bowling alleys. Many fine

hotels and restaurants are to be found at Rehoboth (some of them inexpensive "family" places), as are many exciting nightclubs.

The weather is extremely favorable to the novice pilot in this area, with unlimited visibility almost all the time and very few of the afternoon thunderstorms so frequent in the South. Any apprehensions about the weather can be answered by the Flight Service Station located on the Salisbury Airport, 30 miles to the south, which may be reached over the omni frequency or by telephone.

For a summer full of fun or a weekend's flight, for the city executive or the entire family, the Rehoboth area offers recreation and relaxation for all. ◆

THE AUTHOR

William L. Hill, II, author of "Delaware's 'Gold Coast,' " received a private license in November 1964 and is working toward a commercial license. For several summers, Hill worked at the Rehoboth Beach Airport as a line boy and assistant mechanic. He became interested in aviation while he was a cadet in the Civil Air Patrol and began taking flying lessons during his senior year in high school.

By DOLLY CONNELLY

Islands off coast of Washington combine wilderness and conveniences of sophisticated approach to recreation

'Spellcaster' Islands—
THE SAN JUANS OF WASHINGTON

It is a strange fact that the San Juan Islands of Washington still are in a state of being discovered, though almost two centuries have passed since Francisco Eliza, the Spanish commandant at Nootka on the west coast of Vancouver Island — intrigued by tales of a great inland sea told by still earlier explorers — turned his little fleet of 45-foot sailing vessels north by east inside the Strait of Juan de Fuca. Before Eliza's amazed eyes there arose "an unknown labyrinth of verdant isles set in the tidal flow between the Canal de Lopez de Haro and Gran Canal de Nuestra Señora del Rosario la Marinera."

In our time the age of the outboard brought a new armada to the San Juans: the small boatsman and his family pulled up on uninhabited island beaches to delight again in the sense of discovery. Finally, in the last two decades, the fraternity of sports flyers has discovered the San Juans, often basking in CAVU sunlight in a peculiar "banana belt" lying placid and sun blessed in the protection of great mountains.

Once flyers buzzed sheep off their bumpy pastures, lurching into rutted landings, or landed at low tide on exposed beaches, swiveling wildly as the wheels hit soft sand pockets. This is all changed now. Blakely Island's beautiful grassed and lighted field led the way to construction of small fields on practically everything flat until now there are numerous private strips and good all-year airports on Lopez and at Roche Harbor, in addition to long-existing surfaced fields at Friday Harbor, county seat of San Juan Island, and Eastsound on Orcas Island.

On any weekend, winter or summer, bright-winged private planes fill the parking strips of island landing fields. Blakely Island's fabulous flyers' marina, known as superb to all sports flyers everywhere, draws its aircraft from an entire continent. Blakely, developed by the loving hands of Ola and Floyd Johnson, is an ideal incorporating within its 10 square miles both true wilderness and all the conveniences of a sophisticated approach to outdoor recreation. Its colonists, for the most part sports flyers, may spend the day hauling beach rocks up the

trails to create artistic gardens, but at nightfall they dine by candlelight in the islands' handsomest homes, with half-tame deer peeking in the picture windows and indignant raccoons waiting their turn at the kitchen door.

If this cosmopolitan appreciation of the islands seems strange in an archipelago far more forest and farm than resort, where descendants of Nineteenth Century homesteaders still tend sheep as if they'd never heard of the skyrocketing value of waterfront properties, still more strange is the geologic history of the islands. The San Juans were born by submarine convulsion in the Paleozoic era, when a range of mountains emerged sharply from the sedimentary ooze. Completely engulfed in the last Ice

Age by an immense finger of glacial ice which scooped out Puget Sound in passing, the mountain range was submerged by the weight of ice back into its sea trough. Left above water were only the tops of mountains, 15 mountain peaks with elevations in excess of 1,000 feet and innumerable lesser crests, their highest points deeply striated and polished by ancient glacial action. Plunging ravines became deep fiords, some of them, like Orcas' East and West Sounds, extending inland for miles. The islands still are shrugging off pressure of that burden of glacial ice, still lifting new reefs out of the depths. The slow uplift is apparent in remarkably uniform, wave-cut beaches of honeycombed sandstone ringing many a rugged coast at elevations 20 to 40 feet

Blakely Island, one of the San Juan Islands of Washington. In the right background is 2,400-foot turf strip; right and center foreground show the clubhouse and marina.

PHOTO BY ACKROYD PHOTOGRAPHY, INC., PORTLAND, ORE.

above highest tide lines. These cliffs often are filled with fossilized sea life and tropical plant growth trapped thousands of years ago in sedimentary layers.

The occasional emergence of a new reef from the enormous wash of tidal flow complicates any accurate count of the islands, which varies wildly with depth of tide at which tally is taken. Count of all isolated land areas exposed at deepest minus tides reveals an incredible 786 islands and reefs in Washington's group alone. At high tide the number drops to 457, grouped into 175 land areas of sufficient importance to warrant names. Size range is from the grandeur of 57-square-mile Orcas to lonely rocks.

The record of flight in the islands is uniquely beneficent. The oldest public air carrier in the San Juans, Roy Franklin's Island Sky Ferries, has flown from Bellingham Airport to Eastsound to Friday Harbor, with stops in between as dictated by custom, for 19 years without scratching either customer or freight. Some years back, Island Sky encompassed Seattle's Boeing Field on a thrice-daily summer schedule, so that its service now is from Seattle to the San Juans with stops at Bellingham. This is a boon specifically for the business commuter, who plants his family on an idyllic island beach for the school-vacation months and tends his office daytimes. The Seattle schedule carries an increasing number of business and professional people who come in by airliner, transfer to Island Sky Ferries, spend a few hours in the islands and pop back to Seattle and airline departure the same day.

Pioneer airman Roy Franklin, who has watched over the welfare of island people from his increasing fleet of Island Sky Ferries planes for several million flight miles, writes:

"The islands have not changed for me. This is still the most enchantingly beautiful place in the world. The people who live and visit here still have need for speedy medical aid, for parts for broken-down equipment, for reliable daily transportation. We still make our midnight flights — babies still are being born, people still have heart attacks, kids still fall out of trees. But what a difference! We roar down a lighted hard-top runway with a reliable, roomy ambulance plane, a glowing panel of beautiful gyro instruments and radio gear in front of the pilot. Sure, it's black between here and there, and we have no beams or other navigational aids, but we know that there are lights to show us where to land and that we have the equipment necessary to utilize navigational aids once we hit the mainland.

"Ten years ago I hardly would have dared dream of offering the 40 people on Waldron Island three passenger-and-freight trips daily to Bellingham and three daily to Seattle, but this is the service we provide now from the first of June to Sept. 15, with only small curtailment in winter. I rather think there are few communities of 40 persons around the country which have anything like it.

"Planes on the line now are a 12-passenger twin-engine Lockheed, a six-passenger Stinson, and our four-passenger Cessnas. Island Sky has come a long way since we buzzed sheep off the fields and wobbled in between the ruts. The needs are the same, but the service now has shaped up first rate."

Of four main airports in the islands, Friday Harbor on San Juan Island is the best equipped for the lightplane traveler. It has complete gassing as well as repair facilities. Headquarters of Island Sky Ferries, Friday Harbor field, is 2,400 feet long, hard surfaced and lighted at night. Rental cars — rare in the San Juans — are available at the airport so that travelers can reach several nearby beach resorts and explore the island.

"Summit conference" on Blakely, looking over some of the other San Juan Islands.   PHOTO BY DOLLY CONNELLY

Lonesome Cove Resort is among the most attractive, as it has outboard boats at reasonable rental and is home port of the "'Windsong," a 40-foot Marconi-rigged yawl available for charter. A quaint hotel in town dating back to the turn of the century, of the type with china washbasins and pitchers on dressing stands, is a reminder of the glamorous history of the islands, which once nearly precipitated a fullscale war between England and the United States. San Juan Island is worth exploring from many aspects besides its beauty. At opposite ends of the island can be found locations of the American and British Camps of this comic opera international ownership dispute, known locally as the "Pig War" for its single casualty. [There is a very large real estate and resort development with a good airstrip in the first construction stages at Admiral Cove near Cattle Point at the southern end of San Juan Island. Given another two or three years, this should be an important colony on the island, especially with National Park Service restoration of the American and British camps of the war. — Author's press-time note.] The University of Washington maintains a fascinating marine biology laboratory, open to visitors, near Friday Harbor. There are ancient lime kilns. Small fish canneries still are operated on the island, whose people largely are occupied with salmon fishing, farming, sheepraising and small-scale logging. Write Lonesome Cove, Friday Harbor, Wash., for details on accommodations.

Roche Harbor airfield, near the northern end of San Juan Island, is a good, graded, all-weather strip 4,000 feet long with tiedown area in an island-locked location. The field offers neither services nor gasoline, but nearby is a delightful resort with everything to make a northwest vacation memorable. Heated swimming pool, historic Hotel de Haro and dining salon are open from Decoration Day through Labor Day. Charter boats are available at the small boat harbor, which has moorage for 200 yachts. Bridle trails fan out from the resort to a multitude of uninhabited coves and tremendous high vistas of the adjoining Canadian Gulf Islands to the north. Write Roche Harbor Resort, Roche Harbor, Wash.

On Orcas Island, Eastsound Airport is a good, graded strip, built on gravel foundation, 2,300 feet long and lighted, located at the narrow neck of the double-lobed island. There is no attendant at the airport, which offers neither gas nor service facilities, but within the waiting room may be found a telephone and brochures of a fistful of Orcas Island resorts which promptly will send cars to pick up flying guests. The outstanding resort on Orcas is Rosario, once the luxurious estate of a multi-millionaire shipbuilder, now headquarters of lively fun all year around. Write Rosario Resort, Rosario, Wash., or Orcas Island Resort Owners' Association, Eastsound, Wash.

Blakely has a fine 2,400-foot turf strip with clear approaches over water and is lighted at night when pilots buzz intention to land. Most landings are made to the southwest, as the strip has a fairly good grade for the first 1,200 feet. No aircraft service is offered outside of generous, protected plane parking areas well off the landing strip. Blakely has an excellent clubhouse and restaurant and an outstanding "Skytel," or fly-

Blakely Island deer and friend. Deer roam freely on the San Juans.
PHOTO BY DOLLY CONNELLY

ers' motel. Along the west beaches of the island, near the airport, are about 100 homes of the flyers' colony, used year around. Some of the San Juans' finest salmon fishing grounds are located just off Blakely in the area of Obstruction Pass, which separates Blakely from Orcas Island, and off Point Lawrence, easternmost point of Orcas. Blakely, which rises to 1,050-foot Blakely Peak at its highest point, is a hiker's paradise, rough Jeep roads leading to its two high freshwater lakes — Spencer and Horseshoe — a ghost sawmill town at Thatcher Bay, and to long-abandoned Nineteenth Century homesteaders' log cabins and farms near the southern tip of the island. The beaches and coves are notable for excellent clam digging and profuse numbers of agates which the islanders gather, polish and use in decoration of their homes. Write Floyd Johnson, San Juan Aviation & Yachting Estates, Blakely Island, Wash.

Lopez Island Airport is much used by northwest flyers. It is 2,600 feet long and has tree obstructions on the approaches. It is lighted for operation at night, but there are no service facilities. A telephone at the field will bring Nita or Richie Navarre, owners and operators of Ebb Tide Resort at Fisherman Bay, by car to pick up guests. The Ebb Tide has completely furnished cabins with huge windows overlooking the magnificent sunsets of the San Juans, a lodge dining room and nearby golf course. Seaplanes load at the dock in one of the best natural har-

bors in the islands. Deer, rabbit, pheasant and pigeon hunting are available in season, and Lopez Island beaches are rich in clam and Dungeness crab. Write Ebb Tide Resort, Lopez, Wash.

Private airstrips are located on Decatur, Crane, Spieden, Stuart, Waldron and Shaw Islands, but these offer no facilities or accommodations and may present hazards for the uninitiated, especially in winter, when poorly drained fields tend to develop boggy spots.

There's a serious problem in visiting the San Juan Islands that has no connection with wet landing fields or fir forests on the approaches. It might be summed up as islomania, a catching ailment that has affected visitors ever since Capt. Pickett's Ninth Infantry Battalion set up the American Camp in 1859 near Cattle Point. The islands are full of people who went out "for a week or two" and haven't been shore side since Once they've slept to the gentle susurrus of little wavelets, once they've wakened to watch mountains rise against a paling chartreuse sky all around the horizon from Mount Rainier on the south to the Golden Ears of Canada's Coast Range, once they've heard the joyous bellyflop of homing salmon or the soughing whistle of whales steaming on their way through the islands, they wing back again.

For the San Juans are spellcasters of the first order, a way of life so intimately attuned to the sea and the seasons that, once felt, it is never out of mind. ◆

By ANNE L. CARLING

*Restoration project enables visitors to
get an idea of living styles during
late 1700's and early 1800's*

FLY TO
St. Augustine-
HISTORICAL CITY RESTORED

A carriage tour of St. George Street, restored by the St. Augustine Historical Restoration and Preservation Commission, is in order when one visits this historical area. Buildings along this street contain house museums and craft shops (tobacco and candle making, printing, baking, carpentry and weaving).

Thousands of alligators and crocodiles have been collected at the St. Augustine Alligator Farm, which also houses a complete zoo of Florida wildlife. Featured daily at the farm are 'gator chute-the-chutes and man-alligator wrestling matches.

A costumed guide rests in the patio of the oldest Spanish house.

PHOTOS COURTESY OF THE ST. AUGUSTINE AND
ST. JOHNS COUNTY CHAMBER OF COMMERCE

"We are now arriving at St. Augustine. Please set your watch back 400 years," an airline stewardess is alleged to have stated as the plane set down at the nation's oldest city.

Whether she said it is questionable (since commercial airliners don't land at this ancient city), but one fact is not. St. Augustine, founded by the Spanish on Sept. 8, 1565, is taking its visitors back some 400 years as it presents a living history lesson complete with the inhabitants, homes and crafts of yesterday.

A restoration program begun in 1959 by the St. Augustine Historical Restoration and Preservation Commission, a state agency, is reconstructing and restoring a section of this city as it appeared in the late 1700's and early 1800's. Today, balcony-dotted structures line the narrow streets of San Agustin Antigua, results of this extensive undertaking. Some structures are house museums; others are craft shops where visitors learn how early St. Augustinians earned a modest living.

The old fort, Castillo de San Marcos National Monument; the oldest Spanish house in the United States; the Mission of Nombre de Dios where the city founder, Pedro Menendez landed; and many other interesting points give visitors a further glimpse into St. Augustine's past. For persons with a flair for interior decorating, house museums offer unique ideas of the various periods of the city's history, including Spanish, English and American influence.

Additional museums and attractions range from collections, curiosities and lifelike figures to sites geared to the interest of children and adults alike. Specialized collections ranging from antique toys and guns to store merchandise are also to be seen. For unique views of the city, walking tours, or carriage, train and boat rides are suggested.

Each summer from late June through early September, visitors are afforded an opportunity to relive St. Augustine's founding, as the story of the city's first two years of settlement is told in the outdoor drama, "Cross and Sword." Described as a skillful blending of acting, singing and dancing, the colorful production, written by Pulitzer Prize winner Paul Green, is presented in the 2,000-seat St. Augustine Amphitheater.

During the remainder of the year, the city hosts many special festivals. Its annual birthday party, "Days in Spain," sponsored by the St. Augustine Jaycees, is usually held in late August. A gala fiesta, it includes nightly entertainment, sword fighting exhibitions and colorful booths offering all sorts of delicious foods and unique games.

Easter brings an annual week-long festival highlighted by the "Parada de los Caballos y Coches" (Parade of Horses and Carriages), where horses sport the latest in Easter finery; an Arts and Crafts Festival is usually held Palm Sunday weekend and the Blessing of the Fishing Fleet, on Palm Sunday, brings out the impressive shrimp fleet.

What about relaxation? Miles of white sand bordering the blue Atlantic Ocean answer this question in a most delightful way for ocean and sun bathing, surf fishing or just plain relaxing. Quality restaurants and accommodations, either in the heart of town or at the oceanfront, provide complete vacation enjoyment.

For the city's air visitors, a lighted 6,500-foot runway makes landing at St. Augustine a pleasure; and the Fairchild-St. Augustine Airport (Orlando Sectional) offers many conveniences to patrons. Services include the sale of oil and 80/87, 100/130 octane gas, along with minor airplane servicing. A certificated mechanic is available.

The airport is operated daily from daylight until dark, and a tower, manned by Fairchild Hiller Corporation Monday through Friday from 7:30 a.m. until 4:15 p.m., can be reached on 123.1 or 122.5. Fairchild Hiller is a major industry in St. Augustine involved in airplane modification and engine repair.

A tiedown fee of $1 is charged at the St. Augustine Airport. At present, hangars are available. Free transportation to town is provided for airport patrons, or arrangements can be made for rental cars for those who want a first-hand look at the many points of interest in this oldest city in the United States. ◆

By JANE MAHON

FLY TO

YEAR-AROUND FUN

Florida gets better all the time

as a place to fly and have fun

in winter and summer

The State of Florida, with its relatively even climate and its many and varied attractions, from water sports and fishing, golf and shuffleboard to nightclubbing, is one of the most popular vacation spots in the country.

Florida has in recent years succeeded in making itself a year-around recreation area. And it has gone all-out to attract national conventions, too. Many hotels lower their rates during late spring, summer and early fall in order to attract off-season visitors. The state is ideally situated for year-around comfort — surrounded as it is by water, it has fresh breezes everywhere, in all seasons.

Some Florida cities that have corporate planes landing for conferences and conventions make a particular effort to cater to the flyer, and there are a great number of airport facilities throughout Florida. Check your AOPA Airport Directory for airport facilities in the areas covered in this article. Here are some suggested places to fly to for enjoyable vacations:

At PENSACOLA on the Gulf Coast, anglers can fish from piers and beaches or charter boats for deep-sea game fishing. In addition, there are many fishing camps on the streams and bayous in the area. Other sports for the tourist are skin diving; hunting deer, turkey, quail, dove, duck and geese nearby (November to January for most); and swimming at Pensacola Beach. Things to see are the Pensacola Historical Museum in Old Christ Church for Indian, Spanish and other exhibits; Forts Barrancas and San Carlos, 16th century Spanish; and the Museum of Naval Aviation at the U.S. Naval Air Station, a unique aspect of which is a survival exhibit demonstrating survival in the Arctic and the tropics. Tourist accommodations are reported to be plentiful at Pensacola and Pensacola Beach.

FORT WALTON BEACH is a resort center on Santa Rosa Sound just off the Gulf of Mexico. Swimming and salt- and freshwater fishing are the major attractions. This is a popular stopover for pleasure boats following the Intracoastal Waterway. North of Fort Walton Beach is 800-square-mile Eglin Air Force Base, two-hour tours of which are conducted from the west gate on Thursday afternoons during the summer months. Tickets are available from the Fort Walton Chamber of Commerce.

The FLORIDA CAVERNS STATE PARK is three miles north of Marianna and has limestone caverns with large formations of stalactites and stalagmites. Guided tours of the Caverns are available, and the park has picnicking, golf and camping facilities.

TALLAHASSEE, capital of Florida, is well known for its beautiful gardens with massive oaks and magnolias draped with Spanish moss. The capital building is an imposing structure surrounded by a group of state office buildings to form a distinguished "Capital Center." Florida State University's art gallery and museum feature exhibitions of art and the Carter Collection of American and prehistoric Peruvian Indian materials and displays. Killearn Gardens State Park is 5½ miles northeast of the city and is most interesting during the blooming season from December through April. Picnicking and boating facilities are available at the park.

APALACHICOLA NATIONAL FOREST is a densely wooded wilderness 54 miles southwest of Tallahassee. Supervised hunting is permitted in season. The entire area has been developed for outdoor recreation, including swimming, boating, camping and fishing.

Approximately 54 miles southwest of Tallahassee Municipal Airport is DOG ISLAND. This is a popular fly-in resort area. Swimming, fishing and boating are excellent. The island is connected to the mainland with a ferryboat running to the little fishing town of Carrabelle. Overnight accommodations are available at the Villa, a two-story apartment building with air-conditioned efficiency apartments and camping sites. A quonset hut close to the airstrip houses a small restaurant, an island store, picnic tables and bathhouse facilities for fly-in swimmers.

One of the world's largest springs, located in a beautiful cypress forest, is WAKULLA SPRINGS, 15 miles south of Tallahassee. Glass-bottom boats give visitors the opportunity to see the marine life that abound in this 185-foot-deep spring area. A jungle cruise boat ride takes you through a delightful bird sanctuary.

GAINESVILLE is the home of the University of Florida and the Florida State Museum. Orange Lake, 20 miles south of the city, is noted for its floating islands. There is a 3,000-foot sod strip on the northwest corner of the lake which should be used with caution. Gainesville has excellent facilities for golfing and swimming.

GOLD HEAD BRANCH STATE PARK is 24 miles northeast of the Gainesville VOR in Keystone Heights. Lakeshore camping facilities are excellent. The area is noted for good freshwater fishing and swimming. Boats, campsites and picnic facilities are available.

JACKSONVILLE and the surrounding area provide ample beaches and facilities for yachting, swimming, fishing and golfing. Two dog tracks operate from October through June. Located on 40 miles of beautiful white sand beach between Jacksonville and St. Augustine are Jacksonville Beach, Neptune Beach, Atlantic Beach and Ponte Vedra Beach. At low tide, single-engine aircraft have been seen landing along this area in some of the more remote regions.

At ST. AUGUSTINE, the vacationer can enjoy swimming and other water sports on the

Castillo de San Marcos, completed in 1756, is one of the attractions of St. Augustine. This fort was built to guard the walled city.

St. Johns County beaches, the St. Johns River and at many seaside resort facilities and pools; and he can also enjoy golf, hunting and fishing. Points of interest are Castillo de San Marcos, a fort completed in 1756 which was built to guard the walled city, Lightner Museum of Hobbies and The Museum of Yesterday's Toys.

MARINELAND OF FLORIDA, 18 miles south of St. Augustine, is one of Florida's main attractions. Two large outdoor aquariums, one rectangular and the other round, house a variety of deep-sea life. Underwater portholes allow visitors to see specimens ranging from giant shark to small tropical fish living together as they would in the open sea. There are regular shows held in the adjacent open-air stadium with trained porpoises and whales doing all sorts of tricks. You will have to rent a car to travel from the airport (Fairchild-St. Augustine) to Marineland.

At DAYTONA BEACH RESORT AREA, in addition to fishing and swimming, you can take cruise boats on the Halifax River, and you can visit the Museum of Speed, the Cuban Museum and the Ormund War Memorial Art Gallery, featuring the history of automobile racing, which began there. Other attractions are Animal Land with its exhibit of wild birds and rare animals and Marineland.

Along the entire east coast of Florida, the most conspicuous feature of the terrain is the area surrounding CAPE KENNEDY. While you cannot fly into the restricted area, you can fly close enough to see the huge gantrys at the Cape piercing the blue sky. Although the Cape is closed to the public, it is possible to see missile launchings from a distance of eight or 10 miles on the beach. There is an exhibit of missiles on display in front of the Technical Laboratory at Patrick Air Force Base, which is 15 miles south of the Cape.

The resort community of VERO BEACH is located partly on the mainland and partly on the island that extends into the Atlantic Ocean. There is excellent fishing and boating on the Indian River, which forms the natural divider between mainland and island.

OCALA, an industrial and resort city in the center of the state, has hundreds of fishing lakes and miles of natural forests to lure fishermen and hunters. Open to the public at certain hours are several prize cattle and thoroughbred race horse breeding farms. There are several beaches on nearby lakes, and an excellent 18-hole golf course is open to the public.

SILVER SPRINGS, nine nautical miles northeast of the Ocala VOR, is one of the world's largest springs and is a major tourist attraction in Florida. The springs are formed from a subterranean river and are so clear that objects at a depth of 80 feet are clearly discernible. Electrically operated glass-bottom boats take visitors over the 14 groups of springs and enable them to see numerous varieties of fish, turtles and underwater plants. Around the springs is a beautifully landscaped park with picnic and parking facilities.

HOWEY-IN-THE-HILLS is located in the ridge section of central Florida. Magnificent orange and grapefruit groves, sparkling lakes and rolling hills present a panorama of scenic beauty. This area is on the southern tip of Lake Harris and is known as the Black Bass Capital. The Floridan Country Club offers outdoor recreational facilities, including swimming, boating, golf, riding and tennis.

LAKE APOPKA, northwest of Orlando, is the second largest freshwater lake in the state, and vacationers can rent rustic cypress cottages along the edge.

WINTER HAVEN, located in Florida's central ridge section, is surrounded by some of the state's finest citrus groves. The annual Florida Citrus Exposition held in February exhibits the best of Florida's citrus products

View of Dog Island, a peaceful resort isle, showing 2,800-foot sod strip. Swimming, boating and fishing are good here.

for the season. Recreation in the city centers around Lake Silver which has a beach, amphitheater, two golf courses, tennis courts and swimming. Winter Haven is also the closest metropolitan city to the well-known Cypress Gardens. Besides exploring the junglelike walkways and boat canals in Cypress Gardens, visitors can watch a water-skiing exhibition which is presented four times daily.

LAKE WALES is best known for the Singing (Bok) Tower and the Mountain Lake Sanctuary. Crystal Lake, surrounded by parks, is the recreational center for visitors. There is a tourist clubhouse with facilities for outdoor games. The Black Hills Passion Play, presented at Spearfish, S.D., in the summer, is given here in an outdoor amphitheater.

WEEKIWACHEE SPRINGS is a 137-foot-deep, winding natural spring. An underwater show with acrobatic and ballet dancers is of great interest, and a glass-bottom boat takes visitors on a leisurely ride down a jungle river, during which the boat passes wild animals in a zoo and a Seminole Indian hunting and trading post.

CLEARWATER is on Pinellas Peninsula between Clearwater Bay and Old Tampa Bay. The city of Clearwater and Clearwater Beach form an all-year resort area with

varied types of recreational facilities and are especially popular with family vacationers.

The Greater TAMPA Chamber of Commerce claims that, whatever your pleasure, you'll find it in Tampa. Tampa offers sandy beaches, water skiing, boating, sailing, fishing in the bay or the nearby Gulf, and golf. Sights to see are the banana dock; the shrimp fleet; Fairyland, Tampa's storybook park; and cigar factories. Spectator sports include jai alai, dog racing and horse racing in season.

ST. PETERSBURG is surrounded by more than 200 miles of waterfront. Naturally, boating, skin diving, water skiing and fishing are the favorite sports here. A vacationer can also golf and sail. Sights are Madame Tussaud's Wax Museum, the Ringling Circus, art museums and the Thomas A. Edison home.

SARASOTA is well known as an art and cultural center and has a wide variety of sports and attractions for all age groups. The bay offers ideal waters for boating, and the Sarasota Yacht Club, which welcomes visitors, has its clubhouse on Ringling Isle. The Ringling Museums and the Circus Hall of Fame are a "must" for this area.

FORT MYERS is popular as a west coast winter resort. An annual "Pageant of Light" is held here which honors Thomas A. Edi-

son. The original Edison home, Botanical Gardens and Laboratory have been preserved and are maintained as a national shrine to this famous American. The Florida Marine Museum is a mile north of the city. This museum houses the "Glory of the Sea," reputed to be the rarest and most valuable shell in the world. The Shell Factory, five miles north of the city, has one of the world's largest displays of marine fossils and shells.

SANIBEL ISLAND, 14 miles long and three miles wide, is three miles off the mainland and about 20 miles southwest of Fort Myers. Sanibel has arrays of seashells on its beaches and is a game refuge and bird sanctuary for migratory birds, waterfowl, turtles, and many species of wild game. There are also exotic island flowers and rare tropical birds. At Casa Ybel, Sanibel Island's largest resort, you can water ski, skin dive, spearfish, boat and fish as well as play shuffleboard and enjoy Caribbean cookouts and Hawaiian luaus. There are several hotels on the island that also have family cottage accommodations. Reservations are a must on Sanibel Island.

EVERGLADES CITY is one of the western gates to the Everglades National Park and is popular with sportsmen who use it as a base for fishing and hunting trips. There are several lodges and motels which offer good

Narrow St. George Street is part of the 400-year-old section of St. Augustine, which was founded in 1565. The Museum of Yesterday's Toys (in center of picture) is housed in an 18th-century home.

Exploring the vast sawgrass and hammock flatlands of the Everglades via a skimming airboat opens new vistas for vacationers who want an extensive look at this wilderness area.

accommodations and food. The nearby Ten Thousand Islands group offers excellent beaches for swimming, shelling and surf fishing.

EVERGLADES NATIONAL PARK comprises almost 1½ million acres of wilderness. It is recommended that visitors stop at the National Park Headquarters just inside the entrance to the Park, where Park personnel will explain how to properly see, understand and enjoy the wilderness. At Flamingo Lodge (a 60-room motel 39 miles from the Park entrance on Florida Bay), guides conduct sight-seeing cruise trips. Colorful birds can be seen, as well as opossum, raccoon and otter among the mangrove trees. One can see sea cows, tarpon and saltwater crocodile in the water or along the shore. Beaches stretch for miles along Cape Sable's shore line. Also at Flamingo, guides will take vacationers fishing for tarpon, snook, redfish and trout.

RIVIERA BEACH on Singer Island is at the headwaters of the 18-mile-long Lake Worth. On the south end of the island is Palm Beach Shores, a family vacation center which has motels, apartments, hotels with convention facilities, a modern yacht basin

and clubhouse. For fishing fun, you can go trolling in the Gulf Stream aboard a chartered boat, rent an outboard or just drop a line from bridges or seawalls.

WEST PALM BEACH has a multitude of attractions for the pleasure-seeking visitor. Two fishing grounds are nearby — the Gulf Stream with its deep-sea specimens and Lake Worth with its snapper, snook and smaller pan fish. In 29 parks, tennis, shuffleboard, lawn bowling and other group activities are available. Things to see are art shows, botanical exhibits, jai alai, restaurants and fun spots. There is reported to be a wide choice of places to stay, from luxury hotels and oceanfront cottages to hotels, motels and apartments in the heart of town.

PALM BEACH, across Lake Worth from West Palm Beach, has a public beach area that offers pool and ocean bathing and fishing off a pier. Hotel accommodations and rentals in apartments, homes and motels are reportedly plentiful. Imposing residential sections and fashionable shops on Worth Avenue are of special interest.

DELRAY BEACH is a garden spot — its hotels, motels and cottages are banked in colorful shrubs and set off by bright green

lawns and clusters of palms. Deep-sea and freshwater fishing and golf are available here, as well as swimming and loafing on the miles of ocean beach or at the large municipal pool.

BOCA RATON was once the bailiwick of pirates. Mementos of these days can be seen at Ancient America, as well as Indian burial exhibits. Another spot to cover is Africa, U.S.A.

FORT LAUDERDALE is a city of islands honeycombed by rivers, bays, inlets and canals. Bahia-Mar Yacht Basin is almost a fully contained city within itself. It has numerous shops, restaurants, a club, swimming pool and post office. Many excellent hotels and motels are located on the public beaches, and there is a variety of all resort activities going on day and night.

There are miles of sand beaches open to the public throughout GREATER MIAMI and MIAMI BEACH. The beach at the end of almost every block in Miami Beach is public, and all oceanfront hotels and motels have their own beaches for the use of their guests.

A great variety of rental facilities for boats can be found, for pleasure cruising, fishing or water skiing. Some of the varieties

Ernest Hemingway's home at Key West. This home, in which he wrote many of his major works, is restored and open to the public.

of salt- and freshwater fish that are abundant are tarpon, snook, bonefish, sea trout, snapper, redfish, largemouthed black bass and bream. Hunting is also available in this area. For information on seasonal hunting dates, license cost and hunting areas, contact the Florida Game and Fresh Water Fish Commission, 2531 N.W. 170th Street, Miami.

Among points of interest in the area are the Ancient Spanish Monastery and Gardens at North Miami Beach, Crandon Park Zoo on Key Biscayne, Donnin's Antique Arms and Gun Museum at North Miami, the Gold Coast Railroad and Museum at the University of Miami in Rockdale, and the Muse Isle Seminole Indian Village.

There is a saying that the fisherman is king throughout the FLORIDA KEYS and KEY WEST. The waters of the Atlantic and the Gulf abound with some 600 varieties of fish, from snapper to sailfish, and you can cast your line from bridge, boat or surf.

On the Upper Keys (Key Largo to Long Key) is America's only undersea state park, John Pennekamp Coral Reef State Park. Among the attractions of this undersea park are shipwrecks, living coral and rainbow-hued fish.

An attraction on Key Largo is the Ocean Reef Club, a resort which offers water sports, fishing, golf and tennis and at which guests have their choice of hotel-type rooms, villas and yachtels. It's reported that reservations are a must at the club.

Marathon in the Middle Keys is headquarters for a fleet of colorful shrimp boats.

Other attractions are the North American Indian Museum and a golf course.

On the Lower Keys, you can take a cruise by car over Seven-Mile Bridge and see a panoramic view of the island-dotted waters of the Atlantic and the Gulf. Fishing and shelling are supposed to be excellent, and there is a state park for picnicking and swimming at Bahia Honda Marina.

The atmosphere in Key West is a blend of Cuban, West Indian and Bahamian lore. Key West has a colorful history of rum runners, pirate ships and Civil War intrigue. Of current interest are its shrimping, sponging, salvaging and cigar making, its naval base, dog track and fishing pier. Other points of interest are the Aquarium, Martello Museum of war relics and Ernest Hemingway's home. ◆

By GEORGE R. REISS | AOPA 167067

A Pleasant FLORIDA ISLAND

So you, the private pilot, are seeking the ideal vacation spot to which to fly your personal aircraft for your next holiday? So you would like a place that has everything for the flying vacationist—a good, safe airstrip, away from the headaches of a bustling major air terminal, where your aircraft is safe; a spot off the beaten path where you can loaf and relax—good beach, bathing, weather, food, fishing and interesting history?

Well, Marco Island, Fla., may be your spot. Marco offers virtually everything the vacation-minded flyer might ask, and perhaps more. Plenty air pilots already have found it; most are coming back.

Marco is one of a few hundred saltwater islands, 15 or 20 miles below Naples, lonely and previously inaccessible, except by boat. Marco itself has a perfect four-mile-long white sand beach, a jungle of mangrove swamp, pinelands and sand mounds, relics of the ancient Calusa Indians who lived there centuries before the Seminoles were driven down from the north.

Amid these mangrove swamps, the Deltona Corporation (Elliott, Robert, and Frank Mackle) is building a new Florida vacation colony — streets of beautiful homes, some with canals in their backyards for private yachts; a beautiful vacation hotel; yacht club; country club; golf courses; high-rise condominiums — everything the retired, or simply "tired," folks might want.

Being air-minded fellows, one of the first things the Mackles did to make their dream come true was to set up an airstrip. A 3,000-foot stretch of highway was sealed off, and there it was. The demand has been so great the runway has been lengthened to 4,500 feet, with perfect approaches, and widened to 65 feet, big enough for most twin-engine and some four-engine aircraft.

Parking spaces have been supplied for 20 or more small or medium-size aircraft, or for a few larger aircraft. Unicom (122.8 mc) has been installed. Gas, up to 100 octane, is available; so is telephone service, and it is a one-minute stroll through the palmettos (though a car is available if needed) to one of Florida's most fabulous hotels and dining rooms. The Marco airstrip is a regular stopping off place for plenty of pilots, both the business variety and the "just-for-fun" fellows, too, including some who fly large twins.

"Come ahead, fellows," invites Ray Anderson, chief pilot for the Mackle brothers, who runs the airstrip. "We've got room and we've got fun." The Mackle executive planes often ferry hotel guests to nearby Naples or to Miami, 100 miles across the Everglades.

Naples Airlines has scheduled service between Naples and Miami and makes Marco a regular stop on three regularly scheduled daily flights in each direction. It already operates frequent charter flights there.

This 4,500-foot strip at Marco Beach, Fla., was once part of a highway. Note the high-rise condominium (apartment house) along part of the four-mile white sand beach (top left) and the Marco Beach Hotel and Villas just off the beach.   PHOTO BY THE AUTHOR

A new "vacation colony" is rapidly taking shape. Marco Island once had three tiny settlements — Marco, Goodland, and Caxambus, with a combined year-around population of less than 500. Today, these towns are growing rapidly. New home sites are being developed, swamplands dredged, and new buildings erected. Yacht canals, roads and streets are being developed on the 10,327 acres.

Along the four-mile exotic beach, where you can pick up some of the most startling shells, the $2,000,000 Marco Beach Hotel and Villas have been built. The two-story hotel has 100 rooms, all of which face the Gulf, plus 22 separate villas. Each villa has two bedrooms, two baths, kitchen, a dining room and a living room. Alongside the hotel are a swimming pool, tennis court, and nine-holf golf course.

There is also a $1,500,000, seven-story condominium apartment building which has 48 one- and two-bedroom apartments, a swimming pool and a covered parking area.

A luxury yacht club and marina, post office, 16-unit rental apartment, stores, country club and 18-hole golf course have also been completed.

Below Marco are the virtually uninhabited Ten Thousand Islands and the Ever-

glades National Park; the few beaches on the island south are completely wild and accessible only by boat. However, there is no better snook and tarpon fishing in the country than in the shallow waters of the creeks that wind between the numerous islands. Birdlife abounds, too. Egret, roseate spoonbill, and ibis wade the flats; and one often encounters an occasional anhinga or water turkey. The island even boasts its own eagles' nest.

There are plenty of accommodations — about 10 motels and fishing camps in addition to the palatial Marco Beach Hotel; plenty of charter fishing boats, as well as other attractions. Marco ranks as an extremely interesting "flying vacation" spot. ◆

THE AUTHOR

The author of "A Pleasant Florida Island," George R. Reiss, is a frequent PILOT contributor. A pilot for over 36 years, he is aviation editor for the Youngstown, O., Vindicator. Reiss resides at Niles, O., with his family; and his sons, George G. and John E., have many flying hours.

Airport Hopping Through The

ARKANSAS OZARKS

Tennessee family of four flies Tri-Pacer over family flying with small children is an

As new members of America's flying-family fraternity, we took our first flying vacation recently in the beautiful Arkansas Ozarks. Joe's private pilot license was about six months old, and Mary was a student pilot, serving as copilot and navigator. Our passengers were our two children, Andy, who was three, and David, seven months old. Our plan was to see as much of the Ozarks as possible in five days, and we came home convinced that the flat-topped Ozark Mountains and the many man-made lakes which dot them are even prettier from the air than from the ground.

We made the trip in a rented Piper *Tri-Pacer*. It is not the fastest plane available, but was perfect for landing on short fields and at altitudes higher than we were accustomed to. We had enough room for luggage and for the stroller which we used for the baby.

Since we could cover great distances so quickly, we were never in the plane for more than two hours and our stops were long enough for leisurely meals. Despite the fact that the ground temperature was over 90° most of the time, at a few thousand feet it was a comfortable 75°.

We started our trip at our home in Dyersburg, Tenn., and flew west over the Mississippi River, sighting several long tows of barges coursing up and down the river. Our course over the flat farmlands of eastern Arkansas took us just north of the huge Blytheville Air Force Base where we kept a wary eye out for big SAC jet bombers.

We crossed into hill country as we approached Paragould and checked the weather as we passed over the Walnut Ridge Airport. From there we turned northwest to follow a highway to Hardy, Ark. As we watched the Spring River, a highway, and a railroad running tightly together toward Hardy, we picked out a freight train with a bright red engine heading furiously toward Hardy. Since the track paralleled the many

curves in the river, the train looked like a long snake picking its way through the trees. His speed was amazing until he came to a long grade where we left him far behind.

Near Hardy, we saw Cherokee Village, an immense resort development with a lake, extensive recreational facilities, a country club, and an airport. We circled over the airport and, since it looked deserted and had no restaurant, we decided to go on to Al Gaston's Resort on the White River for lunch. This gave us an opportunity to fly over Lake Norfolk, one of the two big lakes in the Mountain Home area. The many homesites around the lake looked inviting, and we could see water skiers making lazy circles in the calm, blue water. To the north we could see the ferries plodding across the lake in both directions, carrying the heavy traffic of U.S. 62 across the man-made lake. In the distance we could see Bull Shoals Lake, located west of Mountain Home, and it appeared to be a twin to Lake Norfolk.

Just below the Bull Shoals Dam on the White River, we spotted Al Gaston's Resort with its well-marked, 2,400-foot landing strip and its complex of neat pink buildings along the river. Although Joe had never landed on a grass strip before, he made a beautiful landing and we had hardly finished the rollout when a line boy appeared to direct us to the gas pumps. He offered to drive us to the restaurant, but we decided to walk the short distance in the cool mountain air. The restaurant is built almost over the river, kept cool by the water that is let through the bottom of the dam rather than through the top. After a pleasant lunch and a walk down to the dock where the boats for the famous White River Float Fishing trips are kept, we stopped to let Andy try out some of the playground equipment near the swimming pool. The whole complex was so attractive we wished that we had planned to stay there overnight.

We took off and followed the White River

downstream for several miles and then turned south toward Greer's Ferry Reservoir, where we had made reservations to spend the night. As we approached the lake, we saw Sugarloaf Mountain which rolls up out of the lake at a steep angle, forming a most unusual island which is in the process of becoming a game and wildlife refuge. After taking an aerial tour of the lake, we landed at the Heber Springs Airport where Roy Robus, owner of the Rambler Motel, was ready to meet us and carry our luggage to the motel, about a block from the airport.

One of the highlights of our trip was dinner at the Stockholm Restaurant, which is adjacent to the Heber Springs Airport. We were met at the door by a tall, blond woman who greeted us and ushered us to the smorgasbord. She announced that there were 16 meat dishes of various kinds and she hoped we would try all of them. She let us know that she would be insulted unless we came back for more; and after trying small portions of each dish, we were quite willing to have second helpings. After enjoying ample samples of the main course, we completed the meal with huge servings of homemade blueberry pie with almonds. We learned that the restaurant was operated by Conrad T. E. Beardsley and his wife. Beardsley is a retired mining engineer and Mrs. Beardsley is a native of Sweden who came to America as a secretary in the Swedish Embassy at Washington. Since settling at Heber Springs in 1963, the couple has developed the restaurant to such a point that Mrs. Beardsley has shared her recipes in a weekly cooking session on a Little Rock television station.

After breakfast the following morning, Mr. Beardsley graciously took us on an auto tour of Heber Springs and the resort areas growing up around the lake and briefed us on the elaborate plans for a water garden below the Greer's Ferry Dam which had been dedicated by President Kennedy.

By JOE BOYD | AOPA 275151
and MARY BOYD | AOPA 277962

Arkansas mountains and lakes. They conclude ideal way to see interesting travel spots

We had planned to fly to Fayetteville via Lake Taneycomo in southern Missouri, but checking the aviation weather on the radio confirmed our opinion that the weather to the north was to be avoided. We decided to fly on to Fort Smith. On the way we observed the construction activity along the Arkansas River which is forming the Dardanelle Reservoir.

At Fort Smith, we discovered that the general aviation ramp was within easy walking distance of the attractive new terminal building, but we succumbed when the line boy insisted on driving us to the terminal. We had a delicious and reasonable lunch and learned from the complete FAA weather briefing that Fayetteville was now clear after a morning of thundershowers.

We headed north and were in Fayetteville in about 45 minutes.

The following day, we rented a car and spent the day driving through the Pea Ridge National Military Park and the interesting little city of Eureka Springs. Sometimes called Little Switzerland, Eureka Springs was an outstanding resort during the days of railroad resorts and is now undergoing a revival due to the construction of Beaver Lake, still another in the series of huge reservoirs being built in the Ozarks. We stopped to visit the little Catholic Church nestled on the side of the hills which form Eureka Springs. That church is entered through the bell tower.

The highlight of our visit was Onyx Cave, an amazing underground formation just east of Eureka Springs. Our enthusiastic guide was the owner of the cave, Ralph Schmidt, a former marine engineer from Florida. Schmidt and his family had bought the cave less than a year before our visit and were busy developing it into an outstanding attraction for visitors.

Although the cave and Schmidt's commentary were fascinating, we were intrigued by the plans for future development. The fact that the new Carroll County Airport has been completed between Berryville and Eureka Springs, only a few miles east of Onyx Cave, will make it possible for us to make a return visit there with much greater ease.

The fourth day of our trip we flew from Fayetteville, home of the University of Arkansas, to Clarksville where we spent the day visiting relatives. The airport there was unattended and when a windstorm blew up early in the afternoon, we were glad we had carried some rope with us to tie the plane down.

Late that afternoon, we started for Little Rock, but radio reports of thunderstorms there plus the first few drops of rain on our windshield made us decide to land at Con-

Greer's Ferry Dam which forms the lake of the same name. Plans call for the development of an extensive water garden below the dam near Heber Springs, Ark. COLOR PHOTOS BY JOE BOYD

A colorful marina is part of the resort complex on Eden Isle near Heber Springs, Ark. The isle is really a peninsula jutting out into Greer's Ferry Reservoir, one of the newer lakes in the Arkansas Ozarks.

Catholic Church at Eureka Springs, Ark., nestled on the side of a steep hill. Entry to the church is through the tower on the left. Many houses and public buildings in this old resort town have entrances on several levels.

THE AUTHORS

Joseph M. Boyd, an attorney by profession, is a member of the Lawyer-Pilots Bar Association. Mary, his wife, is a correspondent for the Memphis Press-Scimitar. They reside at Dyersburg, Tenn.

way, about 30 miles noth of Little Rock. The accommodating airport manager at Conway, Dennis Cantrell, quickly arranged a motel reservation and transportation to a most comfortable motel and restaurant only a few blocks away from the airport.

One of the funniest incidents of the trip came as we started from our room to the restaurant for supper. The lady in the next room had just parked her car and she asked Mary, who was carrying the baby, if she had our parking space. "We don't have a car, we came by plane," Mary replied. The woman looked all around the motel as if she were looking for a plane, or at least for a parachute, and finally shook her head and

strode off, muttering under her breath, "Damn smart aleck."

The following morning we flew on to Little Rock where we spent the day then returned home between two lines of thundershowers late that afternoon. In fact, we could see a rainstorm less than a mile west of the Dyersburg Airport as we approached the wide concrete runways. We managed to taxi into the hangar as the first drops of rain began to fall.

We arrived home convinced that traveling by plane with small children is one of the best ways for a family to take a vacation and that the Arkansas Ozarks provide one of the most interesting and least crowded resort areas in America. ◆

By NOLA MAE McFILLEN

Fly To SOUTH LOUISIANA Bayous

Once upon a time there was a bold pirate, named Jean Lafitte (also Laffite), who smuggled treasure, fought over booty, and captured pretty maidens in the romantic bayous of south Louisiana. Some people insist that Lafitte was a blackheart; but the people of Lake Charles, La., know he was a colorful and gallant hero, who stole from the rich and buried his treasure under the mossy cypress trees that line beautiful Contraband Bayou, which winds through the heart of that fair city.

Each year in June, the people of Lake Charles revive the romantic, boisterous, pleasure-loving era of Jean Lafitte with a nine-day, colorful celebration called Contraband Days. This gala event features enough skull and bones and blackbeards to chill the spines of all thrill seekers; and it also features enough pieces of eight and pretty female pirates to stir the most sentimental romanticist!

First of all, on a gay day in June, the famous Jean Lafitte and all his revived buccaneers, dressed in their finest silk breeches and waistcoats, with their cocked hats covered with plumes, and their dangling, jeweled earrings, sail boldly through the Lake Charles harbor and dock on the North Beach in full view of all the beachcombers, who've been previously warned of this gigantic pirate invastion. Then Lafitte and his pirates stage a dramatic attack on City Hall, where many duels take place. Finally, they capture the mayor, the chief of police, and all the other unfortunate city officials.

From there on the buccaneers take over, and anything goes! A wild, wild week of treasure hunting, parading, tossing silver doubloons to crowds, capturing pretty maidens, and throwing colorful beach parties, is celebrated because of Jean Lafitte's return. All week, while the buccaneers continue their shenanigans, visitors are grandly entertained by outstanding water ski shows, a beautiful sailing regatta which features a lake full of colorful sailboats, and a majestic boat parade of hundreds of gaily decorated yachts. Motorboat races, sports car races, model airplane flying contests, and many band concerts keep the visitors on the beach, enjoying all this free entertainment!

The highlight of the celebration is the choice of Miss Contraband, who is captured from among the hundreds of female pirate beauties. Then on Saturday night, a gigantic fireworks display lights the sky above the lake with dozens of pictorial presentations. A beach carnival attracts the young at heart continuously.

Occasionally, the mod look creeps in among the skull and bones, especially on the night of the teenage sand hop which is also held on the beach.

At different times during the week there are sky-diving exhibitions, golf tournaments, garden lighting tours, art displays, aircraft and boat displays, and various treasure hunts. All week, two airport operators feature flights over the city, at a special price.

It would be almost impossible for a visitor not to find something to interest him, for the whole city cooperates in making this one momentous celebration. In 1967, Contraband Days will begin on Saturday morning, June 3, and will continue through Sunday, June 11. For a confirmed schedule of this year's activities, write Downtown Development, 429 Broad Street, Lake Charles, La., after May 1.

Pilots flying into Lake Charles for Contraband Days will find two airports just south of the city. The Lake Charles Munici-

'Well, shiver me timbers. If it ain't Jean Lafitte!'

Relive early 1800's buccaneer era during nine-day

Contraband Days celebration at Lake Charles, La.

Pilots will find good general aviation facilities nearby

pal Airport and McFillen Air Park are only two miles apart and both offer rental cars and taxies as well as free tiedowns. Many of the local motels also run courtesy cars to the airports. East Lake Charles Airport (three miles east of the city) has courtesy car, taxi, and car rental services.

The Ramada Inn and the Lakeview Motel are across the street from North Beach, where all the activities take place. They both boast good dining rooms which are open from early morning until late at night. Other good motels include Chateau Charles, Imperial 400, Holiday Inn, and the Belmont.

Since Lake Charles is in the center of good French cuisine, you simply must taste Crayfish Ettouffe, Shrimp Creole, and Lou-isiana Stuffed Crab. These dishes are available in all the good restaurants. The Piccadilly Cafeteria is also a favorite eating spot and features the seafoods listed above.

While visiting Lake Charles, pilots and their families might like to charter a fishing boat and go out into the Gulf of Mexico for a try at the big red snapper, ling, king mackeral, tarpon, and jewfish. There are two sizes of charter boat available. One type carries six people and the other 20. Cost for overnight and one day on either type of boat is about $12 per person.

Lake Charles has three good golf courses and two bowling alleys. Right on the lakefront there is the Imperial Parish Museum. Children will especially enjoy the long hours of fun in the sun that are available on the many beaches to be found in the area.

Welcome to Contraband Days at Lake Charles, La. ◆

THE AUTHOR

Nola Mae McFillen helps her son, Marshall, operate a flight training school at McFillen Airpark (three miles southeast of Lake Charles, La.). This is Author McFillen's most recent contribution to The PILOT; however, longtime readers may recall her "Danger! Female Airport Operators At Work" (September 1961) and "Money-Making Tips For Operators" (June 1962).

Jean Lafitte's life in Louisiana is now, possibly, only legend. He might even have participated in privateering activities of the Barataria smugglers, one of their raids being relived here. In any case, during Contraband Days, "Lafitte" and crew land at Lake Charles and capture the city.

Lake Charles is located on the Calcasieu Lake in southwestern Louisiana. The annual Contraband Days festival is centered on the beaches at that city.

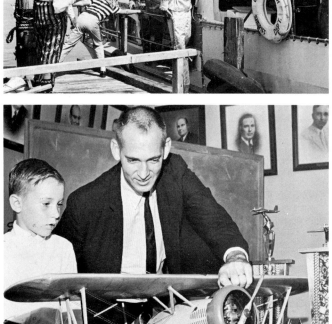

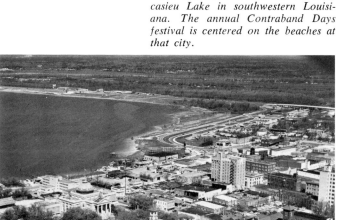

Two highlights of the celebration are a model airplane flying contest and water skiing shows.

By ALLEN F. EDWARDS, JR. | AOPA 21862

MACKINAC ISLAND:
Gem Of The Great Lakes

*Quiet and relaxed atmosphere of historic island off
Michigan mainland has become accessible
to airborne visitors since opening of 3,500- foot airstrip*

Boating is one of Mackinac's popular diversions during the summer months. But there are plenty of other activities available to the vacationist — horseback riding, bicycling, golf and sightseeing, to mention a few.

When the pilot's destination is an island, there is definitely extra satisfaction. No question now that his airplane has all the advantages in time, comfort, and convenience!

No better news reached us one spring than the report that an airport at long last had been built on Michigan's Mackinac Island (pronounced "Mackinaw"). Lying in the blue waters of Lake Huron between Michigan's upper and lower peninsula like a punctuation mark, it enjoys island isolation, yet is but six short miles from the mainland.

The fame of this resort is national. It was designated in 1951 by the Daughters of the American Revolution as Michigan's most historic spot, and it boasts the world's largest summer hotel. However, its greatest attraction is its natural location.

Visitors say the azure blue, crystal clear surrounding waters rival those of the Bahamas for their colors. One can see dimes, 60 feet below, lying on the white sand bottom by the ship dock. A famous international doctor claimed the pine-scented, continental polar air matches only that of

Switzerland for its vigor-giving, pollen-free freshness. Here one can relax in a rocking chair on the 800-foot-long porch of the Grand Hotel and literally drink in the air while enjoying the superb view of ocean ships passing below.

To protect itself from the rush of the Twentieth Century, only horsedrawn carriages are allowed on the island. The pace is leisurely. Visitors heretofore have come and gone by ferryboat or aboard one of the Great Lakes cruise ships that dock at the wharf in the little village.

Recreation is tempered to a pace of relaxation. The golf course is virtually free of sand traps and appears like a rolling field, comprising short fairways, easy shots, and very little rough. Guests have time to reflect on the past as they are taken in carriages to the island's points of historic interest. Slow-gaited riding horses carry one over wooded trails, or two can rent a drive-yourself carriage for a more companionable ride through the park. About the most strenuous activity is bicycling.

We have been visiting Mackinac Island for years, at first driving the hard road miles, then taking the ferry across the straits. If we were lucky and arrived at boat time, the trip over to the island took about 30 minutes. But we often arrived at the dock just as the ferry pulled away, which meant an hour's wait for the next departure.

In recent years, we have flown into St. Ignace on the north side of the straits, taken a 50¢ taxi to the dock, waited for the ferry, then paid $1.35 for a boat ride over.

Leaving early Saturday morning from home, we would be lucky to catch the noon boat; so this gave us the afternoon and part of Sunday to call a weekend.

Sunday was always cut short by having to make a daylight flying departure, and as much fun as the ferryboat arrival was on Saturday, it became an anxiety on Sunday, with its fixed schedule and departing crowds which sometimes exceeded its capacity. So on Sunday, our pleasure was handicapped by the fear of missing that boat which would take us across to the mainland where our airplane awaited. We usually allowed two hours to reach the airport.

Now, one can enjoy Mackinac with a freedom from schedule worry right up to the last minute, knowing his plane is just moments away, parked beside the 3,500-foot hard-surfaced runway. Full weekends on the island now are more practicable. One can arrive early Saturday and remain until late Sunday; or better yet, arrive before dinner Friday.

Visitors must be cautioned that the gasoline engine is not compatible with Mackinac Island living. Neither the residents nor the horses are used to it, nor do they intend to accept it. The airport's presence, however, will be felt only by the additional visitors that are apparent, since it is located well back of the village in the woods. Pilots are urged, therefore, to respect the peace and tranquility which add to the island's charm and to avoid flying too near the residents. One spectacular exhibition could close the field.

Although we come to Mackinac Island with present-day pleasure in mind, we are fascinated by the historical buildings which surround us. One soon finds oneself, guide-book in hand, poking into houses which saw events significant in the history of three nations.

The first white man, Jean Nicolet, came to the straits of Mackinac in 1634 under instructions from Champlain, on a canoe voyage with the Huron Indians.

The island at that time was used principally as a sacred burial ground by the Indians, who came quietly in their canoes to bury important tribal leaders on hallowed bluffs. During the construction of the Grand Hotel, a burial ground was discovered directly beneath the entrance.

Nicolet was followed by religious mission-

Arrival at Mackinac by lightplane is a common occurrence, since the island has opened its airport. Aerial tourists no longer are involved with the ferry, which has been the island's major link with the mainland.

PHOTO BY FRANK FULKERSIN

Mackinac's new airport is expected to be an attractive landing place for fly-ins in the future. One such gathering attracted about 140 planes. The airport is at Lake Huron, about three miles from Mackinaw City on Mackinac Straits, Mich.

PHOTOS, UNLESS OTHERWISE CREDITED, WERE TAKEN BY THE AUTHOR

One of the Island's imposing sights is its Grand Hotel, which was opened in 1887. Although old historically, the Victorian-flavored resort hotel offers visitors modern conveniences and service. The famous old hotel contains 300 guest rooms and boasts one of the longest carpets ever made — it is two blocks long.

When you call a taxi from the Mackinac Airport, be prepared to see a horse-drawn carriage with a "fringe on top" such as shown above. Only horse-drawn carriages are allowed on the island.

aries: Father Jean Allouez, Father Dablon and Father Marquette. Commander LaSalle, hearing of these voyages, brought the first sailing vessel, the Griffin, to Mackinac on Aug. 27, 1679. Then followed Cadillac, Charlevoix, and others whose names grace our monuments.

French rule gave way to British after the defeat of Montcalm on the Plains of 'Abraham at Quebec by General Wolfe in 1759. The Indians did not take kindly to their new governors, and a bloody massacre ensued in 1763. However, time erased the memory of bloodshed, and the wealth of the fur trade rather than conquest soon occupied the minds of both sides.

Of the island's historical sites, the fort is the most spectacular. It is the second oldest fort in the United States. Moved to Mackinac Island from Mackinaw City in 1779, it was first commanded by Major Patrick Sinclair, British lieutenant governor. The move was made as a safety measure against the Americans after title to the island had been obtained by the British from the Chippewas.

After the American Revolution, it wasn't until 1796 that the British evacuated the fort at Mackinac, and then only to move to St. Joseph's Island on the Canadian shore.

On July 27, 1812, the British returned, sneaked in at a point on the west side of the island now called British Landing and moved their cannon to a commanding position above the fort. News of a Declaration of War had reached Detroit and the British fort on St. Joseph's Island, but no such news had reached Lt. Hanks, who commanded Fort Mackinac. Surrender to the British was the lieutenant's only choice to prevent a massacre.

An unsuccessful attempt was made by the Americans to recapture the fort in 1814, but it wasn't until the Treaty of Ghent in 1815 that Americans returned to Mackinac Island. Sixty years later, in 1875, the island became the second National Park in recognition of its beauty and historical significance.

In 1808, John Jacob Astor founded the American Fur Company, and a thriving business followed. At the height of its success, the fur company employed over 400 clerks on the island and 2,000 trappers and voyagers. Many of the company's buildings stand today. In 1842, the fur company closed down. It was replaced by the fishing industry which shipped tons of whitefish and lake trout to the Boston market. It is said that the thick cedar growth in front of the Grand Hotel is nurtured by fish remains dumped below the bluff, where fishermen cleaned the trout before packing them in barrels.

The Grand Hotel is a story in itself. Its operation has been kept on a level of dignity and elegance matched by few establishments in the world. Though closed 81% of the year, the management has still been able to maintain a high level of service at reasonable rates. One should not only read the amazing booklet about the hotel, available at the gift shop, but should view its picture story in the collection of rare photographs hanging in the lower lobby.

The opening on July 10, 1887, was an occasion of splendor. Mrs. Potter Palmer, arriving from Chicago, brought among her equipage three hackney teams, saddle horses, tallyho and carriage. Members of the Swift, Cudahy and Armour families from Chicago, and Adolphus Busch from St. Louis, were also present. Prominent Detroiters included the Whitneys, Algers, Newberrys, the governor, and others who came to spend their summers. The capacity was 1,000 guests, and the hotel was full every night.

Not only is the hotel porch the longest in the world, but the carpet, stretching from the east end of the dining room to the west end of the lobby, is the largest single piece ever produced by the Bigelow-Sanford Company—two city blocks long!

Some 1,200 meals a day are served to employees alone from the kitchens, which boast 75 cooks. The ranges are 47 feet in length. Seven large walk-in coolers and 16 refrigerators store part of the 1,500 pounds of meat used daily, not to mention 250 pounds of butter and 50 bushels of fruit and vegetables.

The hotel has been host to Presidents, actors, writers, financiers, generals, politicians, senators, and thousands of other comfort-loving visitors. Samuel Clemens (Mark Twain) wrote at length at the hotel. The last President to use the suite bearing his seal was Franklin D. Roosevelt, who held a conference there with the Premier of Canada.

The present-day visitor may be a casual tourist, passing a night on his drive southward from northern Michigan holidays. He may be a new husband, hiding a new bride from the busy world. He may be a sailor celebrating a victory in the famous Mackinac Yacht Race which brings sailing fleets from Detroit and Chicago to Mackinac Island each July. He may be a passenger from the SS South American, docking for the day to discharge its package-plan vacationers for shopping and sightseeing.

Or now, since the opening of the Mackinac Island Airport, the visitor may be a pilot and his family who have discovered a gem-like island in northern waters to which they may fly in less than two hours from such cities as Detroit or Chicago, and where they can experience a world of quiet and relaxation unknown in the motorized environment of most resorts. ◆

Here is a partial view of the island as seen from a boat out on Lake Huron. Notice how the Grand Hotel dominates the skyline.

THE AUTHOR

Allen F. Edwards, Jr., is a private, instrument-rated pilot and a frequent free-lance contributor to aviation publications. He and his wife, Terry, who is also a licensed pilot, fly a Beech Model F Bonanza, the second aircraft of that make they have owned. The Edwards' embarked on their plane ownership course in 1932 with a Kinner Bird and have owned a series of Cubs, Aeroncas, a Porterfield, a Taylorcraft, Cessna 140 and others before stepping up to the Bonanza. Formerly sales manager for an automotive supplier, he describes himself now as an investor in various business enterprises.

By VINCENT R. COURTENAY

Although not large, the collection of famous planes at Dearborn, Mich., is singularly significant in early-day flying achievement

Aviation Greats At

HENRY FORD

MUSEUM

Pilots winging into Detroit's Metropolitan, Willow Run, City or other airport facilities, who have a few hours between flights, would do well to hop some ground transportation to Henry Ford Museum and Greenfield Village in nearby Dearborn.

At the risk of sending you on a "pilot's holiday," suffice it to say that this world-famous institution has one of the most singularly meaningful collections of aircraft and associated products in the country.

A word or two to set the perspective on this unique indoor-outdoor shrine of history before talking aircraft.

To begin with, the Museum and Village are located within a few minutes' drive of downtown Detroit. You fly almost directly overhead on southerly approaches (210 Left or 210 Right) to Metropolitan Airport.

Henry Ford founded the Museum and Village in 1929, so that as much as possible of America's history, from Colonial times through the era of mass production, could be preserved. This sounds a little facetious, perhaps, if you haven't seen the Museum and Village, but hear this.

The Museum, a vast 14-acre structure, contains the finest collections of Americana in the world, with something relating to nearly all aspects of the American home and industry through three centuries of history.

If you've ever noticed a building that looks like the twin of Philadelphia's Independence Hall when you've flown over Detroit, there really wasn't a need to recheck your course. That building under your wing was indeed the twin of Independence Hall, down to the last brick. It forms the entranceway for the huge rectangular Museum building.

It contains fabulous collections of American arts and crafts, including America's most comprehensive collections of glassware

and furniture, one of the world's finest lighting collections, staggering displays of basic industrial and power machinery, electronic communications devices, and practically everything that was, or is, part of the American scene.

Adjacent Greenfield Village, some 260 beautiful acres in all, is made up of 100 historic homes and buildings, moved from their original locations around America. These venerable structures are situated on streets of old and are decorated and furnished exactly the way they were when history was made in them.

There is, for instance, Logan County Courthouse, where the great Abraham Lincoln practiced law as a young man. This plain, frame structure, moved from Postville, Ill., contains many objects of Lincoln memorabilia, including the chair he was seated in when he was fatally shot in 1865.

Others include the entire Menlo Park, N.J., laboratory complex of Thomas Alva Edison, where the great inventor said he spent the 10 most productive years of his life. The central building in this group, Menlo Park Laboratory, is equipped exactly as it was when Edison worked there, and contains many of his original inventions. Foremost of these is the world's first successful incandescent lamp, invented in the laboratory in 1879.

The country birthplace of Luther Burbank, stately Webster House, in which Noah Webster compiled his famous dictionary, Ann Arbor House, where Robert Frost resided when he was poet-in-residence at the University of Michigan, and numerous other buildings of historical note also grace the Village Green.

Of special interest to aviation people is the renowned Wright Brothers Cycle Shop, where Orville and Wilbur Wright performed aerodynamic research. It was there that the Wrights constructed components for the

world's first genuine airplane.

The Cycle Shop contains several bicycles popular during the years the Wright brothers operated it, the brothers' original business desk and many of their personal tools. It was moved with the Wright Homestead from Dayton, O., under the supervision of Orville Wright.

In the Transportation Section of Henry Ford Museum, surrounded by remarkable collections of horse drawn vehicles, automobiles, motorcycles, trucks, bicycles, boats, steam locomotives and passenger trains, is the aircraft collection.

It is not a large collection of aircraft, but one of the most singularly important in the history of aviation, ranging from a 1915 Laird biplane through the world famous Piper J-3.

The Fokker Tri-motor in which Adm. Byrd flew over the North Pole in 1926 and the Ford Tri-motor he flew over the South Pole in 1929 are among the historic aircraft displayed. Another is the Junkers *Bremen*, first plane to make the westward crossing of the Atlantic.

The first practical helicopter, the 1939 Vought-Sikorsky 300, can be seen beside the 1931 Pitcairn Autogiro, first such aircraft to be flown commercially in the United States.

Still another "flying first" is the Museum's 1920 Baumann Racing Plane, one of the first aircraft to utilize retractable landing gear and a variable-camber wing system.

Also in the collection is the world's first diesel-powered plane, a 1928 Stinson *Detroiter*. Marking yet another milestone in aviation history is the Museum's Boeing Model 40 B-2, the type aircraft used by United Airlines for the first scheduled transcontinental passenger service in the United States.

In addition to important aviation "firsts," some aircraft in the Museum represent entire plateaus in aviation technology, such as the Curtiss JN *Flying Jenny,* practical and dependable enough to be used as America's standard training plane during World War I.

And all this talk about aviation memorabilia brings us to mention that Henry Ford himself was an aviation pioneer . . . from the production end of things.

His factories turned out the sturdy Ford Tri-motors within walking distance of where the Museum and Village now stand. His efforts were not limited to transport aircraft, and he searched for a machine that would do for aviation what his Model T's had done for the auto industry.

The end result of this search was a limited production of an experimental type of low-wing monoplane, which, conceivably, could have played an important part in "putting the world on wings."

But Ford's test pilot and good friend, Harry Brooks, cracked up while putting the little plane through her paces, and shortly after this Ford withdrew from the aviation industy. A stone marker commemorating pilot Harry Brooks is located on the boulevard of Village Road, directly in front of the Henry Ford Museum.

During his tenure in the aviation industry, Ford constructed the world's first airport hotel, luxurious Dearborn Inn, an early American styled hostelry, within walking distance of Greenfield Village. The Inn overlooks a site formerly occupied by the airport where the old Tri-motors were tested and is a fine place to spend a peaceful stopover.

Ford's participation in the aviation industry had many ramifications. Besides trying to make economy air travel a reality, he supervised some pioneering in the area of air navigation.

His engineers developed, in 1926, America's first radio homing station, heralding in the era of radio navigation. The radio beacon was used at Ford's airfield for many years. It transmitted both constant sound and Morse letter beams and doubled as a ground to air radio telephone system.

The fully equipped radio beacon tower, together with other electronic communications and navigating devices, is displayed in the communications collection in the Museum.

Now, back to the Museum's collection of historic airplanes. Following are descriptive details about most of them:

1915 Laird Biplane

A hot little plane in her day was the Laird biplane of 1915. Built by exhibition flyer E. M. Laird, this ship was one of the first ever to be subjected to a "loop-the-loop," a highly popular specialty. Measuring only 19 feet, five inches long with a 25⅓-foot wingspan, the Laird is powered with a six-cylinder Anzani radial engine rated at 45 h.p. The plane could take off in 125 to 150 feet, climb at 500 to 600 f.p.m. and had a maximum speed of 70 m.p.h. Laird demonstrated this plane throughout much of the United States. In 1917, Katherine Stinson took the ship on an exhibition tour of China and Japan.

1916 Curtiss Flying Boat

This 1916 Curtiss *Flying Boat* shows how such craft derived their name. The mahogany plywood hull is designed for aquanautics as well as aeronautics. Powered by an eight-cylinder V-type Hispano-Suiza engine, most of the top deck is metal surfaced, permitting crewmen to walk all the way around the engine and after section of hull. Succeeded by the Curtiss MF *Flying Boat,* this little ship had a three-place cloverleaf-shaped open cockpit. The later version of this ship, equipped with similar engine, had a maximum speed of 69 m.p.h., and stalled out at 45 m.p.h. Rate of climb of the later version was 238 f.p.m., which is probably only a slight performance improvement over the 1916 model. The ship has fabric covered wings and tail section, and is equipped with metal wing tip pontoons. The fuel tank is located amidships in the hull.

1928 low-wing monoplane, called Ford "Flivver," suspended over Ford Tri-motor.

1920 Baumann RB Racer, one of the first planes to use retractable gear successfully.

1916 J-1 Biplane

This rare old-timer of World War I vintage is a 1916 model Standard J-1 biplane, forerunner of the J-N's that became so popular as civilian ships after the war. This unit is in beautiful condition and was last flown in the 1934 Cleveland Air Races by Ernest C. Hall, who later became director of the Ohio State Bureau of Aeronautics. When Hall donated the ship to Henry Ford Museum in 1938, he commented that he knew of no other J-1's in good state of preservation, and that he alone had flown over 1,000 instruction hours in J-1's during World War I and soloed more than 100 student pilots in them. This particular plane had been originally equipped with a four-cylinder Hall-Scott engine, which was replaced by a Hisso-A engine, made by Wright. The J-1 was designed by Charles H. Day.

1927 Boeing 40 B-2

One of America's first transcontinental airliners, this beautifully conditioned 40 B-2 was one of a 32-ship fleet built in 1927 for United Air Lines. Powered by a rugged Pratt & Whitney Hornet engine, the ship cruised at 105 m.p.h. and had a top speed of 120 m.p.h. Used on the nation's first regularly scheduled transcontinental mail and passenger service, the 40 B-2 has fabric covered fuselage, except for metal enclosed passenger section, which extends from trailing edge of wing to cowling. Pilot's cockpit is open. The enclosed passenger compartment has two bucket seats; is entered through a hatch between upper and lower planes.

1909 Bleriot XI

The museum's 1909 Bleriot XI monoplane is a companion ship to the one Louis Bleriot flew in his epoch July 25, 1909, flight over the English Channel (which took 37 minutes). The Bleriot XI is powered by a 25 h.p. Anzani air-cooled engine. It has fabric covered wing and tail surfaces. Forward section of the fuselage is enclosed with metal skin; aftersection is uncovered.

1928 Ford "Flivver"

Henry Ford was one of America's foremost exponents of aviation—though the fact is not generally realized. His engineers produced this single place monoplane, "The *Flivver*." Designed as a potential "Model T of the Air," only three *Flivvers* were ever built. Ford ordered all work on the experimental craft terminated in 1928, after his chief test pilot, Harry Brooks, died in a crash while putting one of the little planes through its paces. The model in the Museum (and the one Brooks crashed in) has a three-cylinder Anzani engine that develops 35 h.p. The silk covered *Flivver* zipped along at 100 m.p.h., measures 15⅓ feet in length, and had a wingspan of 22 feet 10 inches. Ford developed a superior engine for this craft, a twin-cylinder all-magnesium plant that developed 40 h.p. With the *Flivver*, Ford's entry into the "general consumer" aircraft industry began—and ended abruptly after the death of Harry Brooks.

1920 Baumann RB Racer

Milton C. Baumann constructed the *Racer* in the collection in 1920 and hoped it would win the Gordon Bennett Air Race of that year. (He didn't make it.) Officially designated the *RB Racer*, the high-wing monoplane's fuselage and wings are covered with laminated wood. The wing features a variable-camber system, adjustable to produce maximum lift at low speeds, minimum drag at high speeds. Baumann, in a letter to the Henry Ford Museum, stated that to his knowledge the variable-camber wing system was the first developed and used anywhere in the world, and that his retractable landing gear was the first such system used on a land based plane. The *RB Racer* has only lateral portholes, and, much like Lindbergh's "Spirit of St. Louis," has no provision for forward vision.

1931 Pitcairn PCA-2

The Pitcairn Autogiro, Model PCA-2, first such aerodyne built for commercial use in

1931 Pitcairn PCA-2, first autogiro made in U.S. for commercial use.

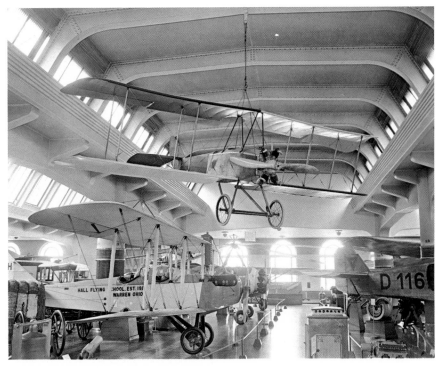

1915 Laird biplane (hanging from ceiling).

1929 Model Ford Tri-motor, used by Adm. Byrd to fly over South Pole.

1916 J-1 biplane, forerunner of the post WW 1 J-N's (Jennies).   COLOR PHOTOGRAPHY BY CARL MALOTKA

1909 Bleriot XI, companion to ship of Channel crossing fame.

America, was delivered to the Detroit News in 1931. Designed by Juan de la Clerva, the PCA-2 made 730 operational flights with the News. The cockpit is fitted with camera mounts. On a still day, the little craft (30-foot wingspan, 23 feet in length) could hop skyward in a 100-foot run. With a 20 m.p.h. head wind, it climbed almost vertically from the ground with practically no forward movement required. The PCA-2 has a normal rate of climb of 800 f.p.m., and top cruising speed of 123 m.p.h. at 2,000 r.p.m. In the event of engine failure, the craft glides to a landing at 20 m.p.h. With stick full back, in a stall, the ship drops at 15 f.p.s. Useful load of PCA-2 was 954 pounds.

Fokker F VIII

The famed Fokker F VIII in the collection was the first aircraft to fly over the North Pole. Adm. Richard E. Byrd and crew made the historic flight on May 5, 1926. The F VIII had 200 hours flying time when Byrd acquired it. Rejuvenation prior to the polar flight included installation of three Wright J-4 200 h.p. air-cooled engines. The ship has fabric covered fuselage and

1939 Vought-Sikorsky VS-300, world's first practical helicopter (suspended from the ceiling).

laminated wood wings with a span of 63½ feet. Measuring 49 feet, two inches, in length, the F VII cruises at 100 m.p.h. and lands at 45 m.p.h. Fuel consumption with full load is 28 g.p.h. allowing a cruising range of 1,500 miles. There is an observer's port topside, abaft of midships.

1929 Ford Tri-motor

The formidable "Tin Goose" has special significance. Richard E. Byrd, pilot Floyd Bennett and crew made the first flight over the South Pole in this ship. Named "The Floyd Bennett" after Byrd's pilot, the ship is powered by a Wright Cyclone 525 h.p. engine and twin Wright Whirlwinds, each developing 220 h.p. The standard Ford Tri-motor (with three Whirlwind engines) performed as follows: top speed, 114 m.p.h.; cruising, 95 to 100 m.p.h.; stalling speed, 59 m.p.h.; and ceiling, 15,000 feet. "The Floyd Bennett" approximated this performance. Wingspan of this 50-foot-long plane is 76 feet. "The Floyd Bennett" was left at Byrd's Antarctic station for five years before being returned to the United States.

1928 Junkers "Bremen"

The 1928 Junkers *Bremen* made aviation history April 12–13, 1928, when, manned by Baron von Huenveld, Capt. Herman Koehl, and Irish Free State Air Force commandant, Col. James Fitzmaurice, it became the first aircraft to make the westward crossing of the Atlantic ocean. A stock passenger and mail transport, the *Bremen* is powered by a Junkers L-5 engine that develops 310 h.p. at 1,500 r.p.m. The six-cylinder in-line unit is water cooled. The Bermen measures 58½ feet long, and has a wingspan of 60⅓ feet. The wings and fuselage are covered with duralumin, the same copper-aluminum alloy that is used in much of the framework. Entrance to the single-engine work horse is through the hinged cockpit canopy. Col. Fitzmaurice, last survivor of the trio of pioneering aviators, died in 1965.

1939 Vought-Sikorsky VS-300

The world's first practical helicopter, the Vought-Sikorsky VS-300, made its debut in 1939 with designer Igor Sikorsky at the controls. On May 6, 1941, after two years of experimental flights and engineering changes, the VS-300, in its present form, established the world's record for rotary wing hovering craft by remaining aloft one hour 33 minutes. Powered by a 75 h.p. Lycoming engine, the single place experimental craft has a fabric covered fuselage. It could fly at 70 m.p.h. forward, and 20 m.p.h. in reverse. Sikorsky delivered this craft personally to the Henry Ford Museum. The little ship provided volumes of engineering information basic to the long line of Sikorsky helicopters that have succeeded it. ◆

First plane to fly over North Pole, the Fokker F VIII.

1916 Model Curtiss Flying Boat with mahogany-plywood fuselage.

THE AUTHOR

Vincent R. Courtenay, author of "Aviation Greats At Henry Ford Museum," started flying at Windsor, Canada, at the age of 15, back in the "viscom" days at that field when you pointed the nose of your plane toward the tower and waited for a green light to send you aloft. He flew Fleet Canucks, Aeroncas and Ercoupes for a couple of years, until the Korean War got him mixed up in the Army and separated him from flying. Somehow he never got back into the cockpit. A writer, he was retained by the Henry Ford Museum and Greenfield Village to do a series of popular features on the Dearborn, Mich., establishments. He has since taken over the managing editorship of the Dearborn Press.

FLYING THE
'HIGH DESERT'

An aerial tour of Great Southwest Plateau region provides

excellent training or reorientation in high altitude operations

as well as scenic splendor and hospitality you'll never forget

By RUTH and DON DOWNIE │ AOPA 188441

Towering red rock jutting up from Lake Powell provide striking contrast to the lake's azure waters.

PHOTO BY DANA DOWNIE

If you go west, young man, the "high desert" area east of Las Vegas is worth a trip. It has some of the most awe-inspiring scenery and some of the most helpful people in the world.

Here's a tour tailor-made for the Las Vegas AOPA visitor who lives east of the Rockies. Airport operators along our high desert route assured us that the best flying weather of the year is in September and October. Our tour, made in one of Cessna's six-passenger *Super Skylanes* (N2536X), was flown the last week in June, when the weather left something to be desired.

With two suitcases, six passenger, and considerable camera equipment, we were at full 3,300-pound gross weight after picking up the tan and white plane from Airflite, Inc., at Long Beach, Calif.

In the following week — and 18 flying hours — we visited an Indian trading post, followed the rising waters of Lake Powell where towering cumulus clouds reflected the red rocks below, and landed at Bryce Canyon (elevation 7,586 feet) and Havasu City (482 feet). Naturally, we flew over the rim of the Grand Canyon and rode the ski lift at Flagstaff, Ariz. We even sat on the ground for an entire day and grudgingly admired a series of vicious thunderstorms that blocked half the horizon at Dinosaur City, Ariz.

"That's about as rough as I've ever seen the weather around here," admitted Gary Ringsby (AOPA 231899), general manager of Grand Canyon Caverns at Dinosaur City. As we talked, we pushed the Cessna under the broad shade ramp of his gas pumps to protect the aircraft from hailstones that were pelting the area. "Later in the year, particularly in September and October, flying weather is fine."

Ringsby has been flying for over 3½ years and has a turbocharged *Apache* in the hangar adjoining his gravel, all-weather 4,200-foot flight strip. The airport is at an elevation of 5,381 feet and is only 40 feet wide, but DC-3's have used it frequently. Both 80/87 and 100/130 fuel are available and there's no tiedown fee. Ringsby's Park Motel has 48 rooms, a cafe and bar with winter rates going into effect Sept. 15. Diners Club cards are accepted. The main attraction is a 45-minute tour through nearby caverns, where an elevator takes visitors down 21 stories to a series of holes in the earth, some 18,000 square feet in size, where the temperature is a dry 56° the year around.

But let's get into this high desert junket as a visitor might travel on his way eastward from Las Vegas. Our first landing wasn't in the true "high desert," but at Havasu City, only 115 miles down the Colorado River. Presenting an outstanding example of modern construction and real estate wizardry far from any visible means of support, it was originally "Site Six," an auxiliary airport for World War II bomber crews training at Kingman, Ariz. Because it was on the backwaters of Parker Dam, a rest and rehabilitation camp was established there. Robert P. McCulloch, outboard motor and chainsaw industrialist, began to expand the area as an industrial resort city. Four-engine *Constellations* have brought prospective real estate buyers from as far away as Chicago for an on-the-spot inspection.

Havasu's City Airport has two 5,500-foot runways (one gravel and one paved), is

The strength and massiveness of Glen Canyon Dam are reflected in aerial view that can't be duplicated from the ground.

lighted and has Unicom, 80/87 and 100/130 fuel. There is no charge for landing, parking, or tiedown. Accommodations include the Nautical Inn (40 rooms at $10 a day single and $12 double), which honors Carte Blanche, Diners Club and American Express cards. The Lake Havasu Hotel has 10 rooms at $12 single and $14 double. Accommodations usually are available only during the week. Reservations are a must.

Both water skiing and fishing are popular, and 14-foot motorboats are available at the marina for $12 a day, $7 for a half day. Largemouthed bass, crappie, bluegill, catfish and trout may be found lurking in Lake Havasu.

From Lake Havasu, it's an easy 95 miles around the corner of 8,420-foot Hualpai Peak to Grand Canyon Caverns. There's free transportation from the airport and motel to the Caverns by tram, where the tour costs $1.50 for adults. Motel rates are reasonable, even during the summer rush, and hospitality is tops.

After takeoff from Grand Canyon Caverns, you can fly southeast over Prescott, northeast over the Grand Canyon, or due east to Flagstaff. The direct hop from Lake Havasu to Prescott has a couple of short lonesome stretches, so a flight plan with either Needles or Blythe FSS is good insurance.

Prescott Municipal is a fully equipped FAA airport, with runways 7,600 and 4,000 feet long, at an altitude of 5,042 feet. The airport is seven miles out of town and has DF equipment for the pilot who doesn't keep his thumb on the map. Sectional charts are recommended for this part of the country, but most local pilots fly in clear weather by using Mt. Humphreys — 12,635 feet high, 10 miles north of Flagstaff — as a navigation aid.

One of Prescott's interesting sights is the Wild West mining town of Jerome that is slowly sliding down the hillside toward Clarksdale, where a huge smelter makes a

Sun-tinted cloud formations over Mormon Lake, near Flagstaff, Ariz., present a striking view that is best captured at sunrise or sunset.

Oak Creek Canyon Airport near Sedona, Ariz., is surrounded by rugged peaks and cliffs, but offers the lightplane traveler an excellent landing surface, good ground services and outstanding hospitality.

To the Downies, Oljato, an Indian trading post in the remote desert country of Utah, was a welcome sight with its smooth and well-kept airstrip.

and dragged the *Super Skylane* in with a little power to clear the overshoot area, then had to use power to get to the gas pit.

Here the red-rock cliffs of the high desert begin in earnest. There's a permanent Wild West motion picture set nearby where many a "horse opera" has been filmed. Since Sedona is a tourist resort area, there are ample accommodations, and a phone call from the booth at the airport will bring transportation.

Next we flew "up and over the rim" to Flagstaff, where the paved Pulliam Airport is 7,012 feet high and 7,000 feet long. Fuel, maintenance, and rental cars are available. The restaurant is open seven days a week. An FAA telephone drop is installed on the airport so that pilots may close their flight plan with Prescott radio.

In an interesting experiment, Meteorologist Paul Sorenson arranged to have the Flagstaff Unicom installed in the Weather Bureau office. This not only assures 24-hour service — aside from the brief periods when outside weather observations are being made — but also puts the weatherman in direct contact with pilots in the area for Pireps that are so essential during the early summer thunderstorm period.

One year-around attraction at Flagstaff is the 6,600-foot Riblet double chair ski lift at the Snow Bowl, 14 miles away. The lift goes from 9,500 to 11,800 feet up the side of Agassiz Peak. There are 22 trails and four areas for beginners. A ride up the lift is $2 for adults and $1 for children.

Other areas of interest in Flagstaff are the Museum of Northern Arizona, Lowell Observatory, and newly created 217-acre Buffalo Park.

Since Flagstaff is really getting into the high desert, operators of Wright Flyte Service, Tex (AOPA 92471) and Beth (AOPA 67034) Wright, recommended a review of the Koch chart for altitude and temperature effects. It is found on the reverse side of most U.S. Coast and Geodetic Survey and state aeronautical charts. Excellent state charts are put out by Arizona, Utah, New Mexico, and others that list areas of interest as well as navaids and commercial broadcast stations. They also include a list of "do's and don'ts" for the high desert that are well worth serious reading.

Utah's state chart stresses that "for each 1,000 feet you are above sea level, it will increase your takeoff run approximately 25% and your landing speed 2%, with a longer run due to your increased landing speed."

The Koch chart showed that our Cessna *Super Skylane*, with a sea level gross weight takeoff roll of 675 feet, would be exactly double at Flagstaff on a 70° day. Frequently, Flagstaff gets a great deal warmer than that, but N2536X and her full load walked right off the field with plenty of room to spare.

The high desert is a fine place to be razor-sharp on short-field landings. Many of the strips marked on the charts are one-way airports. The Utah Airport Directory, for example, lists the Goulding Trading Post at Monument Valley, elevation 5,155, length 3,000 feet, as "Impossible to go around. Must land south, take off north. Cliff at south end." Yet motion picture crews take DC-3's into the airport without incident. [We recommend this as an emergency-use-only landing spot.—Ed.]

fine landmark. We landed at nearby Cottonwood-Clemenceau, a hard-surfaced, 3,600-foot strip at a 3,558-foot elevation, after circling the town twice. The hangar was open and a *Cub* was in the process of being rebuilt, but no one came out to see if we could use a ride. There was a phone inside the hangar and we tossed a coin to decide whether to visit Jerome or continue our flight to Oak Creek Canyon and Flagstaff. Jerome lost.

One way to verify the rental car situation would be to call the Prescott FSS, since

Jerome is only 20 miles from Prescott Airport. Other nearby tourist attractions — by car — are the Tuzigoot National Monument and Montezuma Castle.

The tabletop Sedona Airport at Oak Creek Canyon is one of nature's beauty spots, but don't undershoot it. There are 3,400 feet of paving with a 1,780-foot dirt overrun area to the south. Elevation—4,826 feet. Arthur W. Dick, who handles fuel and rental cars, advised that there's a 70-foot drop from north to south and the winds are generally from the south. We landed uphill

On this particular tour, we limited our landings to paved strips with sufficient length to present no challenge to any modern aircraft. The one flight strip that we did visit by car could be beyond the capabilities of lower powered aircraft. However, we drove to Mormon Lake, Ariz. (elevation 7,180; length, 4,000 feet, dirt), because a recent cloudburst had left the airport muddy. Before flying into this picturesque spot, 20 miles southeast of Flagstaff, check it out for density altitude on the Koch chart. Then doublecheck on the condition of the airport by Unicom or a landing at Flagstaff.

Within 150 yards of the flight strip is the Mormon Lake Lodge. It can handle 55 people in its 12 cabins, four rooms and a studio apartment.

Most visitors at Mormon Lake come for the food. There's no menu; you get steak, beans, parmesan toast and salad. A two-pound steak costs $3.95 and is cooked on a grill made from the boiler of a Civil War locomotive, brick from the Clemenceau smelter, a cultivator's wheel covered with a gravel screen, and a chimney made of stove

oil barrels. The grill produces a really grand meal.

If you can survive a meal like that, it's time to head for the Grand Canyon for a view of one of the scenic wonders of the world. Check with the local "old pro" for proper procedure in leaning your mixture before takeoff from these high fields.

There's a relatively new 6,800-foot paved FAA airport, Grand Canyon National Park, that was nearing completion as we visited the Grand Canyon. The new field is located beside the highway three miles outside the park boundary. At an elevation of 6,610 feet, the airstrip is 6,800 feet long.

You've never really seen the Grand Canyon until you've flown over it or along the edge of the rim. The view was inspiring enough to keep all our passengers — including the teenagers — awake. We headed eastward, crossed the Little Colorado River, talked with Tuba City omni and drifted over the Echo Cliffs toward Page, Ariz. There at Glen Canyon Airport, Mr. and Mrs. Royce Knight have been the operators for the past several years. The airport has a

4,500-foot-long hard-surfaced runway and a 2,000-foot dirt strip. The elevation is 4,292 feet. By the way, the dirt strip (east-west) is used during high winds only. There's fuel in all grades, maintenance and rental cars.

We asked the Knights for destinations that would be interesting to "flat land" pilots, and yet not hazardous to newcomers to aviation. Knight (AOPA 40787) asked, "Have you ever been to a real back-country Indian trading post?" When the six of us shook our heads, he pointed to a circle named Oljato on the map. "It's only 65 miles from here by the time you fly over Rainbow Bridge and the edge of Navajo Mountain. I think you'll like it there, right on the edge of Monument Valley. Then you could go up to Halls Crossing. It's not on your sectional chart, but is on the Utah state chart. You'll find a good-sized trailer camp there and considerable boating activity."

We left a verbal flight plan that Mrs. Knight jotted down, then the six of us climbed back into the *Super Skylane* as a light rain squall blew over the field. However, skies to the east were clear and Knight

An oasis in the high desert country, Dinosaur City golf course gets watered as Cessna Super Skylane taxis in for refueling. Airport manager Gary Ringsby keeps his turbosupercharged Piper Apache in the hangar in background.

prophesied that the rain would blow away long before our return. It did.

Travel brochures say that it's a 162-mile reach from the Glen Canyon Dam to Hite, Ut. About 8,000,000 trout were planted in the lake in 1963 by the Park Service, and fishing was first permitted in 1964. Art Green operates Glen Canyon tours from the marina at Wahweep, five miles from the dam. Trips range from an hour to several days, and combination air-surface tours can be arranged in advance by Page Aviation.

The flight from Page, over Rainbow Bridge and on to Oljato, Ut., was something that we'll not soon forget. Red from the rocks cast a rosy hue on the bases of the cumulus clouds and even made distant lightning look red. Water in Lake Powell and blue skies dotted with puffy clouds made a vivid, almost distorted, color package. Even when you see the results on color film, the contrasts of red and blue are hard to believe.

This part of the country goes almost straight up and straight down, with landing spots virtually out of the question. The big 285 h.p. Continental engine purred smoothly; yet the country below was a subtle invitation to add a little more to the collection plate the next Sunday when flying weather is zero-zero.

Even with two sets of thumbs on the map, we were still surprised to round the corner of just one more flat-topped mesa and see a 4,200-foot blacktopped flight strip, fenced to keep Navajo sheep and cattle outside. The name, Oljato, was in white on the side of a red cliff with "122.8" adjoining. This modern aviation assistance just didn't seem real this far out in the high desert, but there it was.

A quick punch on the mike and Edward Smith (AOPA 119859) replied, "36 X-ray. Wind calm. Normal landing uphill to the southeast."

We spiraled down, dragged the airport and swung back to the north before landing. On a low-power approach, you can't see the runway until you're within a quarter mile because of a bend in the canyon, but the adjoining valley is amply wide and flat for a go-around.

We landed on the smooth runway and taxied into the parking area. Smith and his 14-year-old daughter, Wyona, came out to meet us. Smith and his family have operated the trading post for over 15 years, and he learned to fly in 1955 when it still took eight hours to drive to Flagstaff. A paved road to the east has cut his driving time to 3¾ hours, but the flight in his Cessna 182 is only 1:10.

Each visitor gets a "takeoff run and rate of climb table" with a density altitude chart on the reverse side just as soon as he climbs out of his airplane. There's also a "back seat pilot's license" for younger passengers. Smith sells 80/87 fuel at 45.9¢ a gallon and 100/130 at 49.9¢, which was cheaper than at some of the larger towns.

If you were to walk into the side door of the one-story combination home and trading post that nestles beneath the trees at Oljato, what's the last thing you'd expect to see? There in one corner was a fully operable Link trainer that had been swapped for Indian rugs.

"I taught Wyona how to 'fly' in the Link," Smith said, smiling quietly. "She's had dual instruction here and with Tex Wright at Flagstaff. She's ready to solo now, but we'll

Old Grand Canyon airport, 6,400 feet above sea level, has two fine sod strips and will soon be supplemented by a new airport nine miles closer to the Canyon, under construction by FAA. Note the tractor-towed refueling rig.

just have to wait until she's 16."

The main items of barter at Oljato are Indian blankets, many of which are sold directly to visiting pilots, eliminating any middleman. However, you can purchase turquoise and silver Indian jewelry, a kerosene lantern, a saddle, or a new wagon wheel.

"They don't manufacture wagon tongues any more," commented Smith, "so we have to make them out here."

Between 100 and 200 Indian families live within a 25-mile circle of the airport, and there's a tribal meeting hall adjoining the trading post. The field is always available for emergency ambulance flights.

"The hardest thing I have to do here is to try to talk pilots out of buying gas," Smith said. "Many visitors forget that we're fairly high here and it does get hot. I always advise a pilot to take just enough fuel to make his destination with a good safe reserve. That extra couple of hundred pounds of fuel can make a great difference in the way an airplane operates up here."

The Smiths have a gun collection that practically tells the history of the Wild West. While there are no regular eating or overnight accommodations, Smith does admit that he has "some cots that we can stack down the hall and a huge 'pilot's coffee pot' in case someone is forced down by weather or maintenance."

Good motel accommodations can be had at Goulding's Monument Valley Trading Post, just six air miles east, and a new motel has opened at Kayenta. Smith cautioned that the Kayenta strip was made on "gumbo" that could be slippery following a cloudburst. "I believe that a power line is being constructed across the west end of the strip, so take a good look at it before landing," Smith advised. "Naturally, keep a sharp lookout for cattle and sheep."

Whether you purchase an Indian blanket or perhaps a piece of native jewelry, watch

Indians bring in items for barter, or merely pass the time of day with flying talk, the Smith family with their unpretentious old-time trading post will leave vivid memories of the Wild West as it is today.

Just another 19 air miles northeast of Oljato is the 5,000-foot gravel strip marked on the charts as AZ Minerals Company, altitude 5,320 feet. The town of Mexican Hat is five miles farther east along a paved road.

While we were touring this high desert area, Murray Hillman (AOPA 135086), his wife, Dena, and their two daughters, Denise and Bonnie, spent two days visiting Mexican Hat with N4022D, a 1957 Cessna 182.

"The dirt strip had a little grass on it, but the surface was in good shape," Hillman reported. "There are no obstructions for miles and the prevailing wind favors a downhill takeoff from the north end. There's a wind sock, two chain tiedowns and cables anchored into the ground for additional aircraft, but carry your own ropes. There is no runup pad or fuel. It is possible that 80/87 fuel may be available at Mexican Hat in barrels, but plan to fuel at Oljato, or perhaps Blandings.

"There's no phone at the flight strip, so 'buzz' town fairly well, and a car from the San Juan Trading Post will come out from Mexican Hat.

"We spent two full days there and had a most enjoyable time."

James and Emory Hunt operate the trading post, a 22-unit air-conditioned motel, cafe and Canyon Country Scenic Tours. Motel rates for two range from $8 to $12, and the daily Jeep tours have a minimum charge of $35, or $11 a person for four or more. Carry your own lunch. Tour director Hunt will furnish the drinks and cold watermelon. Canyon Country Scenic Tours use new high-wheelbase GMC station wagons that "will go places that you can't take a Jeep," according to Hunt. The 8.50–5:30 tour is arranged in a circle to put the sun

Cessna Super Skylane in which Downies made their high desert flight is parked next to automobile entrance at Grand Canyon Caverns, Dinosaur City, Ariz.

Lake Havasu, Ariz., a World War II military rest camp, has become a popular resort area for fishing, boating and other water sports, largely because of the presence of the airport.

in the right place for photography of the unique rock formations throughout the entire trip.

Hillman reports that overnight trips are available with sleeping bags, equipment and Dutch oven cooking, complete with sourdough biscuits, at $25 a person. A two-day combination Jeep and boat trip takes visitors to Rainbow Bridge and return. Other Jeep tours visit areas with picturesque names like Muley Point; the Goosenecks of San Juan Gorge, where the river turns more than six miles to gain one mile toward the Colorado; the 300-room Indian cliff dwelling at Poncho House Ruin; and Garnet Ridge, where you can pick garnets right off the ground.

Shadows were lengthening from the high sand cliffs when we again filled 2536X and made the 35-mile hop to Halls Crossing. The strip was a mile away from the trailer court and seemed to offer no photographic opportunities to put both aircraft and scenic background together. We circled twice and followed our verbal flight plan down the Colorado River to Fage. A meteorologically beautiful line squall, complete with frequent cloud-to-ground lightning, covered the 7,600-foot-high Kaiparowits Plateau, and we picked our way through scattered rain squalls until we were able to talk with Mrs. Knight on Unicom.

At Knight's suggestion, we stopped at Kanab City, Ut., the next morning on our way to Bryce Canyon. There's a fine 5,300-foot paved runway there and a 2,640-foot gravel strip with a pay phone to call for fuel or transportation. Norman Cram is both town marshall and airport manager. Any of the 13 motels in town will furnish free transportation from the airport.

Kanab is a delightful place. A permanent western fort has been built near the airport, and three separate film companies were working in the area during our visit. More than 50 films have been made near Kanab, including "Drums Along the Mohawk," "Buffalo Bill," and a TV series.

Floyd Marshall, owner of Aikens Lodge, showed us the area, where livestock and timber vie with the tourist trade. A landing here would provide a relaxing pause from the rigors of the "big town" or any qualms at flying the isolated back country.

The surface wind was picking up dust from the south as we took off for Bryce Canyon, Ut. Using sailplane ridge-soaring technique, we kited up the side of the Pink Cliffs with the rate of climb pegged at 2,000 f.p.m. The *Super Skylane,* with its conical cambered wing tips and extended stabilizer, smoothed out the bumps nicely, and not an ice cream carton was required.

After circling the jagged red spires at the Bryce Canyon resort, we called the FSS and were given 20-knot surface winds directly down their east-west runway. When we requested fuel, we were met at the gas pumps by Jerry Bartlett (AOPA 280039), who doubles in brass as airport manager and owner of the Pink Cliffs Motel and Cafe, just one-quarter of a mile from the airport. His 10-unit motel has rooms from $7.50 to $12.50 and "the closest beer to the park." His *Tri-Pacer* is kept in a picturesque log hangar that was built at Bryce Canyon during the days of the depression.

There are no rental cars at Bryce Canyon, but you can borrow "The Green Hornet," an aging Chevrolet sedan. FSS operators keep this car available, and visiting pilots always keep the gas tank filled. A local "kitty" and donations from Utah's airport tax provide an occasional tire or repair. Thus, if you want to drive the 3½ miles into the Park, you have "wheels" to make it. However, either Jerry or Mrs. Bartlett is always glad to pick up visitors. And don't miss the homemade pie in their cafe. Such a trip could be hard on a weight watcher if it weren't for the rough weather in the summer.

FSS supervisor Ken Shake explained that Bryce Canyon has an omni communication setup that will work most areas of the high desert. Shake pointed out that the omni (112.8 mc) and one remote receiver tuned to 122.1 are located on a 9,000-foot knoll to the west of the airport. By transmitting on 122.1 and listening to Bryce Canyon omni, a pilot can keep in communication over many areas that might otherwise be very lonesome. While we were in the FSS, we were able to hear clear transmissions from an aircraft working Tuba City omni from southeast of that station — and Tuba City is 115 miles distant.

Bryce Canyon is one of the highest airports in the United States (elevation is 7,589 feet). We were faced with the option of taking off uphill into a 10–20-knot head wind with rising terrain to the west, or going downhill into a gentle valley, pushed by a strong tail wind. Each of these situations is different, and many pilots prefer the downhill, downwind takeoff. However, the *Super Skylane* had power to spare so we enjoyed the leisurely mile-and-a-half taxi and turned into the wind. Factory specifications call for a 1,115-foot roll and 2,205 feet to clear a 50-foot obstacle at this density altitude. With the help of the gusty wind, we were able to better those figures appreciably.

Once we reached the edge of Sevier Canyon, we picked up a ridge wind and "coasted" skyward. Flying under a "street" of cumulus clouds also helped. Within 10 minutes after takeoff we called in at 13,500 feet and were still climbing. As soon as the 11,307-foot Bryan Head and the Cedar Breaks National Monument just north of Zion National Park had been passed, we began a steady letdown, since there was no oxygen aboard. From 10,500 feet, we were able to maintain good communications with Bryce Canyon from Mormon Mesa, 125 miles distant.

Next stop, Las Vegas and then home. There are many other airports of interest in this area, however. The ghost towns to the north of Las Vegas [see September 1963 PILOT] make a fine trip by themselves. Ask any of the local operators and they'll outline a trip to fit your own personal taste.

However, try to include some of the high desert. This remote island of the Southwest is at its best when seen from the air — and there's more than enough high adventure to keep you awake. ◆

FLIGHT PLAN TO 'LEVIS AND SPURS'

Sixty-three air miles west-northwest of the Phoenix Vortac (115.6) is Wickenburg, Ariz., center of the dude ranch country.

Within a five-mile radius are 20 of the finest dude spreads in the Southwest. They offer programs from bunkhouse accommodations, family-style eating, roughing it — even poking cattle — to resort ranch living.

Two dude ranches, Rancho de los Caballeros and the Flying E, have landing strips long enough to take light twins. Rancho de los Caballeros has Unicom on 122.8.

We packed four of our brood into a 1961 Cessna *Skyknight*. With son Peter flying shotgun, we took off from the Oakland, Calif., airport for Rancho de los Caballeros with a brunch stop at Santa Barbara.

Over Monterey the air was smooth and cool. At 55% power, the engines sounded like Casals stroking a long cello note. Offshore Big Sur lay scattered clouds. A brisk quartering wind furled the sea.

We made a 45-minute transit at Santa Barbara. Flight time had been 1:15 from the Bay area.

We crossed Palmdale at 11,500 feet and put on oxygen masks. To the right was a dishwater-gray overcast. At Hector we climbed to 19,500 feet to stay on top. Our ground speed checked at 258 m.p.h.! A Phoenix weather sequence gave 4,000 feet with broken clouds and 30 miles visibility.

Fifteen minutes out of Needles (115.2) on the 110° radial we saw a froth of low rolling white clouds lather the distant mountain tops. One corner of the horizon broke into bright sunshine; the other held the rain curtain of a cold front.

Peter tuned in 290° on the Phoenix VOR (115.6) and set up a cross-radial of 350° on Buckeye (110.6).

By CHUCK BANFE | *AOPA 164119*

'An Arizona dude ranch should be on every pilot's yearly flight plan,' author says. You'll find some good ones around Wickenburg, Ariz.

Flying over the airstrip at Rancho de los Caballeros shows the proximity of the strip to the ranch buildings. The ranch will accommodate 100 people.

A Sunday morning chuckwagon cookout was the highlight of the Banfe's dude weekend.

We began our letdown. As we passed through 10,000 feet an immense landscape took shape and rolled toward the Vulture range, south of the dude center. We began to make out tiny mesquite trees and cactus as footballs and walking sticks and fire hydrants and telephone poles.

Ahead of us was Wickenburg. We overheaded the town. Four miles south-southwest would be Rancho de los Caballeros. Checking our position with a 290° radial on Phoenix (115.6) and 350° on Buckeye (110.6), as advertised, the two strips were close together. Flying E had a large, whitewashed "E" at the southwest end. To the left was Rancho de los Caballeros' shorter parallel runway.

We made one circuit of the field and landed to the southwest. Wires strung across the final approach path were well below the glide path. A hill rose off the far end of the runway.

In three minutes the *Skyknight* was secure and we were pulling up in front of a well-tended hacienda.

The family, June (wife), Susan, Petey, Juli and Nicky, washed the altitude off their hands and faces. Bob Roshone, head wrangler from South Dakota, took the children out to meet their horses. For the long weekend they would be under his spur. They would eat, ride and play together. It would leave us free to mingle with other adults, but not out of reach.

We met the ranch's girl Friday, Peach Curnow, at the El Toro bar. It was beautifully done in an antique Spanish decor, combining all of the colors of the desert sunset. Frank Welch, the bartender, was an Irishman turned cowboy from Boston. He sported a red knit vest and frontier pants.

Edie and Dallas Gant are the owners and operators of Rancho de los Caballeros. Lean and sandy, Dallas *was* a cowboy despite his pressed levis. "We have a nice landing strip now, for most aircraft up to small jets," he said.

"There has been a tremendous increase in the number of dudes in planes," said Edie. "Our strip always has a few aircraft on it. When flying clubs come down here, we're really loaded. Not long ago, Cessna brought distributors in from all over the country. There were 35 of the top ones with their wives. Air Oasis has been here with 74 aircraft. The Skylarks from Fullerton, Calif., came in with 50 planes. There was a 99's family fly-in from Fresno recently. Santa Monica's Fly-For-Funsters had a nice group. Los Amigos de Viento from Sacramento filled all of the tiedowns when they came in."

Dallas pointed out that Wickenburg is no more than one day's flight from almost any airport in the United States. "Not only that," he added. "Even though this is CAVU country, we have excellent VOR and ADF facilities."

Though the late luncheon snack was served with informality, Dan Blocker, of "Bonanza," never saw such eatings. Later Dallas introduced us to the chef, Langill Stanley, who works during the summer at the Narragansett By The Sea in Kennebunk Beach, Me., with his brother, Ted, as assistant chef. The brother act has become famous in the West.

Meanwhile, down at the stables, cowhands were saddling the horses. All four children were astride by the time we arrived — even Nicky. He was to get some dual in the corral before soloing on the trail.

June and I took the afternoon ride. We wandered among the cholla. Now and then a deer, a jackrabbit, or a Gambel quail with its feather eyeshade came into view. Peach pointed out the "jail tree," a relic of calabooseless times; its iron shackles dangled from its trunk. It was the Old West in all its splendor.

After we returned, the family took a dip in the pool.

An old railroad bell clanged chow time. We parted company. The children went to their dining room and we ate in the main dining room.

That night we bunked early. Off in the distance we could hear the bleating of a lonesome burro.

The next morning, not long after dawn, I joined the children for breakfast. As per flight plan, son Peter, the rogue, acted up. I was about to reprimand him when wrangler Bob cut in ahead. "Pete, knock it off! Down with the chow pronto or no riding." Pete went rigid as a plebe and shoved his food down.

The morning ride was two hours long. The afternoon was two or more, depending upon how long one could sit. Before dinner we swam or played tennis; in the evening we relaxed in the enormous Spanish sitting room with tall, beamed ceilings flanked by lean wooden pillars. Mesquite logs burned in the fireplace.

The highlight of the dude weekend was the Sunday morning desert cookout. Juice, rolls and coffee were served in the large living room. Wagon wheels were chandeliers and the fireplace was copper-hooded. At the corral we split into three groups; the walkers, lopers and fast trotters. In two hours everyone converged miraculously at the desert chuckwagon site as if on cue.

All 60 horses were tethered. Smoke curled from the fire, and steam twisted upward from the coffeepots. The breakfast in the shadows of the Vulture mountains was fabulous.

We returned to the ranch, packed our gear and prepared for our departure. We filed with Phoenix ATC to Palm Springs, Salinas and Oakland.

At cruising altitude, the children dropped off to sleep, one by one. The long dude weekend had been better than TV dreams.

Not too expensive and just a few hours away, an Arizona dude ranch should be on every pilot's yearly flight plan. ◆

Chuck Banfe "unloads" his family from Cessna Skyknight at Rancho de los Caballeros. The children were "under the spur" of Bob Roshone, head wrangler from South Dakota, for the weekend, so their parents were free to mingle with other adults.

Sun-bathing and swimming in the warm-water pool are popular pastimes, particularly after a couple of hours of horseback riding.

By H. V. MILLER

*Carefree, Ariz., an easygoing travel spot, bids
visitors have a light-hearted, happy-go-lucky time.
Let only the sun mark time here*

TAKE A
CAREFREE
FLIGHT

Elsa Kirk, a New York City Mooney owner, wades a pool surrounded by native cacti and other desert flowers.

Looking out over the Carefree Inn to the golf course and airport in the background.

The only landing obstructions at Carefree, Ariz., are stately saguaro cacti that cover the rolling hillsides. Since Carefree has what the Chamber of Commerce proudly refers to as the largest sundial in the Western world, it's to be expected that the town is referred to as the area "where the sun marks time."

The 105-room Carefree Inn, complete with 4,000-foot airstrip, is the largest of the resorts in the area. The decomposed-granite flight strip is 130 feet between the lights and slopes 2% uphill to the northeast. There are 15 tiedowns, fuel, rotating beacon and Unicom. Jack and Ruth Mallery manage the airport that has been in operation for the past six years.

Just about the only distraction in landing at Carefree's fine airport is the visitor's tendency to admire grotesque saguaro cacti while coming in on final approach. When Robert H. Weston (AOPA 135003) of Glendora, Calif., and I stopped in recently while ferrying a new Cessna *Super Skylane* out from the factory, we found the unique shapes of the cactus to be a fascinating sight.

Carefree is 25 miles northwest of Phoenix, Ariz. The luxury winter resort at the inn, part of the Western International Hotel chain, has 80 terrace rooms with private sun patios overlooking a central swimming pool, built-in refrigerator bar, television and radio in each room. Naturally there's air conditioning and oversized twin or double beds. Rates for two people are $25 per day without meals between opening day and Jan. 15. During the season, until April 15, the rate is $36 per day. Then the charge drops back to the lower rate until closing on July 1. If you want a modified American plan (breakfast and dinner), add $8 per day per person. The full American plan is $11 per person.

The Carefree Inn also has five two-bedroom and five more one-bedroom cottages, complete with kitchenette.

There's plenty to do in and around Carefree. Aside from the sun, splendor and hospitality, fly-in visitors can use the large, free-style, heated outdoor pool; two wind-free regulation tennis courts; paddle tennis and shuffleboard; Ping-Pong; horseshoes; badminton and cards.

There's the championship Desert Forest Golf Course between the inn and the airport. Greens fee for this 72-par 6,926-yard, 18-hole course is $5. Electric carts for two persons rent for $7, and club sets are available for another $2 — just in case you didn't want to overload your airplane. PGA Professional Stan Graff is in charge of the course.

It's a five-minute drive to Hube Yate's riding stables where one-horse-power mounts bring $3.25 for the first hour and $2.75 each for two or more hours.

Rock hunting and searching for artifacts of the Hohokam Indians are Carefree pastimes that appeal to many visitors. The nearby town of Cave Creek "boasts of everything from cabins to mansions and from frontier features to the most modern conveniences," advises the Chamber of Commerce somewhat shyly.

Weekly events at the inn include chuck-wagon breakfast rides, night rides, steak barbecues, fashion shows, golf tournaments, holiday celebrations and hunting and fishing parties. Carefree adjoins the Tonto National Forest and is within 15 miles of the Verde River and Bartlett Reservoir.

Carefree Inn has Avis Rent-a-Cars, 24-hour valet and laundry service, baby sitting on request, a beauty salon open daily except Sunday, newsstand, and cigar and gift shops that are open daily. Reception and dining rooms can handle up to 400 people.

At the nearby planned community of Carefree, where there are more than 1,500 year-around residents, a huge sundial is the dominant feature. The gnomon arm on the sundial is 62 feet long and rises 50 feet in the air. The face of the dial is 90 feet in diameter and has a circumference of 284 feet. It's equipped with tubes to heat water by solar energy for an adjoining office building.

Near the sundial, visitors can stop at the International Restaurant with separate, yet interconnecting, dining rooms and a capacity of 350 people. There's cosmopolitan food from noon 'til 10 p.m., and the Mediterranean Room's cocktail lounge is open 'til 1 a.m. Dancing is scheduled on weekends both at the Carefree Inn and the International Restaurant.

Shopping centers include Sewell's Indian Arts Shop at the Carefree Inn or "Quien Sabe? South American Imports," "Dos Cabesas, Imports from Mexico," (literally, "two heads") or the "Ho Hum Nursery" downtown.

If you happen to be flying a helicopter, there's even a heliport just south of the sundial. ◆

Carefree Airport's manager, Jack Mallery, fuels Cessna 206 as George Boyd (center), Director of Sales, and Bob Weston stand by.

Main swimming pool at the Carefree Inn.

PHOTOS BY THE AUTHOR

127

By JOAN STANDLEE

Texas couple moseys—via Cessna 140—over to Arizona corral where wintertime temperature is reported usually in the 80's with sun shining a good percentage of the time

SADDLEBACK RANCH

Cal and I found ourselves with a week's vacation, but with no plans. We started thumbing through our worn copy of Places To Fly. Ah! What better fun than a dude ranch?

After writing for reservations we drove to Stinson Field (San Antonio, Tex.) to take a look at 4269 November. She was dusty and sad looking, but a little washing soon had her gleaming. We were ready to go — so we thought! At the last minute, we found that our reservations had not been confirmed. With some disappointment, we leafed through some travel folders. There were a few phone calls then the takeoff. We pointed the nose west to Tucson, Ariz. We would spend a few days at the Saddleback Ranch 16 miles northeast.

The rising sun welcomed us in a blue-white sky as we climbed out on the 280° radial of the Stinson omni. It had been many months since we'd flown our red and white Cessna 140, too long. The pleasant hum of the well-tuned engine was the only sound at 8,500 feet, lulling us into perfect contentment.

Bucking a 20-knot head wind, the miles slowly drifted by. At midmorning we were suddenly aroused from our lethargy by what felt like an invisible hand slapping us about the sky. We were approaching the mountains east of El Paso. Since the mountains were almost 7,000 feet high, 8,500 feet was not a comfortable altitude at all. We climbed to 10,500. The turbulence at 10.5 was almost as rough: up a thousand feet, then down, then up again. We had to fight hard to maintain a semblance of an even altitude. The mountain peaks were jagged and snow covered. How fast the wind would be roaring through those passes! At times we felt as helpless as a feather being blown about. Then suddenly we were clear of the turbulence. We were off our radial a little so corrected to "zero in." When the dim outline of El Paso appeared in the distance, we were only too glad to RON.

We were up early the next day, ready to once again tackle the mountains, this time wiser in their ways. Soon the outlines of Tucson began to take shape.

The coffee shop at the RONtel was a welcome sight. No sooner had we finished coffee than we found a car from the ranch waiting for us. The outskirts of Tucson lay clean and neat in the warm midmorning sunshine. As we drove through them, owner-manager Jack Rowin told us a little about Saddleback Ranch. It nestles in the flower and cactus covered Santa Catalina Mountains at the foot of a hill that is shaped like a saddle. It is a working ranch as well as a guest ranch, and Jack has some cattle in the mountains behind it. The ranch accommodates 26 people, catering mostly to professional people who come from as far away as Canada, New York, and Chicago for its famous western hospitality and excellent cuisine. Like most guest ranches in Arizona, Saddleback is usually open from Oct. 15 to June 1.

At the entrance we received a big smile and a warm welcome from Nancy Royal, who said, "We're so happy you were able to get here before lunch. Would you like a swim first?" That sounded great to us and we were soon in the pool.

After drying off in the sun, we went in to a delicious lunch of cold roast beef, several salads, and nut bread. While we were chatting over coffee, wranglers Joe Carr and Jerry Byrnes appeared, looking the perfect image of western cowboys — sun bronzed, tall, lean, and born in the saddle!

Guests at Saddleback ride in small groups with a wrangler. After an hour's rest, we headed for the corral to find Joe and Jerry

The author (riding Scooter), wranglers, and another guest prepare for a trail ride.

saddling a group of good-natured, well-kept horses. Scooter was to be mine. Although he was the homeliest horse I've ever seen, he was a joy to ride. Riding through the giant cactus-covered desert and flower-covered mountains on 4,500 acres of ranch land in the dry Arizona air was pure pleasure. Joe and Jerry pointed out interesting spots and gave us tips on how to keep from bouncing so hard in the saddle! After the

ride there was another swim and then a cookout on the trail.

To describe a cookout on the trail seems well nigh impossible. There was warm camaraderie, a crackling fire, good food, a purple sunset, and songs to the accompaniment of a guitar; and at the end, the tired, comfortable, content feeling that follows a wonderful day.

The next morning I awoke to discover

that my ambitious husband was already up and hiking up the mountainside. I was content to lie still, awed by the perfect silence of the Arizona morning. Imagine! To hear absolutely nothing except the occasional chirp of a lonely mockingbird! I looked out and everything was still — giant cacti and tall green trees standing motionless in the cool morning sunshine. No movement anywhere. What perfect peace.

After a delicious breakfast of hot cakes, eggs, and sausage, we groaned about our "saddle sores" and prepared for another delightful ride, this time high into the mountains above the ranch. Our group was a "medium fast" group. We just sat and allowed our horses to pick their own way up the rocky mountainside. Below us we could see the entire Tucson valley, and above us we could hear the rush of water in the canyon.

For the more ambitious guests at Saddleback Ranch, there is a golf course 10 minutes away, trips to the Old West shops on the outskirts of Tucson, get-togethers and square dances at neighboring ranches. Manager Jack will even arrange side trips for surf or deep-sea fishing off the Gulf of California. Activities may be planned or unplanned to suit the desires of the individual. One can be busy with many varied activities or just relax, away from the pressures of city living and the business world.

The food, whether it be hot cakes and eggs prepared by chef Cindy or thick, juicy steaks charcoaled by Jack, would delight any gourmet. Never have we eaten so well!

It was difficult to tear ourselves away from the beauty and peace of this land and the delightful people who had made our stay so pleasant. As we climbed out over the desert we could see spirals of sand being lifted and whirled high into the air. So this is the "blowing sand" that one occasionally reads about. We pushed 69 November a little higher, thinking we'd soon be above the "dust line" and have better visibility. But we never reached "on top," finally leveled out at 11,500 feet. We knew we should go no higher. Visibility was still a good 20 miles and the turbulence was only occasionally severe. We could see the "dust line" above us, at about 13,000 feet.

With a 20-knot tail wind, we reached San Antonio in six hours with only one stop, El Paso.

Our little 140 has been to many vacation spots in the southern part of the United States and in Mexico, but our trip to Saddleback Ranch turned out to be the best fly-in vacation we've had. We think you might enjoy it too. Land at Tucson International or the small strip 1½ miles from the ranch. ◆

Lounging at Saddleback's pool could be one of the visitor's favorite pastimes.

Ranch buildings at Saddleback. To the left is a gigantic saguaro cactus, the blossoms of which are Arizona's State flower.

PHOTOS BY THE AUTHOR

THE AUTHOR

Army Nurse Joan Standlee met her husband, Cal (AOPA 104312, U.S. Air Force), in Frankfurt, Germany; he was her flight instructor. They now reside at San Antonio, Tex., and have flown their Cessna 140 "across most of the southern United States, the Bahamas and Acapulco under both VFR and instrument conditions," Joan said. She has logged about 200 hours, and Cal has approximately 3,000 hours.

By DON DOWNIE | AOPA 188441 and DANA DOWNIE

LEADVILLE:

COUNTRY'S HIGHEST LANDING SPOT

Care in operating at high-altitude airport required, but a visit to colorful Colorado mining town is well worth it. Horace A. W. Tabor, onetime mayor of Leadville, made his fortune there

Harrison Avenue, Leadville's main street, at dusk. In the days of the Old West, Leadville was known as California Gulch and was the home of Horace A. W. Tabor, American miner and capitalist.

Leadville, Colo., has the highest altitude paved airport in the United States. The 4,800-foot runway is 9,927 feet above sea level and is surrounded by some of the best fishing, hunting, skiing, 24-hour-a-day mining activity and Western frontier folklore in the entire nation.

However, there are people-and-plane problems in operating at these altitudes. On a 70° F summer day, the density altitude at Leadville is a whopping 13,000 feet, and you'll be able to draw only about 55% horsepower on take-off with unsupercharged engines.

Incidentally, people operate much the same as power plants in this rarefied air. Don't plan to run up three flights of stairs during your first day in town. And, to the uninitiated, one after-flight drink will do the work of two in Leadville.

There's a wealth of fascinating Western information to be gained near Colorado's "City In The Clouds." First, however, let's get on the ground. Our visit to Leadville was completely spontaneous. We were returning from a trip farther east with George Buckner, Piper's western regional manager for multi-engine sales, in his turbocharged Aztec C, N5781Y. Buckner is an avid angler who "just happened to have" his fishing gear in the nose baggage compartment so we planned to land for a day of fishing at the Taylor Park Reservoir where the Forest Service maintains a flight strip. However, the entire valley west of the Sawatch Mountains of the Rockies was under clouds so we headed northeast, tentatively for Lake Granby, 40 miles west of Boulder, Colo.

We picked our way between the peaks at 13,000 feet and soon saw the inviting Lake County flight strip at Leadville. Nearby lakes looked as though they might have their share of Rocky Mountain rainbows (they did!), so we called Leadville Unicom to check on the situation.

No one answered since there wasn't a Unicom transmitter in town at that time. By the conclusion of our visit, a two-way Unicom was on order and is to be operated by Jack East, owner of radio station KBRR (1230 kc, 250 watts, 16 hours a day, "The Voice Of Fun").

Both approaches to the Leadville Airport are free of obstruction. While the up-slope to the north of the Arkansas Valley makes the airport appear to slope up, it's actually 40 feet higher at the south end, according to Leadville Cessna 182 pilot Stephen Narans, president of the Silver King Inn. His modern motel and the Holiday House will both furnish ground transportation for visiting pilots.

There's a telephone booth and western-style restrooms at the airport. At the time of our visit there were only five tiedowns and most of these were in use by local pilots. Additional tiedowns and parking areas are planned, but for the moment, bring your own tiedown kit.

A look through the local telephone book confirmed that there was neither a taxi nor a rent-a-car office at Leadville. However, Buckner soon found out that both the Hockett Ford and Gibson Chevrolet agencies will rent demonstrators at about $10 per day and 10¢ per mile. John Hersch (AOPA 171710) manager of the Gibson

Chevrolet agency, sold Cessnas at Cortez, Colo., for 4½ years before moving to Leadville. There is no local flight school at the airport, but Hersch has taught several local residents to fly.

Fuel is available in town only in emergency. However, most visitors to this high-altitude resort prefer to take off with only partial fuel to keep their gross weight to a minimum.

During winter months, Lake County road grading equipment keeps the airport open year 'round. Lights and a rotating beacon were to be installed soon. The airport was completed in 1962 by joint county-FAA funds and is the site of many high-altitude tests of military STOL aircraft and helicopters. A Lockheed C-130 has used the field for high-altitude evaluations.

There's a good gravel road to Highway 285 and it's only two miles into town. Once you hit town, you're strictly on your own. This high-altitude area of the Rockies has just about everything that a tourist could want. The Chamber of Commerce is located on Ninth Street just east of Harrison and has a number of good brochures covering the area. You'll find out that Leadville's history dates back to 1859 when placer gold was found in the area. Rich gold and silver deposits were discovered in the 1870's and the mining rush was on. Leadville was Colorado's second largest city in 1878. More than one billion dollars of mineral wealth has been produced in Leadville in the past 100 years.

Today the American Metals Climax Mine, 12 miles north of Leadville, employs more than 2,800 people to produce more than 66% of the free world's Molybdenum ("Moly"). The mine operates 'round the clock to process 45,000 tons of raw ore daily. Tours are available during certain months.

Leadville has a number of excellent skiing facilities during winter months. Cooper Hill, 12 miles to the north, is considered to

be Colorado's best family slope and is operated weekends only through April. Baby sitting, ski rental, instruction and ski patrol services are available. Aspen is 58 summer — and 140 winter — surface miles to the west. (Check with the nearest FAA FSS at Eagle, with a remote Vortac at Kremmling on 113.8, for the condition of the 6,500-foot Sardy Field at Aspen where elevation is only 7,773 feet. Unicom is available.) The new Vail Village is 37 miles north of Leadville and Breckenridge, 45 miles to the east, is the site of a new ski and recreation center.

Ice skating is available in Leadville itself while sled and toboggan slide areas are nearby.

Back in 1886, Leadville residents spent more than $100,000 on a huge five-acre Ice Palace. The building had octagonal towers 90 feet high and was constructed with 5,000 tons of ice. Inside there were a 90×180 foot skating rink, dance hall, dining room, gaming rooms, curling alleys and "all types of concessions advertising their tinseled wares." Statues in ice depicted life in a mining camp.

For your first day at 10,000 feet without an oxygen mask, try a leisurely tour of Leadville itself. There's the Healy House and Dexter Cabin, open from June through mid-October by the Colorado Historical Society. The Tabor Opera House is open during the summer months for tours. This fabulous auditorium was built in 1879 and featured all the "big name" performers of that era from New York and other eastern cities.

To pilots living in cities where the May Company does business, it is of interest to note that David May opened his first store in a tent at Leadville in 1877.

Visitors can see the Matchless Mine where H. A. W. Tabor became one of the world's richest men. Later, his widow, "Baby Doe," guarded the mine for 35 years because her husband had cautioned her not to sell it. She was found frozen at the mine one winter.

The Unsinkable Molly Brown spent most of her adult life at Leadville and was a famed survivor of the Titanic disaster. A booklet by former Denver Post writer Caroline Bancroft tells the story of The Unsinkable and her life at Leadville.

Today, a series of water development projects is expanding the economy of Leadville: $178,000,000 are programmed for the Flyingpan and Arkansas diversion project and another $65,000,000 are being spent on the Homestake water project to supply the towns of Aurora and Colorado Springs. A 5½-mile 9⅔-foot horeshoe tunnel through the Continental Divide will carry this water, and power plants will be incorporated in the system. An important by-product of these water systems is the enlargement of Twin Lakes and Sugar Loaf. Government officials predict that 2,000,000 visitors will visit this

Tabor Opera House at Leadville, which reportedly cost $500,000, opened Nov. 29, 1879. Performers there on the "Silver Circuit" out of New York have included Florenz Ziegfeld's Mamselle Napoleon, Houdini and Thurston, Sousa's Marine Band, Shakespearan Actor Lawrence Barrett and many others.

area as soon as marinas, campgrounds, motels and night clubs are completed.

As a purely personal aside, who needs a night club when you can stand on the edge of Crystal Lake (or any one of more than 300 lakes in the area), watch the change in color of the sunset (or sunrise, if you prefer) and see rain or snow squalls pass by while fishermen like George Buckner reel in those hungry golden trout. Mother Nature presents one of her best floor shows over the Rocky Mountains near Leadville.

The hunting season, usually for deer or elk, opens in mid-October and closes early in November.

If you're the summer season traveler who really doesn't enjoy those big piles of snow, put Leadville on your date book for the last weekend in July and make your reservations early. The last Sunday in July 1967 is the date of the 19th annual World's Championship Pack Burro Race. The 23-mile event is run alternately between Leadville and Fairplay, over the 13,182-foot Mosquito Pass. Fastest time for the event is three hours, three minutes, 23.1 seconds, with a $1,000 prize for the winner. There's also a women's division with a $300 first place.

Jack East explained that six members of the Cornell track team entered one year and only one of the college men was able to finish the race. The program states, "each contestant is required to walk, run or even carry his burro, but is not allowed to ride at any time. No persuasive implements are allowed to further increase the progress of the burro." East remembered that one winner had been disqualified after judges found needle points planted in the end of his 15-foot lead rope.

"The burro is equipped with a regulation pack saddle and 25 pounds of weight. In addition, he must exhibit certain old-time prospector's equipment, such as a gold pan, pick and shovel."

The burro race is the highlight of the annual three-day Lake County Fair, with a livestock and horse show, rodeo and, of course, a dance.

Leadville has grown from a population of 4,000 in 1960 to more than 15,000 today. A new $4,500,000 school construction program is under way that includes a dual-campus junior college (Central Colorado Mountain College) with classes to begin in the fall of 1967 at both Leadville and Glenwood Springs.

When you're finally ready to depart, make sure that your passengers haven't filled your baggage compartment with the weighty mineral souvenirs of Leadville. Unless wind conditions dictate otherwise, local pilots recommend a takeoff to the south since the valley falls off slowly to 8,080 feet at Buena Vista, 7,484 feet at Salida and then it's downhill all the way to Pueblo.

If you enjoy flights to unusual, off-the-main-path destinations, you'll make a second call at Leadville. ◆

Crystal Lake, a delightful fishing spot, is six miles south of Leadville. These fisher folk think a possible catch is worth enduring a rainstorm.

The entrance of Tabor's Matchless Mine, which is now a museum, is being inspected by Jack East, owner of KBRR (1230 kc) radio station. Here "Baby Doe" Tabor gained fame for her long vigil, hoping the mine would again make her wealthy. "Baby Doe" died in poverty in a cabin beside the mine March 7, 1935.

Piper regional sales manager, George Buchner, shows off a golden trout he caught at Twin Lakes, south of Leadville, Colo.

The Healy House Museum, which was built in 1878, has been restored by the Colorado State Historical Society. The adjoining building, Dexter Cabin, is called "the stiffest and most exclusive private poker club."

OPERATION HAZARDS AT 9,927 FEET

Neither people nor airplanes operate with peak efficiency at high altitude.

"If you write about flying into Leadville, Colo., you're going to be the indirect cause of some serious airplane crashes, no matter how strongly you explain the problems of high-altitude flying," said veteran lightplane designer John Thorp (AOPA 22461). "Many lightplane pilots seem to feel that they have the right to use any airport on the map, whether or not they or their equipment are capable of doing the job. There's a feeling of 'the greater the hazard, the greater the challenge.'"

The airport at Leadville is 9,927 feet above sea level and the highest full-sized airport in the nation. It is frequently used for both military and civilian high-altitude tests. On a warm day of just 76°F, you can expect a density altitude of 13,000 feet and you'll be able to draw about 55% of sea-level power on takeoff with an unsupercharged engine.

"You can't afford to fly well at 13,000 feet," continued Thorp, "since this type of performance would penalize other flight characteristics of the design. I'd recommend that no pilot fly a two-placer into a field this high unless he does it solo, with partial fuel and little or no baggage. A four-place plane at this altitude should be considered as a good two-placer with the same limitations."

Takeoffs, climbouts, approaches and landings on the highest paved airport in the nation are going to be a great deal different from those at sea level. The safest advice to any non-mountain-flying pilot is to take his own — or rented — airplane to 13,000 feet and see exactly how it performs with gear down and takeoff flaps. This experimental flight should include the exact amount of weight in passengers, fuel and baggage that you plan to use in the high mountains. If your plane won't climb at a minimum of 300 f.p.m. under these conditions, *don't* go to Leadville or any of the other high-altitude flight strips of the area.

The 300-f.p.m. minimum was set by FAA a number of years ago and changed to the best angle of climb that approximates this rate; 300 f.p.m. is only five feet per second and the pilot of any low-powered aircraft or sailplane well knows that five f.p.s. of "soft" air (downdrafts) is extremely common. Have just a little wind passing across those high ridges and the vertical currents far exceed this 300-f.p.m. figure.

If winds do exist, determine their direction and fly on the "upwind" side of the valley to take advantage of any updrafts. For example, if you're flying north up the Arkansas River Valley toward Leadville with 14,260-foot Mt. Evans on your right and 14,431-foot Mt. Elbert on your left and have a wind blowing from the west, fly the right-hand side of the canyon to look for updrafts. And, if the turbulence or wind conditions are extreme, this is a fine time to practice that 180° turn and work your way back to Colorado Springs. Should you be approaching from the north, try Denver. From the west, Grand Junction's Walker Field is down at 4,858 feet above sea level, while a pair of airports in the Rifle-Glenwood Springs area are below 6,000 feet. Then take a rental car and look up at the scenery for the last leg of the trip.

High-altitude takeoffs and landings should carry the same mixture-leaning as cruising at altitude. Always lean your engine for maximum r.p.m. at full throttle before starting your takeoff roll. Some pilots establish their maximum high-altitude power just before landing and leave the mixture set at that point for the subsequent takeoff. The disadvantage to this system is that the landing might be made during the cool of the evening when the density altitude was comparable with actual altitude. If the takeoff were to be made at midday with a warmer-than-normal temperature, the mixture would be too rich for maximum performance because the density altitude of the airport would have risen.

If you're flying a turbocharged aircraft,

mixtures should be kept lean during runup to avoid stalling. Once the throttles are advanced on takeoff, the mixtures should go rich since the exhaust-driven turbine will be up to speed and developing sea-level horsepower.

If you suspect icing conditions and have a non-fuel-injected (carburetor) power plant, make your complete runup with full carburetor heat or alternate air source. Then turn off the heat, adjust the mixture for maximum power, reapply heat briefly to clear out any ice that may have formed and then close the carburetor heat for actual takeoff. Since FAA requirements call for a 90°F temperature rise at 30°F with full heat applied, this would rob the engine of about 20% of its power. Even on a "normal" 23°F day at 10,000 feet, you can pull only about 60% power. Take away that 20% for carburetor heat and you're down to 48% power and really sagging on takeoff. Fuel injected engines do not have this icing problem, but they should be leaned for maximum power before takeoff just as the carburetor type.

While the airplane itself doesn't know it and the indicated air speed remains the same as at sea level, things happen faster during high-altitude landings — and slower on takeoffs. At 9,927 feet, your air speed correction is almost 20%. Thus, if you cross the fence on a landing at 80 m.p.h. indicated, you use the same 80 m.p.h. indicated at altitude, plus perhaps an extra 5% insurance for a strange airport. However, what you see outside the cockpit will be going by at 80 plus 20% or about 96 m.p.h. After touchdown, this higher actual speed becomes a definite factor during rollout. Once your wheels are on the ground, all rollout figures must be based on true air speed rather than indicated air speed so, on a "normal" day, you're going to have to come to a stop from an equivalent 96-m.p.h. approach; not an 80-m.p.h. one.

High-altitude takeoff rolls are going to be longer, much longer, than those at sea level. When you have only 50% of your sea-level power available, you double your takeoff distance. In addition, at 10,000 feet, the liftoff speed will be 20% faster and some of that 50% power must be used to accelerate the airplane to the higher rolling speed.

"The takeoff distance might easily be infinity at 10,000 feet," computed John Thorp. "You might never get going fast enough to take off. If you can climb 300 f.p.m., you probably have enough excess power to 'hack it.'"

High-altitude operation should include the same cautions used in short-field flying at sea level. Make sure that there's no frost or ice on the aircraft. Run up carefully and lean out for maximum power. Then apply power briskly and start with a sweeping turn if there's room. (The Leadville Airport is too narrow for this procedure.) Things aren't going to happen very fast anyhow, but make absolutely sure that you're not dragging your brakes during this long takeoff roll. Pick a go/no-go point before takeoff and don't change your mind. If you don't have sufficient flying speed by the time you reach your go/no-go point, abort the takeoff, taxi back and either send all your passengers downhill by bus or wait 'til much later in the day or the next dawn when the temperature is cooler and the density altitude much lower. The Pilot's Operating

Manual of each type of aircraft lists both high-altitude performance to be expected and go/no-go distance for a balked landing. Check "the book" for your particular airplane.

Don't try to force the airplane into the air. This takeoff procedure works poorly enough at sea level. The higher you go, the worse it gets. From an aerodynamic standpoint, aircraft with a lighter span loading (longer wings) will generally get off the ground at altitude better than designs with a short span. This is about the only situation where span is important.

Since the power curves and performance specifications differ with each design, it is impossible to talk about specific models and their performance unless all are listed. In general, however, the airplanes that have lots of power available will have the least amount of trouble at altitude. However, a "clean" design will also help getting into the air.

Since effective wing loading increases with angle of bank, all turns in the pattern should be made more shallow than those at sea level. Planes loaded out of center-of-gravity (C.G.) limits will affect only the stability and controllability, but don't tempt a high-altitude field with any plane approaching heavy weight.

The FAA has a film titled "Density Altitude." This 29-minute color movie traces the flight from a sea-level airport in Louisiana to a fishing spot in the High Sierras. It is available without charge from the FAA Film Library, P.O. Box 25082, Oklahoma City, Okla. 73125.

One prudent approach to Leadville — or any other new flying situation — is to talk with an experienced flight operator at your last point of refueling before going into the really high country. Show him your airplane and the load you have aboard. Give him an honest report on your personal flight experience and ask him if he feels that your proposed flight is safe for you. If he suggests that you ship most of your baggage ahead and leave your auxiliary fuel tanks empty, heed his advice. If he suggests the possibility of having your passengers come out by bus or bringing them out in two successive flights, why not give it a try? And, if he says "don't go," why not wait for better weather, a more powerful aircraft and/or a lighter load?

Don't be influenced by urgency or passenger's suggestion. John Thorp commented, "My wife thinks that I can fly at any altitude. She may push me into killing us yet. We plan to come home from the Midwest via Canada and the Grand Tetons. 'We have an airplane. It can go anyplace — so let's go and quit dragging your feet,' she says sweetly."

There's a Koch chart for altitude and temperature effects on the reverse side of all sectional charts. Since your navigation in the canyons of these high mountains should be by sectional map anyhow, take a look and see how your proposed flight checks out on this "Koch chart."

The nearly two-mile-high airports of the Continental Divide are wonderful places to visit. They are certainly no place to go to practice flying. As in parachute jumping, you have to be right the first time. ◆

Landing facilities are available near restored Eighteenth Century American town for pilots who want to fly there with their families

WILLIAMSBURG, VIRGINIA

By RICHARD A. REPP | AOPA 137848

A pilot winging southeast from Richmond, Va., needs no tourist guide to know that below him is some of the most inviting country in the world. As one flies over this historic area, there may be an overwhelming attraction to "drop anchor" and visit.

It was in 1607 that the captains of three tiny ships, Susan Constant, Godspeed, and Discovery, first dropped anchor here; and the history of the United States as an English speaking nation began. Here, jutting like a peninsula into the blue of the James River, lies Jamestown Island, where the four-month sea voyage ended, and the first English colony in America was established.

Jamestown is just one point of what is referred to in the area as the "historic triangle." A few miles east is Yorktown, scene of the decisive Revolutionary War battle that brought America victory and independence. Cornwallis surrendered to Washington here in 1781. Both Yorktown and Jamestown are now the locations of parks which

The windmill at Williamsburg is still in use. The grinding operation is performed exactly as it was almost 200 years ago.

The first permanent English Colony in America was established in 1607 at Jamestown Island, Va. The settlement was capital of Virginia until 1699, when Williamsburg was made capital.

Eighteenth Century offenders of the law were locked in pillory at the gaol (jail) and subjected to public ridicule. Here, the author is made to pay for a "slightly rough" landing in his Twentieth Century flying machine.

re-create conditions from the days of old, including a glass blowing demonstration and sailing replicas of the three original ships.

The highlight of the area for the modern visitor, however, is at the northern tip of the triangle, five miles from Jamestown. This is Colonial Williamsburg, restored over the last 35 years by a Rockefeller endowed organization to the glory it knew as the capital of the Virginia colony in the exciting era of the Revolution. George Washington, Patrick Henry, Thomas Jefferson, and other leaders went to Williamsburg to lay the foundations of our government.

Today is yesterday in Williamsburg. The numerous homes, shops, and other buildings open to the public are staffed by costumed hosts and hostesses who lend authenticity to the colonial atmosphere. Walk through the town and you'll find it a backward step — about 200 years. ("Airplane? What's that?") Or tour it by carriage, manned by an Eighteenth Century coachman. Watch the colorfull militia, complete with fife and drum corps, muster on the Market Square; hear their muskets and cannon fire; dine on the

excellent fare of the inns and taverns which offer Eighteenth Century specialties served in the manner of the times. Do, in fact, whatever you like, but don't speak too loudly of independence, for it's 1770 and the British flag still flies over Williamsburg!

To date, 83 colonial buildings have been restored, and 48 major and several hundred dependent buildings reconstructed on their original sites. More than 80 acres of public gardens have been re-created. A major attraction is the Raleigh Tavern, where the patriots frequently met. The governor's palace, powder magazine, and gaol (jail) with its public stocks are places to give your camera a workout, too. Backing up these buildings are a dozen craft shops, where the blacksmith, wigmaker, gunsmith, and other colonial artisans practice their trades just as their forebears did.

Virginia was the largest of the colonies, extending as far west as the Mississippi River; and, as its capital from 1699–1780, Williamsburg, ranked in importance with Philadelphia, New York, and Boston. Within her walls, Patrick Henry delivered his fa-

mous Caesar-Brutus speech in support of his Resolutions against the Stamp Act. Here also, May 15, 1776, the Resolution for Independence was adopted. This document proposed that the colonies declare themselves free and independent of Great Britain and influenced the better known July 4 Declaration of Independence in Philadelphia. Jefferson's famous Bill for Religious Freedom was also introduced here.

Standing within these same walls today, the visitor finds the barrier of time between the Twentieth and Eighteenth Centuries shattered. This magnificent historical perspective alone is reason enough to make Williamsburg one of the country's most fascinating places to fly to.

Aerial visitors are happy, too, to find themselves at no disadvantage for not having their cars. Automobiles aren't even permitted in the restored area during most of the year.

Instead, courtesy buses run every few-minutes, connecting with all parts of the restored area and with some of the motels and hotels in the area, as well as with the Information Center just outside the restored area. The Center should be the first stop for all visitors. A dramatic color film, "The Story Of A Patriot," is shown there throughout the day and provides a meaningful introduction to the old town.

Accommodations, by the way, are reasonable, ranging from $6 per couple at guest homes to a $23 maximum for lodging at the luxurious Inn. Many motels have pools, and Williamsburg boasts two fine golf courses.

Let the 116° radial out of Richmond be your path to the past. Or, if a more leisurely course is your cup of tea, or you don't feel like navigating by dead reckoning, the meandering James River will lead you the 40 miles. Coming from the south, Williamsburg is situated 45 miles northwest of Norfolk. Caution should be exercised in passing over the Norfolk area, however, because of the high density of military air traffic.

Best access to Williamsburg is from Central Airport, a 4,200-foot turf strip two miles north of town (see Norfolk Sectional). The field is attended days, and flyers may obtain 80/87 and 100-octane fuel and major repairs. Lights and paving are in the offing.

For hard-surfaced runways, lights, and "grope slope," Patrick Henry Field at Newport News, 17 miles away, is the best bet. Rental cars and limousine service to Williamsburg are available at this field.

No matter what means of travel you use, however, the important thing is that you have come. This will prove a refreshing journey — one that will reward you richly with enjoyment, understanding, and an increased appreciation of our country's heritage. ◆

THE AUTHOR

Richard A. Repp was 16 years old when he soloed at Wayne Major Airport, Romulus, Mich. Mr. and Mrs. Repp visited Williamsburg many times before moving there when he enrolled in the Law School of the College of William and Mary.

In the scenic savanna country of North Carolina is a resort that caters especially to geese and pilots. The wildlife, hospitality and relaxation to be found at that resort are as unusual as its name.

Here, close to the vacationland coast and 40 miles southwest of Kitty Hawk, scene of the Wright brothers' historic flight, is secluded Lake Mattamuskeet, with a lodge situated at a wildlife refuge. No ordinary place is this, as pilots flying to the area will know from the moment they behold the broad blue waters of the lake, the clustered cypress trees, marshes, tangled pine groves, and canals left over from a bygone era of glory. In winter the great water birds dot the sky and fleck the lake with wings of blue, gray and white. In summer, marsh and songbirds abound. Fat turtles lazily sun themselves, and deer and small game are plentiful. Fish, numerous and varied enough to satisfy the most ardent fisherman, may be found in the lake and canals. In the less traveled areas about the refuge bear, boar, and an occasional alligator may be seen.

On the southern shore of the lake, set at the junction of two canals, is the lodge. A picturesque structure with red-tiled roof and 120-foot-high observation tower, the appearance of the lodge belies the facts that it began existence as a pumping station and that the tower served originally as a chimney. The conversion was a good one, and the result is a comfortable lodge with accommodations for 50 people. Hearty meals are served in the large dining room. From what could most closely be called a lobby, French windows open onto a long balcony from which you may fish, bird watch, or simply sit back and enjoy the scenery. A large trophy room with a gallery and massive fireplace is available for guests and group gatherings.

Inversely proportional to the quality of this unusual resort, however, is the cost of its enjoyment. A room with private bath plus three excellent meals goes for the unheard of rate of $7.50 per day per person! Nor do surprises cease with that. The lodge provides free transportation from the airport, and guests are invited to take boat or auto tours of the refuge without charge.

As previously indicated, the planners of Mattamuskeet never intended that it should be what it is today, and its history is one of experiment, defeat, and rebirth. The area, dominated by extensive swamps, savannas, and low pinelands, relegated agriculture to the ridgelands. Thus, the idea of draining the 40,000-acre lake intrigued people for some time. The feasibility of the project was enhanced by the shallow depth of the lake, which averages only four feet, and in 1914 large-scale drainage was begun. Through a network of canals which crisscrossed the lake bed, water was pumped out of the lake and into Pamlico Sound, and the reclaimed land farmed. A small model community called New Holland was constructed on the former lake bottom. While the fertile soil yielded good crops, the cost and hazards of keeping the lake drained, coupled with the depression, saw the failure of the undertaking in the early 1930's. The lake refilled, and the birds reoccupied their old habitat.

In 1934 the U.S. government acquired

MATTAMUSKEET, N.C.

By ANNE H. CUTLER | *AOPA 241867* and *RICHARD A. REPP* | *AOPA 137848*

Sportsmen, wildlife enthusiasts and those seeking relaxation and hospitality should enjoy this spot

Lake Mattamuskeet provides refuge for a number of snow geese each winter. A few of these birds take off for a local formation flight.
FISH AND WILDLIFE SERVICE PHOTO

137

ABOVE: Fishing is permitted at Mattamuskeet except during the waterfowl hunting season. Black bass, white perch, and bream are caught frequently.

RIGHT: This modified Stearman has been used as an agricultural plane on the refuge at Mattamuskeet. Although a landing strip is located at the refuge, visiting pilots are requested to use the airport at Fairfield, on the north side of the lake.

FISH AND
WILDLIFE SERVICE PHOTO

The red-roofed structure with tower (center) is the lodge, which accommodates up to 50 visitors. Lake Mattamuskeet, in the background, is 15 miles long and four feet deep. Crossing the lake is a causeway which links the refuge with Fairfield, N.C.

PHOTOS BY THE AUTHORS
UNLESS OTHERWISE CREDITED

much of the land around the lake and established there a waterfowl sanctuary. Since then the operation has been run and further developed by the Fish and Wildlife Service of the U.S. Department of the Interior and has been directed at protecting the waterfowl and getting the maximum production of waterfowl foods out of the lake and bordering marshes. At Mattamuskeet one can see the largest assemblage of Canada geese on the Atlantic seaboard and more whistling swan than one would normally see in a lifetime. Many varieties of duck, geese and swan that in summer scatter across the northern rim of the world from Labrador to Alaska come down the skylanes in the fall to refuges such as this to find the conditions they need to survive. Spectacular mass flights of these birds between the time of their arrival at the refuge in the fall and their departure in the spring are a thrilling sight for visitors. Summer species to be seen include the American eagle, while others such as the great blue heron and the egret are year-around residents. In the evening, the bird songs provide a melodic concert of the finest quality, a song unheard by city ears.

A refuge not only for birds, Mattamuskeet today is one of the fast disappearing places where a person can really "get away from it all." Informality and tranquillity are the prevailing atmosphere, and just relaxing frequently the prevailing pastime. Hiking is popular, however, as is fishing in the lake and canals (the lodge will pack a picnic lunch for you at no extra cost). Black bass, white perch, and bream are caught most frequently. Fishing is permitted throughout the year except during the waterfowl hunting season between mid-November and mid-January. Two areas have been set aside for managed hunting during this period. About 35 blinds are maintained, each the responsibility of a guide. Hunters are required to have a North Carolina hunting license, a daily lake hunting permit, and a Federal duck stamp. Blind fees, including a guide, boat, and decoys, are $15 per day for two hunters, $21 for three, and $24 for four.

Feathered air visitors to Mattamuskeet are free to land wherever they choose, but pilots are requested to restrict themselves to the use of Mattamuskeet Airport, a 3,600-foot turf strip which serves the town of Fairfield. While the field, situated on the 59° radial of New Bern (EWN), is not attended in the strict sense of the word, it is well maintained; and 80/87 octane fuel is available there. It is recommended that pilots provide their own tiedown equipment, if desired. With advance notice of your ETA the lodge will have a car waiting for you at the field. There are no landing or tiedown fees.

A lake, a lodge [Mattamuskeet Lodge at New Holland, phone 919-926-4211 — Ed.], a lot of good food and congeniality, Mattamuskeet is an interlude to the pace of daily living. It is a place well worth flying to. ◆

THE AUTHORS

Anne Cutler began flying in 1962. She is currently a private pilot, having logged about 250 hours, and resides at Williamsburg, Va. Coauthor Repp wrote the Places To Fly article, "Williamsburg, Virginia," which appears elsewhere in this volume. That article was quite a hit with fly-to-see travelers, we have heard.

By CHARLES H. BALL

Visits to historic fishing and trading ports of Massachusetts are rewarding to summer tourists. Flying vacationists will find ample ground facilities for such visits

The Clipper-Ship Country

Romance of the clipper ships and the "thar-she-blows!" type of whalers still lingers at Massachusetts historic seaports, but the fishing fleets of today are very real. The masts and spars of fishing vessels against the sky is a sight that tourists to New England never cease enjoying. This mast-and-spar scene was taken in the Princetown Harbor, a takeoff point for the Grand Banks fishing grounds. PHOTO BY JOHN W. GREGORY

It would be quite enough if coastal Massachusetts offered only the magnificence of her natural splendors — the sun, the sand and the sea — to the summer visitor. But these are just the surface attractions, albeit enticing ones, of a shore line that speaks with each washing wave of the nation's heritage and early history. And though "the wild New England shore" was forbidding to the Pilgrims, it beckons to the private pilot and his family today with a good network of airports and an abundance of reasonably priced accommodations.

On this trip, the past — with its whalers, fishing fleets and sleek clipper ships — comes alive in the historic seaport communities of Plymouth, Provincetown, New Bedford, Gloucester, Nantucket and Martha's Vineyard. The present is well taken care of, too, whether the choice is swimming, sailing, deep-sea fishing, golfing or simply lazing on the beach, breathing the salt air and dreaming of succulent lobsters and clams.

Where to begin? It doesn't really matter, because all of the Bay State's coastal sites are within easy reach of each other. It doesn't matter, either, whether you settle down at a home base, flying off in easy hops on day trips, or whether you put down for a day or so, or more, at each spot. From June to September the whole area brims with attractions and with New England hospitality, which has been a mark of the region, despite the usual stories of Yankee reserve, from the time the Pilgrims and Indians welcomed each other as brothers at the first Thanksgiving feast.

At Plymouth, in fact, Pilgrims will still welcome you in person, dressed exactly as the original settlers were in 1620. In this and other ways, the town inspires as profound a sense of history as you're apt to encounter anywhere.

Walk the streets and read the markers where the Pilgrim homes stood; stand where Myles Standish drilled his Pilgrim guard; pace the decks of the Mayflower II, the replica of the original ship that was sailed across the Atlantic from England in 1957; see how the Pilgrims lived in a visit to *Plimoth* Plantation, a reproduction of the Pilgrims' village as it was in 1627; and gaze upon Plymouth Rock, the symbolic cornerstone of the nation.

Every Friday in August, at 5 p.m., townspeople in authentic costume assemble to the beat of drums, each marcher representing one of the Pilgrims, man, woman and child, who survived the rigors of the first winter. Then they march under arms to the site of the fort on Burial Hill, thus reliving the weekly procession of the Pilgrims to their worship place.

Plymouth Airport, five miles southwest of the city, has two paved runways (3,000 and 2,500 feet). The airport is attended from 8 a.m. to sunset and is lighted for night flying. There are rental cars at the airport plus taxi service to the city. Accommodations at nearby motels range from $6 to $25 a night, and the wise traveler makes advance reservations.

If the children are along, a side trip out of Plymouth takes you to the famed Edaville Railroad in South Carver, where the clang of a bell and the blast of a steam whistle send you off on a six-mile journey through cranberry country. There's also a replica of a nineteenth century village and the

Gloucester's Fishermen's Memorial, shown here, is focal point of memorial services held every year, honoring departed fishermen. Flowers are thrown into the water in front of the statue and carried out to sea by the tide. The monument featured prominently in the movie version of Rudyard Kipling's "Captains Courageous."

PHOTO COURTESY OF MASSACHUSETTS DEPARTMENT OF COMMERCE

Just the mention of the name "Gloucester" stimulates a mind-picture of hardy fishermen, clad in oil skins, standing up to and taking all a "no'-easter" can throw at them. This is a contemporary view of Gloucester harbor where fishermen, every bit as hardy as those of the last century, go out to battle the elements and the cod.

PHOTO BY GERALD S. CURHAN

chance to have a chicken barbecue dinner among the pines.

Forty-three miles southwest of Plymouth, standing as a gateway to Cape Cod, is the industrial and port city of New Bedford. Like Gloucester, it is a community that has known sorrow in the hopeless wait for men who will never return from the sea. It is a brave past. The feeling can be captured by following the Moby Dick Trail to the Old Whaling Museum, the Old Wharf, Fort Phoenix in neighboring Fairhaven, the Old Candleworks and the Captain Winsor Home, among other landmarks. For the youngsters, there's the Children's Museum and the Lincoln Amusement Park, also the Battleship Massachusetts in nearby Fall River.

If possible, schedule your visit to New Bedford for the weekend in August when the famous Scallop Festival takes place in Marine Park. This annual event attracts some 30,000 people to sample New Bedford scallops and view the famous fishing fleet at the waterfront. In August, too, there's the Summer Festival featuring the theater, plays, and lectures.

New Bedford Municipal Airport, located 2½ miles north of the city center, is a trunk field with two 5,000-foot runways and a 24-hour control tower. Two-way radio is required. There's a restaurant and pilot's lounge in the administration building. Accommodations and prices are those of any large city, offering a wide range of choices.

Still on the mainland, but just barely, is Provincetown, at the tip of Cape Cod. It has earned a reputation of being way out in temperament as well as location, but few find the arty flavor objectionable — it's more likely to be a pleasant change, and to stand at Race Point, overlooking miles of white sand and a heaving sea, is reward enough for any traveler.

Provincetown, like Plymouth, dates back to 1620. It was here, any native will tell you with bursting pride, that a party of Pilgrims en route to the Plymouth settlement came ashore. By the late 1600's, a substantial village had been established; and by the 1800's, Provincetown was the focal point for the New England fishing industry as a provisioning base, port and market. The town's character bears the stamp of its Portuguese residents, descendants of the fishermen who came from the Azores in the 1800's.

Trying some of their native specialties, such as coivas, linguica and Portuguese bread, is a must. So is a visit to the 255-foot Pilgrim monument and the Provincetown museum. The town is rich in art galleries, art schools, handcraft and antique shops, and good restaurants, as well as bearded young men and bare-footed, or sandaled, tawny-haired girls.

New York, New Jersey and Connecticut flyers are everyday visitors to the Provincetown Airport, which is two miles northwest of the town. It has a paved 3,500-foot runway. If you're a surf fisherman, you never have to leave the field. A world's record for striped bass, since broken, was set a few years ago by a fisherman casting into the surf on the beach parallel to the runway. There are rental cars available at the airport. Prices in town go from $5 to $25, and higher, depending on whether your taste is for a room, an apartment or a hotel suite. Again, reservations are advisable.

Summer's fun in Massachusetts extends

Picturesque is the description usually applied to North Shore, Rockport, which is a few miles up the shore from Gloucester. Amateur photographers consider this Rockport view as one of the most desirable camera subjects.
PHOTO COURTESY OF MASSACHUSETTS DEPARTMENT OF COMMERCE

Mayflower II, a replica of the original Mayflower which brought the Pilgrims to the New World, is one of the tourist attractions at old Plymouth, Mass. The vessel was anchored only a short distance from the historic Plymouth Rock, when this color picture was made.

off-shore to the islands of Martha's Vineyard (10 miles south of Cape Cod and 27 miles southeast of New Bedford) and Nantucket (30 miles at sea and 55 miles from New Bedford).

"Of all the earth's surfaces," it is said, "the islands are the aristocrats." Both of these islands lend support to the claim. Martha's Vineyard, the larger of the two, is 21 miles long and 10 miles at its greatest width. Across this acreage woodlands, beaches, fishing villages, old New England towns, rolling hills, towering dunes and magnificent cliffs blend into a restful vacation paradise.

There are three airports — Katama Airpark two miles south of Edgartown on the eastern side of the island; Oak Bluffs Airport one mile south of Oak Bluffs in the northeast section; and Martha's Vineyard Airport four miles south of Vineyard Haven on the north side.

Katama has four turf runways up to 4,000 feet and a taxiway that leads to a beach parking area. For a small fee, you can be swimming just minutes after leaving your plane, and because just about everyone on the beach is interested in flying, the company is unusually good.

There are bicycles and rental cars for the two-mile trip into Edgartown, the oldest settlement on the island and a one-time whaling port, with narrow tree-shaded streets and the stately homes of old sea captains. Pilots can stay right at the airport at Katama Shores, which has a restaurant, lounge, view of the ocean and rates of about $125–$200 a week. There's a taxiway from the runway to the hotel. There are guest houses and hotels in Edgartown, where the rates range from about $10 to $30 a day. Again, here and elsewhere on the islands, make reservations.

Oak Bluffs Airport has two turf runways, the longest 2,200 feet. It adjoins the Island Country Club, which has a challenging 18-hole golf course, tennis, swimming, a restaurant and motel units priced from about $25 a day.

Both the Edgartown and Oak Bluffs fields are privately operated. The Martha's Vineyard Airport, run by the county, has the only paved runways on the island, the longest 5,000 feet, and is equipped for night operation. There's a restaurant at the airport plus rental cars and taxi service.

A bit farther away from it all, and another fine vacation retreat, is Nantucket Island, where the first settlers arrived in 1659 to begin what has become a pilgrimage of many thousands to the island each summer.

Once the whaling center of the world, Nantucket reaches back into history for its restfulness. Main Street was paved in 1837 with cobblestones from Gloucester; the Jethro Coffin House was built in 1686; handsome elms that were planted as long ago as 1851 line Main Street.

There is much that appeals to the younger set, too, as evidenced by the boys and girls

One of the most popular places in New Bedford with visitors is the old Whaling Museum. One exhibit there is the Lagoda, a 54-foot, half-scale model of a New Bedford whaleship, shown here.

COLOR PHOTO COURTESY OF THE WHALING MUSEUM, NEW BEDFORD

who come in waves all through the summer. Rates for rooms start at about $7 per night.

There is ferry service between the mainland and the islands, if you want to try your sea legs. For the flyer, however, Nantucket Airport is two miles southeast of the town of Nantucket on the southern edge of the pork-chop-shaped island. It has two paved runways, 5,000 and 4,000 feet, approach control and a tower manned from 7 a.m. to 11 p.m.

At other times, Airport Advisory Service is available from the Nantucket Flight Service Station, which also operates the Island Reporting Service, an overwater guard for aircraft entering, flying through or leaving the islands and lower cape. The area em-

visibilities may be much poorer than over reporting stations. In other words, keep informed through all available pilot reports and stay alert to rapidly changing conditions.

At some of the busier fields, weather warning signs equipped with flashing red lights are activated, on advice from the Nantucket FSS, whenever weather below VFR minimums occurs or is forecast.

The FAA warns against beach landings. They are hazardous "and should not be attempted by anyone but a pilot experienced in this type of flying."

Back to the tour — and to Gloucester, the only community mentioned that does not have an airport. However, Beverly Airport, 15 miles northeast of Boston, is just 17 miles

You can't leave the Gloucester area, of course, without a visit to neighboring Rockport, a town so famed for its natural beauty that its Number 1 motif, a view of the harbor, is one of the most oft-painted scenes in the world.

Rockporters are proud craftsmen, too, and a walk down Bearskin Neck brings into view a wide variety of skillfully made, handwrought objects in a succession of gift shops.

The town's famed inns, guest houses and cottages have rates ranging from the princely to the moderate.

The excellence of the food — the fresh fish and mouth-watering lobster — cannot be described adequately.

For summer theater buffs, there is no

Pier and part of the skyline of today's Provincetown, a favorite Cape Cod spot of the summer colonists. The Pilgrims are said to have landed here before they went on to Plymouth and disembarked.

PHOTO BY JOHN W. GREGORY

braces about a dozen airports, including Hyannis, Chatham, and Falmouth on Cape Cod.

To initiate the system in the air, the pilot calls Nantucket radio on leaving the mainland, or when skirting the coast line, and asks for "flight following" protection.

Radio contacts are made every 10 minutes or more often. If the aircraft doesn't report within 15 minutes after an estimated checkpoint over the mainland or an island, search action is started.

On the ground, the area's busier airports are connected to Nantucket by fastline interphone service for weather briefings, flight plan exchanges and collection of weather observations.

The FAA's Nantucket FSS Information Bulletin gives a detailed rundown of what to expect in the area. It can be obtained by writing to: Federal Aviation Administration, Flight Service Station, Memorial Airport, Nantucket, Mass. 02554.

Some specific weather hazards encountered in the area bear emphasis, however. During midafternoons, as the sun lowers, sea fog moves over the area, reducing visibility to nil. Although the area may be reporting ceilings above VFR, overwater ceilings and

and a 20-minute drive from Gloucester. Arrangements can be made for a ride in a courtesy car.

Gloucester, again, embodies all the best traditions of a seafaring community, sending out its fishing fleet not merely to hover about the home coast but to range far and wide, and often perilously, in a tradition of adventure that moved Rudyard Kipling to write Captains Courageous.

The fisherfolk are mainly of Portuguese or Italian ancestry. The Italian fishermen honor their patron saint, St. Peter, each year, in a fiesta that has fireworks, games and street decorations climaxing in the blessing of the fleet. Another annual event is the International Dory Race between Gloucester and Lunenberg, Nova Scotia. (These events are held, normally, in June of each year.)

There is much to see in Gloucester — the vessels of the fishing fleet moored beside weathered wharves, colonial houses, artists painting with unconcern for onlookers along the sidewalks, art galleries, intriguing gift shops, museums, even a castle, and fine old churches that harken back to the days of the fight for religious freedom.

There are plenty of hotels, motels, guest houses and cottages.

richer circuit to follow than up and down the Massachusetts coast.

Finally, all the airports mentioned, it might be noted, are covered by the Boston Sectional — which should be something of a hint for those wanting to shake the sand from their hair for a day or two.

Boston is the place to go. And though the city fathers and the boosters have taken to calling it the New Boston, fortunately it's still the same old, wonderful town. ◆

THE AUTHOR

Charles H. Ball, author of "The Clipper-Ship Country," is aviation editor of the Boston (Mass.) Traveler. He has soloed a Cessna 150 and hopes to get his private ticket before long.

Inexpensive fun and nearby lightplane facilities are awaiting flying vacationers when they fly to Oklahoma state parks

Horseback riding at Roman Nose State Park, near Watonga, Okla. This park is in the old Cheyenne-Arapaho Indian reservation and got its name from Chief Roman Nose of the Cheyenne.

Lake Murray State Park has 21,000 acres surrounding a lake where you can swim, boat, fish and ski.

State parks abound in Oklahoma, where the living is easy and the fishing is good. Here are four of them which have numerous attractions for flyers, including lodging accommodations. Detailed information on airport facilities is given at the end of the article.

LAKE MURRAY STATE PARK

This 21,000-acre park surrounding a lake has swimming, boating, fishing and skiing. For children, there are a nursery, playgrounds and babysitters. Accommodations include a 55-room lodge; 86 villas, 32 are housekeeping units; and three dining rooms. Airports accessible to Lake Murray State Park are Ardmore Municipal, Lake Murray State Park, Lake Murray State Airpark and Winrock Farms-Turner Ranch Division.

QUARTZ MOUNTAIN STATE PARK

The 46-room lodge at Quartz Mountain State Park is reached over a scenic road carved from the solid granite mountains. The dining room of the lodge overlooks the lake and mountains. Sixteen cottage units are air conditioned and furnished for housekeeping.

Among facilities for fun at this park are a nine-hole golf course, fishing for bass, crappie, catfish and other game fish in the 6,180-acre reservoir, swimming in a sand-beached lake or a concrete pool, water skiing, boating, hiking, dancing and shuffleboard. There are two children's playgrounds and an amusement park, and two youth camps are available for organized groups.

Free camping facilities are available and include shelters and restroom and shower buildings. A 10-unit trailer park has utility hookups.

Airports accessible to Quartz Mountain State Park are Altus Municipal, Hobart Municipal, Hohman, Ponder Field and Sayre Municipal.

ROMAN NOSE STATE PARK

Roman Nose State Park, Watonga, is in the old Cheyenne-Arapaho Indian reservation and got its name from Chief Roman Nose of the Cheyenne. Members of the Roman Nose family still live near the park.

A nine-hole golf course roams over and through the canyon and is reported to be challenging. The swimming pool is constructed of natural rock and is filled with water from the "Big Spring" that feeds the canyon and the two fish-stocked lakes. Rowboats may be rented. Other recreational assets are horseback riding, picnic and camping areas and a children's playground.

On the rim of the main canyon, overlooking Lake Boecher and Lake Watonga, is 20-room Roman Nose Lodge. Other accommodations, in addition to rooms in the lodge, are housekeeping cabins and cottages. There is also a youth camp with dormitory-type sleeping accommodations and dining room and kitchen facilities.

Clinton Municipal, Thomas Municipal and Watonga Airports are accessible to Roman Nose State Park.

SEQUOYAH STATE PARK

Sequoyah State Park fills a wooded peninsula jutting out into 19,000-acre Fort Gibson Reservoir in northeastern Oklahoma. Water sports predominate at 3,000-acre Sequoyah —fishing, water skiing, boating, and swimming in a pool or at a sand beach. A nine-hole golf course runs along the lake shore.

FLY TO FOUR

Oklahoma State Parks

Western Hills Lodge overlooks the water of the reservoir. This lodge offers a choice of rooms in the lodge or cottages. Less than a mile from the lodge, in the park, is a 2,500-foot paved strip which has tiedowns. Transportation to the lodge can be arranged.

The lodge has planned entertainment, including dancing, stage coach rides, horseback riding, breakfast and moonlight trail rides, hayrides and chuckwagon feeds. There are supervised activities for children, and individual baby-sitters are available.

Shuffleboard, badminton and table tennis are offered at the lodge. Park playgrounds have a softball field and shuffleboard, as well as play equipment. Also in the park are two tennis courts and an amusement park.

Accessible airports are Sequoyah Park, Hatbox Downtown, Tulsa International, Tulsa Riverside, Sequoyah State Park and Wagoner.

Some of the airports near the four state parks follow.

Altus — Altus Municipal (Oklahoma City Sectional), four miles north of the city. Runway 17-35 is 4,000 feet, concrete. Some of the services available are fuel, tiedowns, runway lights, Unicom and taxi. The airport is attended in daylight.

Ardmore — Ardmore Municipal (Oklahoma City Sectional), 11 miles northeast of the city. There are four runways. Among services available are fuel, major repairs, beacon, and weather information. The airport is attended 24 hours.

Ardmore — Downtown Ardmore (Oklahoma City Sectional), one mile south of city. The paved runway is 3,000 feet. Fuel, minor repairs, weather information, beacon and runway lights are available. Airport is attended in daylight.

Ardmore — Lake Murray State Park (Oklahoma City Sectional), eight miles south of the city. There's a 2,500-foot asphalt runway. The airport is not attended.

Clinton — Clinton Municipal (Oklahoma City Sectional), three miles northeast of the city. There are three runways, 3,200 feet, paved, and 2,500 and 2,050 feet, sod. Among services available are fuel, minor repairs, beacon and runway lights, weather information, Unicom, hangars and tiedowns, taxi. The airport is attended 24 hours, seven days.

Hobart — Hobart Municipal (Oklahoma City Sectional), three miles southeast of the city. There are three asphalt runways, all about 5,300 feet long. Some of the services available are fuel, major and minor repairs, hangars and tiedowns, beacon and runway lights, weather information and taxi. The airport is attended 24 hours, seven days.

Western Hills Lodge in Sequoyah State Park. Less than a mile from the Lodge, in the park, is a 2,500-foot paved strip, and transportation to the lodge can be arranged.

Lone Wolf — Hohman (Oklahoma City Sectional), one-half mile east-southeast of the city. There's one 2,600-foot oil-and-rock runway. Services are fuel and courtesy car. The airport is attended irregularly.

Mangum — Ponder Field (Oklahoma City Sectional), one mile north of Mangum. The runway is 2,500 feet, turf. Services available include fuel, hangars, tiedowns, weather information and minor repairs. The field is attended 8 a.m. to 6 p.m.

Muskogee — Hatbox Downtown (Little Rock Sectional), two miles west of the city. The two paved runways are 2,800 and 3,800 feet. Among the facilities available are fuel, major repairs, beacon and runway lights, weather information, hangars, tiedowns and taxi. The airport is attended 7 a.m. to sunset.

Sayre — Sayre Municipal (Oklahoma City Sectional), eight miles south of the city. The runway is 5,000 feet, concrete. Some of the services available are fuel and tiedowns. The airport is not attended.

Sulphur — Winrock Farms-Turner Ranch Division (Oklahoma City Sectional), six miles east of Sulphur. The runway is 2,200 feet, asphalt. The field is not attended. [This is a private airstrip; use at your own risk. — Ed.]

Thomas — Thomas Municipal (Oklahoma City Sectional), one-half mile southeast of the city. There's a 3,000-foot paved runway. Among services available are fuel, tiedowns, weather information and courtesy car. The airport is attended during daylight hours.

Tulsa — Tulsa International (Tulsa Sectional), 6½ miles northeast of the city. There are five paved runways, 10,000, 7,100, 6,360, 4,160 and 3,690 feet long. Among services available are all kinds of fuel, major and minor repairs, hangars and tiedowns, beacon and runway lights, weather information, limousine, bus, taxi and car rentals. Two-way radio is required. The airport is attended 24 hours.

Tulsa — Tulsa Riverside (Tulsa Sectional), six miles south of the city. There are two runways, 4,000 feet, asphalt, and 1,700 feet, turf. Services available include fuel, hangars and tiedowns, beacon and runway lights, weather information, taxi and car rentals. The airport is attended 24 hours.

Wagoner — Sequoyah State Park (Little Rock Sectional), seven miles east-southeast of the city. The runway is 2,500 feet, asphalt. Among services available are runway lights, weather information, tiedowns, Unicom and limousine. The airport is not attended.

Wagoner — Wagoner (Tulsa Sectional), 1½ miles east of the city. The runway is 2,800 feet, sod. Services include tiedowns and taxi. The field is not attended.

Watonga — Watonga (Oklahoma City Sectional), adjacent to the city northwest. The runway is 2,200 feet, asphalt, with a sod overrun. Among services are fuel, major and minor repairs, runway lights, weather information, tiedowns and taxi. The airport is attended irregularly. ◆

A SKIER'S PARADISE

Author feels this story about Alta, Utah, will 'make one fire up the bird, wax his skis and go west.' We hope you agree

If you're a real skier and a real pilot, then Alta, Ut., is the place to go. Not only does Alta challenge the Alps in every respect, its fabulous ski runs and powder snow are only 45 minutes drive from the huge Salt Lake City jet airport.

Nowhere in our travels have we found such superb ski facilities and complete flying facilities so close together.

Like us, you probably prefer to fly pretty close to the main routes over the vast and lonesome West. Not only were the airways oriented for their better terrain, but they offer the comforting feeling of a few human beings below, towns, superhighways, well-equipped airports, and radio aids.

We're easterners (Michigan), and we depend upon and trust our Continental 225 implicitly; but we do get a sort of lonesome feeling between Tuba City, Ariz., and Alamosa, Colo., or Pocatello, Ida., and Casper, Wyo. In winter, with everything clean and white, the vastness of the Great Divide Basin and the Green River Valley seem ever so great.

Looking down at towns like Kemmerer or Eden, Wyo., we wonder if the residents realize how far they are from their nearest neighbors. The long, straight black ribbon of Highway 2, cutting across the Nebraska plains, is a mighty long jump between watering stops, filling stations, and human beings. One flies hours that seem like eternities between check points, and often these are simply little round, white buildings with a white cone on top, spotted in the barren wasteland of erosion and clay, sand and lava that cover half our nation.

Alta is on the main line. One of the first transcontinental airways (V-6 New York to San Francisco), still following the same route of the wagon trains across the Rockies, accompanies the new four-lane superhighway 80 through Rawlins, Rock Springs, the Bear River Divide, and into Salt Lake City. Frequent VORs make navigation easy, and many of the small towns have radio stations,

if you want to play with your ADF and get a "positive" on a check point.

Many still shudder at the thought of flying over the Rockies, but a few trips will prove that the mountains aren't nearly as foreboding as one might imagine. Actually, they run in bands or appear as limited ranges which can be circumnavigated easily. Further, with a little altitude, one can usually see over and beyond each range to more comfortable terrain. The percentage of time

spent over a hazardous surface is really small, and with a little planning and an early start, Salt Lake City can be reached in one day from many parts of the United States.

Winter flying provides denser air for high-altitude takeoffs, so where one stops to load up with gas is not as critical as in the summer. Coming from the east, we have usually made Scottsbluff, Neb., our rest stop where Bluff's Aviation will be glad to top your tanks. Eighty octane is 41¢ per gallon, and

The author's wife, Terry, and trick ski performer Art Furrer. Chin-deep powder attracted Furrer, who is a certified Swiss ski instructor, to Alta. Look for him in Warren Miller's film, Skiing On The Wild Side (1967).

World-renowned skier Alf Engen (left) runs the ski school at Alta. He and fellow enthusiast Lowell Thomas survey ski runs.

By *ALLEN F. EDWARDS, JR.* | *AOPA 21862*

motels, transportation available, etc. This does make a difference in getting under way the next morning. Further on, Rock Springs Airport with its ILS appeared way out in the boondocks, and that was the only other choice. The operator at Rawlins gladly drove us into town to an excellent and inexpensive motel then picked us up in the morning, and with our six gas tanks only down a few gallons, we were embarrassed not to buy fuel from such a nice guy.

Our ship hauls 90 gallons which would have carried us all the way from Detroit to Rawlins, nonstop. Now with almost full tanks, tips and all, everything was still within limits, even at the 6,784-foot level of the airport. It proved no problem.

One should be a little philosophical about knocking off for the day. Compulsion to complete the trip in one day, to get there, to tell everybody how far one went all at once, leads many to foolish decisions and sometimes disastrous conclusions. It was obvious we couldn't reach Alta that day and would have to spend the night at Salt Lake City had we pushed on. Rooms are cheaper in the country; one can see the spectacular scenery in the daytime, which otherwise would be missed; and dinner too late is never good for sleeping.

There's something about an early start that makes one feel one has something extra out of each day that late starters miss. The world is fresh and still, the air smooth and calm, the visibility crisp, clean and invigorating. Night has dissolved the frustrations of yesterday; our minds are clear, the sky brand new; we feel good. We always seem to make extra distance in the morning hours that we never quite accomplish in the evening. Perhaps we're more patient with the world, our plane, our navigation. Anyhow, it was no time before we were on the ground at the enormous Salt Lake City Airport, and the phone call made at breakfast to the Alta Inn had a Wagoneer waiting for us on the ramp.

While Denver has the Rockies in the western distance, Salt Lake City has them right over her head. One leaves the city limits in the foothills of the Wasatch Range and in a few short miles is heading up the canyon to Alta.

This is the area that can have 30 inches of powder snow a night! The canyon drive up to Alta has been buried frequently by avalanches. However, this hazard is being alleviated by a second road on the south side of the gorge which is not under the sun-drenched face of the north side.

One is not aware of the ascent as one drives, but Alta is 8,603 feet above sea level and 4,400 feet above Salt Lake City. Incidentally, Alta is pronounced like the "a" in "altitude," not like the "a" in "all." There is no town. It is simply the end of the road.

Four inns face the most spectacular ski complex in the United States: the Peruvian Lodge (now officially the Alta Inn), the Alta Lodge, the Rustler, and the Goldminer's Daughter. Edwin Gibbs, proprietor of the Alta Inn, says he changed the name at the request of the Chamber of Commerce, which offered him advertising support if he did. However, old-timers and even newcomers will probably always refer to it as the Peruvian, and mail still comes so addressed. We like the name Peruvian, too; guess we're old fashioned. Accommodations here — 157.

there is a refund of 2½¢ from the state upon application. After Scottsbluff, the land rises rapidly, putting Medicine Bow, Rawlins, and Rock Springs above 6,600 feet. So a gas stop at Scottsbluff (BFF) permits a full-load takeoff almost 3,000 feet lower.

Leaving BFF and proceeding westward, it's a bit lonely as far as Medicine Bow, but here the airway is joined by U.S. Highway 80, and you have the comfort of its company all the rest of the way. We stopped for fuel at BFF late in the afternoon, then got an uncertain weather report with thundershowers over the Uinta Mountains just east of Salt Lake City. This report, plus oncoming darkness (and you can't stop sunset), dictated a stop for the night and completion of the job in the morning.

We selected Rawlins, a wise choice. In our aerial library on board we always carry the AOPA Airport Directory, which tells how far the airport is from town, names of

Snowy peaks rise above the challenging ski trails. Alta, well over 8,000 feet above sea level, can get 2½ feet of snow in one night.

Future ski experts — the children of Edwin Gibbs, owner of the Alta Inn.

Lifts at the Alta ski resort rise directly from the lodges. The ride up and descent over the alpine runs usually take about an hour.

The Green Trail, which features long runs over snow and pine covered terrain, is just the other side of this mountain.

The Alta Inn (nee Peruvian Lodge) has a new top floor. That space provides about 50 more accommodations for lodge visitors.

PHOTOGRAPHS BY THE AUTHOR

As Terry, my skiing wife, says, "You'll never find the 'jet set' here — nobody would pay any attention to them and their fancy clothes."

Alta is just for good skiing, excellent food, comfortable lodging, and wonderful people.

The lodges are simple and complete, definitely family style. Much of the help at the Peruvian are young couples, real ski enthusiasts. Their little tots run up and down the halls. If you don't keep your door locked, you may wake up in the morning to find a two-year-old sitting on the foot of your bed grinning at you. We didn't lock ours. While waiting on table, mother may be spooning Gerbers into her high-chaired baby as she passes. Father may be working behind the sumptuous buffet at meal times, helping around the lodge or on the ski patrol. Meals are served promptly, cafeteria style, in the Peruvian, then personally checked at the table by the chef, Bob Wagner. If he feels you haven't taken enough, he may disappear into the kitchen and return with slices of rare roast beef, turkey, or what have you. Nobody goes away hungry.

Most everyone returns to the lodge for lunch, 12:30 to 1:30. At 2 o'clock everyone is back at the lifts ready to get a full afternoon of skiing. By 4:30, it's time to run down to the lodge, leave one's skis in the ski room, get out of the long Johns and beat a hasty path to the hot outdoor swimming pool. Sort of makes one chuckle to enjoy such contrast — to be sitting in the soothing hot water outdoors watching the last ones come down the snow-covered mountain on skis.

Utah is a dry state; no bars, no liquor sold over the counter and very mild beer. A bottle club arrangement permits guests to enjoy a couple of short drinks before dinner, but the bell rings at seven, and the roast beef is pulled off at eight; so the cocktail hour never takes over, and everyone gets a hearty meal. The place is pretty quiet after nine. Believe me, after Alta's alpine runs, one doesn't wish to waste one's strength in late hous — the mornings are too much fun.

The reputation for unusually deep, powder snow has kept many, used to groomed slopes, from attempting the challenge of this resort. Recognizing this, new lifts to more gentle heights have been installed, and packers have made other runs most enjoyable for the average skier.

Our greatest pleasure came from the spectacular long mountain skiing that one can find only at Alta and possibly one other resort in America. About one hour is required for the round trip up the lift to the top, then back through the bowls, the pine trees, down the rolling Green Trail and back to the lift again. For those who want greater thrills, Ted Johnson will teach you how to handle chest-deep powder snow. Like riding in goose feathers, one learns to sit back and plane through the fluff, throwing up a cloud like the bow wave of a Chris Craft at full blower.

Alf Engen of world renown (50? 60? he won't tell) is in charge of the ski school. It is a challenge to any soft, office-conditioned American to meet this example of what we could be like with more attention to our physical well being. Alf was my childhood hero, pictured on a can of jumping ski wax which I used when jumping on my college ski team. Not only was Alf 10 times a national champion jumper, he won slalom, downhill, cross-country and combination championships with a versatility unmatched by any other skier in the world. Skier Of The Century award in 1950 and Skier Hall Of Fame in 1956 are but two of the many honors bestowed on this athlete. Dedicated to physical fitness, he is the picture of health, the envy of the weak, the example of the man tuned to the great outdoors. In the evening, he delights in feats of strength in competition with his young ski instructors and will pick up a heavy wooden chair by gripping the top cross-bar in one hand and holding the chair legs straight out to one side. Try that with two hands! He shakes hands gently.

Another enthusiast is Lowell Thomas. These two men have learned that winter is no time to remain indoors. Both Alf Engen and Lowell Thomas have been instrumental in developing fantastic plans to construct an aerial tramway across the mountains. Work has been started on this tramway which will be part of the new Wasatch Mountain State Park.

Five major ski areas are within a 14-mile radius of Salt Lake City center, and all within a five-mile radius of each other. By 1970, all resorts will be interconnected by a series of gondolas, lifts, and tramways. The first link of this system will connect Heber, Alta, and Brighton with a jig-back tramway and two gondolas. Park City, likewise, will be included. It is presently known for one of the most unusual ski lifts in the world. An old mine shaft drilled laterally into the mountain takes one to a central elevator which then carries the passenger right up to the top of the mountain. The entire ride is inside.

Completion of present plans will permit the greatest variety of skiing in the world on terrain equal to anything the Alps can offer.

We have reported on Sun Valley, and we still think that is an excellent all-around resort accessible to flyers, but it's different. A complete resort, Sun Valley probably has more of everything except the intimacy of Alta; and nothing can top the spectacular Uinta Mountains of Utah.

We flew over to Sun Valley in an hour and a half from Salt Lake City (about eight hours by car), which makes for a well-rounded ski package. Our next jaunt will probably be to see the new development at Jackson Hole, Wyo., which also has an excellent airport. We've been to Jackson in the summertime and must admit the trip will take you over some long, lonesome, uninhabited stretches. More on this one later.

In the meantime, we wonder how anyone could do better than Alta, with its convenience to a major airport, its accessibility over a safe route, and its fabulous, fabulous skiing. Reservations are absolutely essential. ◆

THE AUTHOR

Allen Edwards has been a pilot for 34 years. He wrote "Mackinac Island: Gem Of The Great Lakes," which appears elsewhere in this volume. Allen and his wife, Terry, who also is a licensed pilot, reside at Grosse Pointe, Mich.

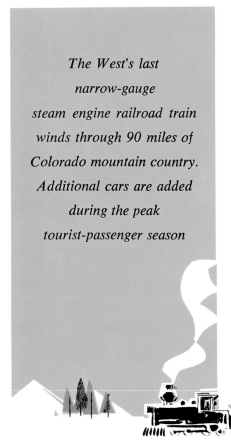

The West's last narrow-gauge steam engine railroad train winds through 90 miles of Colorado mountain country. Additional cars are added during the peak tourist-passenger season

Durango, Colorado

By DON DOWNIE | AOPA 188441

What modern pilot wouldn't be charmed by travel on a narrow-gauge railroad built in 1882? For this picturesque contrast, fly to Durango, Colo., then ride the Silverton, the last of the narrow-gauge steam railroads of the West. This colorful reminder of the Old West runs daily from June 2 through Sept. 30, with a second section added during peak tourist months. The day-long excursion costs only $6 per person ($4.25 for children five to 15).

No matter what route you take, the flight to Durango is over some of the most scenic country of the Rocky Mountains. My daughter, Dana, and I visited Durango during a ferry flight to the West Coast in a 100 h.p. Cessna 150 after a colorful two-hour, 13-minute flight across the Sangre de Cristo Range from Trinidad. A section of the Denver and Rio Grande's narrow-gauge railroad still extends eastward from Durango, over the 10,022-foot Cumbres Pass, to Alamosa. Occasional "rail fan" trips are still made over this section of track and, after having flown the route, I'd certainly like to travel it behind an old steam engine.

La Plata Airport, 17 miles east of Durango, has 7,000 feet of lighted, hard-surfaced runway at an elevation of 6,684 feet. The omni is located on the airport and there are regular Frontier Airlines flights. Gregg Flying Service ("Pappy" Floyd — AOPA 12816 — and son, James) takes care of transient traffic and has a "hot-line" in the office to the FAA FSS at Farmington, N.M., 40 miles to the south.

The Greggs have tiedown space on their oiled ramp for 21 aircraft and plan to ex-

The fiesta grounds at Durango, Colo., where a rodeo is held each August, appear in the center of this photograph. One residential area is in the foreground, and the La Plata Mountains are in the rear.

PHOTOS BY LES TINKER

150

The Silverton always draws a crowd. Here, spectators are watching the train at the station in Durango.

Skiers enjoy the slopes of Purgatory, a ski center north of Durango.

pand to 40 this season. Tiedown is "$1 per night per engine and payment of 10 days storage covers for the remainder of the month." Inside storage is limited, with a fee of $4 for singles and $6 for twins.

Floyd Gregg estimates that more than 180 planes visited Durango in the summer of 1965 specifically to ride the steam train. "While a definite count is not available for past years, I can safely say that we are getting at least 25% more tourist planes each season," Gregg explained.

"Some weekends we really have a madhouse around here, so we are happy to make reservations in advance for any service from hotels to train tickets. We request that visitors advise about what they expect to pay for lodging since all classes are available. Write to Box 866, Durango, or phone 303-247-4632.

"Ground transportation is by cab or rental car. We expect to have a deal worked out whereby the fly-in customer may rent a car at the field and turn it in downtown if he is not going to need it for a day or two. Then he can pick up a car in town and drive back to the field. In any event, there will be a dozen rental cars available, but this does not mean that reservations are not in order during the busy season."

Airline limousine fare from the airport is $2 should your arrival coincide with Frontier.

Cab fare was $4.80 for two persons with a $2 charge for each additional passenger.

During the summer season, Durango sports a Gay Nineties, Far West atmosphere with good evening entertainment of "mellerdramas," a rustic open-air theater featuring Navajo Indian dancers and illustrated talks by Forest Service rangers.

Other tourist attractions include Mesa Verde Park, fishing, boating and big game hunting in the fall. The Purgatory Ski Center, 30 miles north of Durango, has "poma" and chair lifts. Skiing here "promises to be the best in the state since the runs are on a north slope and should maintain real good snow throughout the season," said "Pappy" Gregg. The season will probably run through April 15.

However, the Number 1 tourist attraction in Durango during the four summer months is the 90-mile round-trip ride on the Silverton's "journey to yesterday." This lone but lusty survivor of narrow-gauge (three-foot gauge versus the standard four-foot, 8½-inch gauge) mountain railroads begins its eighty-fifth year of passenger and freight service. During 1965, 72,546 passengers were carried. In three successive days at the peak of the season, more than 1,000 passengers filled the two full sections and additional observation cars. So, reserved tickets are advisable.

Much of the credit for the continued operation of the Silverton must go to Conductor Alva Lyons, who happened to be aboard the train when we rode. He's spent his life on the narrow-gauge and, aided by local residents, rail fans and a decision of the Interstate Commerce Commission, he convinced the Denver and Rio Grande Western Railroad to keep the Silverton line open as a tourist attraction. The railroad's Advertising Manager, Ed Roe, says "Conductor Alva Lyons is certainly as much a part of the train as the locomotive."

Between his informative monologue over the train's public address system, Lyons stated that he might retire "one of these days." Durango's visitors hope he doesn't.

Fourteen years ago 3,444 persons took this scenic trip. In 1963, for the first time in history, a narrow-gauge railroad ran two sections to keep up with the midsummer demand.

Some of the coaches, wooden originals built before 1880, are "probably the world's oldest transportation vehicles in public use today," according to Conductor Lyons. Eight all-steel counterparts are almost exact replicas of the wooden coaches.

The Silverton's engines are K-28 Mikado "sport models" with a tender that carries 5,000 gallons of water and eight tons of soft coal. Unless you want coal dust in your hair

and "clinkers" in your eyes, bring sunglasses and a washable scarf, cap or hat.

The 45-mile trip to Silverton takes 3½ hours. Cinders & Smoke, a mile-by-mile guidebook of the Durango-to-Silverton narrow gauge, quotes The La Plata Miner of June 23, 1883 — 11 months after the completion of the railroad — as follows:

"There are in Silverton five hotels, 10 restaurants, 34 saloons, five blacksmith shops, eight laundries, six tobacco, fruit and candy stores, four livery stables, two bakeries, one theater, three dance halls, one photograph gallery, five assay offices, two newspapers, 18 lawyers, one bank, four doctors, two dentists, three mining offices, nine mining engineers, 294 dwellings, two hardware stores, two furniture stores, two harness shops, four meat markets, three drug stores, three jewelry stores and four millinery and ladies stores."

Perhaps it's because the leisurely, 13-m.p.h. pace is so different from flight in even the slowest airplanes, but there's a nostalgia to these old narrow-gauge trips that may be of particular significance to many pilots.

For an ideal flying trip back into the lore of the Old West, make it Destination Durango. Both on your en route flight, and lumbering along the bottom of the narrow Animas River canyon in the old narrow-gauge coaches, it's a trip you'll never forget.   ◆

This spectacular picture shows the narrow-gauge train, the Silverton, winding down through the Animas River valley on its 90-mile round-trip between Durango and Silverton, Colo.

THE PHOTOGRAPHS OF THE SILVERTON WERE SUPPLIED BY THE DENVER AND RIO GRANDE WESTERN RAILROAD

By IRA HARKEY | *AOPA 235348*

MAMMOTH CAVE
NATIONAL PARK

There's a spelunker's paradise in south-central Kentucky that's close to a general aviation airport. Echo River, Frozen Niagara, the Maelstrom, and Bottomless Pit are a few attractions to be found at the cave

PHOTOS BY W. RAY SCOTT, NATIONAL PARK CONCESSIONS, INC., UNLESS OTHERWISE CREDITED

Onyx cascades and gypsum formations help form Frozen Niagara. Discovered in 1923, this is the most massive formation in Mammoth Cave, being 75 feet high and 50 feet wide.

In 1798 a Kaintuck sharpshooter stalking a bear came upon an opening in the earth leading to what since has become one of the world's most celebrated natural wonders, the 175 miles of winding underground passageways now known as Mammoth Cave.

Airplane travelers of 1967 won't have to tail a bear to this outstanding geographic marvel of the eastern United States. Instead, they can stalk the 327° radial from Crossville Omni, 27° radial from Nashville Omni, or 250° radial from New Hope Omni to land at the up-to-date municipal airport at Glasgow, Ky., some 16 miles south of the cave.

I visited Mammoth Cave to show its wonders to my daughter, Amelie, 14, and son, Dale, 13, first writing to Mammoth Cave National Park, Mammoth Cave, Ky. 42259, for brochures on accommodations and tours, and to Glasgow Municipal Airport for information on services and car rentals. Our two-day visit went without a hitch. The airport, located along Victor 5 east between Nashville and Louisville (Nashville Sectional) at 720 feet has a 3,000-foot elevation, asphalt runway and an ample terminal building from which to call for your rental car. Both 80/87 and 100/130 octane fuel are available, but only minor repairs may be had and those only by special arrangement.

Open all year around, the cave since 1936 has been part of the 51,351-acre Mammoth Cave National Park, one of 31 national parks administered by the Federal government through the Park Service. Formed through the ages by underground rivers and surface seepage, the miles of intricate natural tunnels and great domed vaults are filled with beauty. Hundreds of thousands of stalactites and stalagmites — from tiny needles to giant columns and broad flowing sheets of curtainlike material — show their browns, yellows, reds, blues, greens and purples to some 500,000 awestruck visitors annually. Gypsum crystals in the form of unbelievably lovely "flowers" cover the ceilings and form friezes in many rooms. Ancient Indians gathered these flowers (for what purpose is not known) and at least one of them gave his life in the gathering. His mummified remains were found in 1935 on a ledge where he had been trapped by a shifting boulder. The mummy, perhaps 1,000 years old, is on exhibit at the park.

At the cave's lowest point, 360 feet below the surface, flows the Echo River, at places 60 feet wide, in whose cold water live a tiny white fish (*Amblyopsis spelaeus*) and a crayfish, both blind, their eyes having disappeared over the eons of darkness. Eyeless beetles and crickets with fragile legs like a daddy longlegs' cling to the cavern walls. Darkness is total in the depths, as tourists discover uneasily when their guides turn out the lights. Until about 25 years ago the cave was not wired for electricity. Lighting was by torches carried by the guides who were expert in pitching skill. They would place small kerosene-soaked wicks on the end of a stick, light the wicks with their torches and toss the flaming missiles across scores of feet to roost on tiny ledges or in tiny crevices, in order to light the way ahead or to show their charges some phenomenal shape or color in the cave's formations. My guide told me there are still one or two old-timers who can throw "the torch." "All of us younger ones practice it from time to time,

Amelie and Dale, the author's children, await Dad on the apron in front of the main building at Glasgow Municipal Airport.

PHOTO BY THE AUTHOR

but none of us are really any good," he admitted.

Mammoth Cave has attracted visitors for more than 150 years. During the War of 1812, a saltpeter mine was opened in the cave to supply the young United States with the nitrates necessary to the manufacture of gunpowder. Wooden vats and water pipes made of bored-out oak and poplar trees remain as they were when the mine was abandoned in 1814.

During the summer there are five different cave tours available, lasting from 90 minutes to seven hours, costing from $1.50 an adult to $2.85. Any child under 16 goes free when accompanied by an adult who has paid the tour cost. During the winter, three of the tours are available, requiring from 90 minutes to 4½ hours. On the longer tours in all seasons, a pause for lunch is made in the Snowball Room, 267 feet underground, where the ceiling is covered spectacularly with white puffs of gypsum.

The cave country is a place for all seasons. During the summer the verdant Kentucky hills are lush with forests containing about 80 different types of trees and shrubs. In the autumn the reds, browns and yellows are brilliant, and in the spring the return from slumber is beautiful. During the winter only pines, cedars and other evergreens remain in leaf, allowing breathtaking vistas across the valleys. Winter temperature averages 39° and roads are kept open always.

Temperature down under is a constant 54°, cool in the summer and warm in the winter. There are some steep climbs on some of the cavern tours, so the "unhale" should check with guides before buying the wrong tickets. Footing is generally good, paths having been worn safe by the feet of the millions who have gone before. But, ladies, don't wear high heels or those flimsy flats unless you want sprung ankles or mighty cold feet. Everyone should take a sweater even on the hottest day above ground.

All activities are not underground. Topside there are nature trail hikes, boat rides, color slide shows of cave and surface beauties, and illustrated lectures on how the caverns were formed. There are public showers, a camp store, picnic areas, a Kentucky crafts shop and a coin-operated laundry. For surface crawlers there are trailer parks.

Accommodations in summer range from rustic woodland cottages for $4.25 a day, plus $1.50 for each additional person, to the swank air-conditioned New Mammoth Cave Hotel at $9 single, $13 double and $2 for each additional person in the same room. In between are the Sunset Point Motor Lodge, $12.50 for three to a room, $14 for a family unit for four; the venerable Old Mammoth Cave Hotel, a rambling frame structure, from $5 for one to $10.75 for four; and hotel cottages, $7 for one, $1.50 for each additional. A 10% discount can be earned on most accommodations by booking for a week. In the winter, only the new hotel and the motor lodge remain open.

Meals, at unresortish prices, may be taken in either the coffeeshop or the dining room at the new hotel; that is, if you don't carry a barbecue rig in your plane. Service is rendered expertly and cheerfully in the summer by college students on their vacation breaks. Dress everywhere in the park and its facilities is shirtsleeve informal. Missing, strangely in an area where the summer temperature averages 88°, is a swimming pool, and there are no swimming holes on either the Green or the Nolin Rivers that wind through the park's emerald hills.

From Glasgow Airport you will drive northwest over good roads about 16 miles through the gently swelling hills of south-central Kentucky. (Glasgow is about 80 statute miles south of Louisville Standiford and 74 statute miles north of Nashville Metropolitan.) The drive is pleasant, but warning: do not heed the authoritative arm signals of certain sharpies who stand by the

Exhibitions on history, geology and archaeology can be seen in the Visitor Center from which all cave tours depart. All visitors must be accompanied into the cave by a guide.

The Onyx Chamber at Mammoth Cave, where natural formations in pits, rivers, and domes may be viewed along a winding passageway that is over 150 miles long.

road near the National Park boundary and attempt to "direct" you off the highway. These men wear uniform-type outfits and caps that, at first glance, make them appear to be police officers. If you stop you will be hustled through a cave that is *not* Mammoth Cave. The state of Kentucky should terminate this fraud. Official Park Service signs will tell you when you have entered the park and are en route to the genuine Mammoth Cave.

My first trip to this wonderland was made when I was a lad of 10 in 1928, when getting there was half the fun and also half a day's project, to reach the cave from Glasgow Junction (now Park City), which is on the Louisville and Nashville Railroad main line. A pygmy of a dinky engine named Hercules pulled one wooden car the nine miles from the junction to the cave, huffing mightily over the snaking narrow-gauge tracks, enveloped in a choking smoke screen. I was overcome with nostalgia to find Hercules and the bright red car on display near the park headquarters where they have been enshrined since their retirement in 1929.

My children were fascinated by the relics. They who travel by Mooney at up to 160 miles an hour listened politely to my remembrances of travel by Hercules at 18 miles a day. Amelie said something about how funny things must have been "in the olden days" and I felt like a relic myself, ready to be stuffed and put on view beside Hercules. I gained back my status as a contemporary piece the next day, however, when we racketed down Runway 7 at Glasgow Airport and I rotated gracefully and winged us back home. ◆

By R. E. PENDLEY | AOPA 37008

Enjoy roughing it at airstrip camping sites in scenic western mountains. Three specific areas described

FLYING TO

Mountain Campgrounds

Camping beside a stream or lake in the high mountain country of the American West is surely one of life's most delightful experiences. This country features sensational scenes of great rock outcroppings among specimen pine and fir trees standing before towering mountains whose patches of snow are dazzling in their contrast against the blue sky. Few things can lift spirits as much as landing several trout from the clear,

icy waters at the very edge of a camp in this country and cooking and serving them in a matter of minutes. After dinner, there is the peace of the campfire until bedtime. Before dropping off to sleep, campers looking up from their sleeping bags are treated to the sight of millions of stars shining down through the boughs with a brilliance not seen in lowlands.

Although there are in the great National

Parks and Forests of the West thousands of square miles of scenery like that just described, attempts to enjoy them are often disappointing. Visitors in automobiles are usually restricted to "designated camp sites." Such camp sites have become so crowded in recent years that visitors must check in with park officials early in the morning in order to find space for their automobiles and sleeping bags for the following night. Too often,

Mark and Alan Pendley use the hand-powered cable car to cross Indian Creek.

the "designated camp site" is a hodge-podge of autos, camper trucks, sleeping bags, cardboard boxes, milling people, transistor radios and outhouses (clean and well-built, but still outhouses). To be sure, beyond all this there is the aforementioned scenery, but its enjoyment is largely lost.

As with many people here in the West, my two sons and I backpack into the high country, often across 12,000-foot passes, in order to escape the crowds and camp where we please. This takes a lot of effort and time and a degree of physical condition that is becoming less accessible to me with each passing year. For our 1965 summer trip, I decided to investigate the possibilities of flying into an airstrip in a mountain wilderness area in my flying club's Cessna *Skylane,* with the hope of camping in relative solitude near the airplane.

A study of sectional charts of the western mountains revealed a number of landing strips in the remote, central Idaho primitive area. The Idaho Department of Aeronautics was wonderfully accommodating in responding to my request for information on flying into this area. The department forwarded descriptive information on the suitability of a number of landing strips for camping. A booklet with detailed information on, and recommended procedures for flying into, each airport and landing strip was also included. On the basis of this information, I selected Indian Creek Landing Strip (La-Grande Sectional) because it appeared to offer the desired surroundings and was well within the capabilities of the *Skylane* and my airmanship.

Late in August, my sons, Mark and Alan, and I departed Long Beach Municipal Airport in N2220G, which was loaded with 165 pounds of sleeping bags, plastic tarpaulins, food, cooking utensils, a Coleman stove, and fishing tackle. Comfort-allowing gear can be carried on this kind of trip that can't be carried on a backpacking trip. About six hours after takeoff we landed at Hailey, Ida., where there is a long (5,200-foot), smooth, turf strip. We filled our tanks here before beginning the final one-hour leg into the primitive area. The field is only a mile from the center of the village, to which we hiked in order to buy fishing licenses, pick up fire permits, and obtain advice from the U.S. Forest Service Ranger Station.

We took off late in the afternoon for the final leg to Indian Creek. Shortly after penetrating the mountainous area, all VOR signals were lost, and navigation became a matter of compass, clock, and chart. Since the mountains are dense in this area and most of their peaks are near 10,000 feet, the flying was mostly along deep, rather steep-walled river valleys. Our visual reference was therefore confined to a fairly small area. We came to a critical point where the canyon we were flying along branched off into three separate canyons. The chart indicated that the correct one was the middle one, but the shape of the entrance didn't look much like the contours on the chart. Comparison of the compass readings with the airplane aimed at the canyons in question confirmed that our course should pass down the middle canyon.

Shortly, we were without doubt proceeding downstream along the Middle Fork Salmon River. Right on schedule, Indian Creek (elevation 4,662 feet) showed up 5,000 feet

Alan casts at the edge of the white water.

down in the canyon below us. The strip is parallel to and located almost on the bank of the river, which winds through the forested mountains that rise from the river banks to 9,000 feet. The river is almost straight for some distance upstream, but it makes a fairly sharp bend from the downstream end of the strip. A wind sock is provided on the strip, and it indicated a slight preference for an approach from downstream. This required that the glide be performed along the canyon out of sight of the field. As we came around the bend at what seemed like a sufficiently low altitude above the rocks and trees along the canyon walls, we found that we were too high. However, overshooting is no problem. We continued past the airstrip and along the river until we had enough altitude to turn comfortably between the canyon walls for another pass.

The second time all went well. Although the deforested area of the strip is quite wide, the well-marked landing surface that has been cleared of stones is just wide enough to serve its purpose. The field is astonishingly long (5,200 feet), and we used only a fraction of it. We taxied to the upstream end, where several concrete and chain tiedowns have been provided by the U.S. Forest Service.

Actually, the wind was so light that we could have made the much easier approach from upstream where the field would have been in sight continuously during a long straight-in.

A hundred paces from the tiedowns, we found a marvelous camp site on the bank of the river. The view upstream from this point is beautiful. The river makes a slight, graceful double bend which provides a sparkling foreground to the green wooded slopes beyond. The river is about 150 feet wide, and it rushes downstream across a boulder bed. The water is cold and crystal clear.

The river banks are forested with large lodgepole pines and Douglas firs. There is almost no undergrowth, the forest floor consisting of a pine needle mat. Firewood is abundant. Insects were practically absent. Each morning after breakfast, we loaded a pack sack with lunch, fishing tackle and rain gear and hiked two to three miles up- or downstream, fishing promising holes along the way. We found a number of places where water cascading through a restriction of stone narrows had eroded deep, blue-green pools, or where a bend in the river had accomplished the same thing. The rainbow, native cutthroat, and Dolly Varden trout found in these pools wait for food to be washed down to them from the riffles at the upstream edge. We had these pools all to ourselves, seeing only one other fisherman in four days, and he was on the opposite bank. Spinners and flies were both effective.

We also enjoyed a day's hike up Indian Creek, a tributary which empties into the Middle Fork near the flight strip. To get to the trail, which is on the opposite side of the creek, we used the quaint, hand-powered, two-place cable car which has been provided by the Forest Service. We found a large level meadow inside a generous bend of the creek that we decided, for sure, must have been the scene of an important Indian camp in historical times.

The Forest Service chart indicates that there are Indian paintings on stone walls at several points downstream, the closest about six miles. Persons with sufficient time should, by all means, pack their sleeping bags downstream for overnight to see these paintings, which, unfortunately, we could not do.

Each day we had a brief light sprinkle from the midafternoon cumulus buildup. The days were cool, the nights crisp, with the wind very light or calm. The clouds were scattered, nights and mornings.

The Skylane is shown at the Three Rivers, Calif., landing strip with the mountains at the entrance to Sequoia National Park visible in the background.

We departed Indian Creek for Bradley Field, Boise, late in the afternoon on the last day of our stay. The motel and restaurant at this excellent airport, adjacent to the tie-down area, provided the pleasure of a shower and a night's sleep on a mattress before we left the next morning. The motel's proprietor is accustomed to receiving unshaven guests seriously in need of a bath.

A number of other landing strips are available in the Idaho mountain country, some of which adjoin or have on the premises accommodations for persons who wish to enjoy the ordinary comforts of civilization while being a short hike from solitude and great fishing or hunting. The Department of Aeronautics can provide descriptive information on a number of such areas.

Although they are not in a wilderness area such as is Indian Creek, I can recommend two other scenic and pleasant landing strips suitable for an outing: Trinity Center in Northern California (Mt. Shasta Sectional), and Three Rivers (Mt. Whitney Sectional). Overnight camping is available at both places.

A fine surfaced strip with spacious tie-down area is adjacent to the village of Trinity Center on the western shore of Trinity Reservoir. The lake is brilliant blue and is surrounded by beautiful forested mountains.

There are many miles of undeveloped, wooded shore line. A telephone is available at the strip from which one may call Scott's Marina, one-half miles south, for rental boats.

Three Rivers landing strip is very near the entrance to Sequoia National Park. Two hundred paces from the airplane parking area, visitors find a small stream containing a number of rapids and small waterfalls. The stream is bordered by large shade trees (principally oak and sycamore) and a well-maintained spacious campground. The elevation is low (850 feet), consequently, the weather is pleasantly warm in the summer, and the stream is warm enough for swimming. About one-half mile downstream, this stream merges with a larger one that comes down from the park. Near this confluence, the water flows across a large, smooth granite surface and plunges into a turbulent pool. Those swimmers who manage to keep to the right of the slightly submerged rocks enjoy exhilarating floats over this natural slide.

The landing strip is closely bordered on each side by sizable hills. Although I understand many pilots land in the direction going up the valley, I felt better about flying over descending terrain in the event of an

overshoot and therefore made a downstream approach. In addition, the wind sock indicated a slight preference for this approach. Pilots making their landing approach in this direction should be alert to the fact that the gradient of the valley results in an upward component of the wind, which reduces the airplane's glide slope markedly, and the pilot experiences a hazardous desire to slow his airplane. In addition, a low hill and corral at the upstream end prevents landing at the runway threshold. The field is short and you don't like losing this extra runway length.

Three Rivers is not far from Mineral King, from which pack trips may be made into the heart of the Sierra back country.

Of the three landing strips described, Trinity Center is the easiest to maneuver into. Because of its length, Indian Creek is not too difficult when you adjust to the psychological impact of flying between walls of trees. The Three Rivers strip is the tightest — you must be just about right to get in. Pilots who know their airplanes and faithfully observe the excellent advice on mountain flying issued by the Idaho Department of Aeronautics can expect a safe and marvelous time when flying to any one of the three strips. ◆

Borrego Springs, California, offers many recreational pursuits.
Among them, rest and relaxation are prime commodities

Pilots Invited To DESERT RESORT

By ALLAN PALMER | AOPA 162681

Entrance to desert park which is location of Borrego Country Club.　　　PHOTO COURTESY OF UNION-TRIBUNE PUBLISHING COMPANY

On the eastern side of the coastal mountains of far-southern California lies a semibowl opening on the Salton Sea. Here is Borrego Valley, where serenity is sold.

About 1,000 people live here, but that is misleading. As the summer heat fades the number begins to climb; and if put on a graph, the line would rise and fall with weekends and holidays like the horizon of the High Sierras.

This is San Diego County's desert resort, without the status symbols and ambitions of Palm Springs. Nor does it have such an illustrious history. Major development began little more than a decade ago.

First, some vital statistics. The 3,500-foot, lighted, paved runway is 28 miles from Thermal Vortac on the 185° radial. In between are the Santa Rosa Mountains, up to 6,623 feet. It is easier on the family plane to fly around the point of the mountains and approach from the east, through the open side of the bowl. The desert floor rises slowly from the below-sea-level Salton Sea to 520 feet at the airport.

From San Diego Vortac it is 63 miles, at 45°. The highest point along this route is 5,993 feet.

Dots on the desert floor noted by the approaching flyer are mostly private homes. Much sand and space separate neighbor from neighbor. Street patterns mark the expanses, with the shadows of structures only here and there lending shading to the aerial picture.

There are more abuilding — homes, apartments, stores. A million-dollar shopping center and 28-unit apartment complex were recently completed.

The valley, however, is 30 miles across and there is no difficulty in finding solitude. For the vacationer — from fog and smog, or snow and cold, or the city's traffic noise and rush of commerce — Borrego is a moment of calm and rest.

Most have come on wheels, but flying is being encouraged. At the county-owned airport the lessee operates a restaurant and bar and a nearby motel, the Molina Verde. Hospitality at other motels includes transportation from the airport. The Borrego Springs Chamber of Commerce will answer telephoned or written queries with late information. For example, Ray Freelund, operator of Stanlunds Motel, keeps a courtesy vehicle for flying guests. When reservations are made, an arrival time should be noted and a

car will be sent. Desert weather rarely causes a change in ETA.

Other motels of note include La Casa del Zorro, Borrego Village and Hacienda del Sol. Only La Casa del Zorro has its own dining room. Reservations are necessary during the season — from Labor Day to Memorial Day. The greatest influx is from November through February.

Rest and relaxation are the major commodities. Tours in rented Jeeps and hiking are popular. If hikers are also rockhounds, opportunities are endless. De Anza Country Club golf course is for members, but the Borrego Springs Park has a nine-hole and a three-par golf course.

However, all such pursuits run second to just soaking up the warm clear sunshine in the desert quiet. ◆

THE AUTHOR

Allan Palmer, author of "Pilots Invited To Desert Resort" is a San Diego newspaperman. He has written several articles for The PILOT in the past. A private pilot since 1949, Palmer was once a fixed-base operator in Colorado.

Restaurant, adjacent to a tiedown area, at the Borrego Valley-San Diego County Airport.

PHOTO BY THE AUTHOR

160